A Beginner's Guide to the
MCMI-III

A Beginner's Guide to the
MCMI-III

Dan Jankowski

Foreword by Theodore Millon

AMERICAN PSYCHOLOGICAL ASSOCIATION
WASHINGTON, DC

Published by
American Psychological Association
750 First Street, NE
Washington, DC 20002
www.apa.org

To order
APA Order Department
P.O. Box 92984
Washington, DC 20090-2984
Tel: (800) 374-2721, Direct: (202) 336-5510
Fax: (202) 336-5502, TDD/TTY: (202) 336-6123
Online: www.apa.org/books/
Email: order@apa.org

In the U.K., Europe, Africa, and the Middle East, copies may be ordered from
American Psychological Association
3 Henrietta Street
Covent Garden, London
WC2E 8LU England

Typeset in Meridien and Frutiger by World Composition Services, Inc., Sterling, VA

Printer: Port City Press, Baltimore, MD
Cover designer: NiDesign, Baltimore, MD
Production Editor: Catherine Hudson
Project Manager: Debbie Hardin, Carlsbad, CA

The opinions and statements published are the responsibility of the authors, and such opinions and statements do not necessarily represent the policies of the American Psychological Association.

Library of Congress Cataloging-in-Publication Data

Jankowski, Dan.
    A beginner's guide to the MCMI-III / Dan Jankowski.
        p. cm.
    Includes bibliographical references and index.
    ISBN 1-55798-843-9 (alk. paper)
    1. Millon Clinical Multiaxial Inventory.   I. Title.

    RC473.M47 J36   2002
    616.89'075—dc21   2001046349

British Library Cataloguing-in-Publication Data
A CIP record is available from the British Library.

Printed in the United States of America
First Edition

With endless love and dedication—To Helen

Contents

7
_____

The Psychological Report: Scripting the Results   139

Foreword

What a welcome idea, a brief and intelligently organized instructional text on the clinical profession's recent and currently second most-used diagnostic inventory for adults with moderate levels of mental disorder. Now in its 25th anniversary year, the Millon Clinical Multiaxial Inventory (MCMI) is the only test published in the past half century to have broken into that august category of the 20 most frequently used psychological instruments.

Dan Jankowski has provided a highly informative and readable synopsis that has been carefully designed for use by advanced undergraduate or graduate students in introductory testing or advanced personality assessment courses, not only in clinical psychology but also in counseling, psychiatry, social work, and education. Instructors may use the text as a foundation for students who are able to devote as little as one- or two-hour sessions to the inventory or have it serve as an anchor for an expanded several week period, depending on course goals or the level of student future responsibilities.

The book is organized in a logical sequence of subject areas. Dr. Jankowski establishes first a solid foundation for students by setting down the essentials of the test's guiding theory, followed by a thoughtful articulation of the structure and composition of the inventory; both have been done in a graceful and illuminating writing style, easily followed and understood by students with minimal previous preparation.

Especially valuable are the three "interpretive" chapters, the first devoted to issues of validation and distorting response patterns, the second to the distinguishing features of the inventory—that is, its personality disorder Axis II scales—and the third to the classical clinical syndromes of Axis I. These interpretive chapters are elaborated and integrated with great clinical sensibility and sound judgment, providing students with a firm and wise foundation for their own use of the instrument. The final basic chapter illustrates the form and substance of a clinical report, done with special reference to the place and purpose of the MCMI. This chapter will furnish students with a guide and a comprehensive framework for organizing and writing "multiaxial" reports of optimal utility.

The numerous case illustrations, self-testing exercises, and practical steps that Dr. Jankowski provides the student throughout the text and its appendices make this beginner's primer a superb addition, one that will find a valuable niche in the well-established and growing body of books on the MCMI.

Theodore Millon, PhD, DSc

Acknowledgments

In a work of this kind, it is necessary to rely on previous authors. I am grateful to Dicandrian, Inc., the American Psychiatric Association, the American Psychological Association, John Wiley & Sons, Drs. Othmer and Othmer, and Drs. Choca and Van Denburg for their permission to reprint original materials.

I extend my appreciation to the professional editorial staff of the American Psychological Association, who readily accepted the manuscript and brought it to publication. A note of thanks also goes to Dr. Neil Bockian for his helpful consultation in refining certain aspects of the text and to Dr. Eliezer Schwartz, for—among other things—introducing me to the learned works of Dr. Millon.

Finally, I am indebted to two special people whose support and assistance have been indispensable. I personally thank and acknowledge Ms. Donna Baker and Dr. Theodore Millon. Ms. Baker meticulously edited the text numerous times throughout its revision process, allowing the printed word to come alive through her mastery of the English language. To Dr. Millon, I extend my deepest and most sincere gratitude for his continued support and valued review of this book and also for the wealth of personality theory I have acquired from his writings over the years. Without their generous support; the realization of this book would not have been possible.

Introduction

As an adjunct professor teaching objective personality assessment, I have felt for some time that a basic instructional book could facilitate the learning process of the MCMI-III. I contacted Dr. Theodore Millon with a proposal to write such a textbook, and he encouraged me to do so and has enthusiastically supported me throughout this endeavor. What resulted was *A Beginner's Guide to the MCMI-III*.

For the student in clinical psychology and related fields of counseling, education, social work, and psychiatry, *A Beginner's Guide to the MCMI-III* provides a concise approach for learning the MCMI-III. The practicing clinician can also find it to be a valuable resource companion, occasionally called on to reference specific material in the instrument. Nonclinicians such as attorneys in forensic settings or administrators in hospital positions who wish to gain a basic familiarity of the MCMI-III mechanics may likewise find it useful.

The book is designed not only to provide a basic understanding of the instrument but also to assist in developing interpretive skills. Although various books have been published on this instrument, the versatile and user-friendly format of this book is particularly well-suited for classroom instruction. It may also be used independently as a self-tutoring guide. To reinforce the beginner's understanding of the fundamental knowledge, each chapter contains *Test Yourself Exercises*. Using these exercises, the student can review material as well as apply it to practice the interpretive cases. More often than not, practice is the best of instructors.

Although this book can be used as a self-tutoring guide, it is important to note that it is not a substitute for the *MCMI-III Manual, Second Edition*. Reference to the manual is necessary not only to obtain procedural information but also to gain a fuller understanding of the impressive psychometric development of the MCMI-III.

My guiding objectives in writing this book have been twofold: to provide the reader with an understandable primer and to preserve the integrity of Dr. Millon's subject matter, meaning, and theory to remain consistent with his theoretical system. *A Beginner's Guide to the MCMI-III* incorporates Dr. Millon's rich theoretical framework and reflects his developing ideology.

Millon's Clinical Multiaxial Inventories have grown in popularity since the introduction of the original version in 1977. The current edition, MCMI-III, is particularly useful in diagnosing personality disorders and identifying existing syndromes within the psychiatric population. Grounded in Millon's theoretical framework, the MCMI-III's rich interpretive value is reinforced by the fact that its 175-item self-report format closely parallels the classification of disorders found in the *Diagnostic and Statistical Manual of Mental Disorders* (4th ed.; American Psychiatric Association, 1994). Concordance with the *DSM-IV* not only strengthens the diagnostic dimensions of MCMI-III but also increases the utility of Millon's guiding theoretical system among clinicians.

One of the many strengths of the MCMI-III is its systematic link to a comprehensive, rationally based theory. Chapter 1 traces the progression of Millon's theory from its early biosocial–learning roots to his recently developed evolutionary theory. An overview of Millon's 8×14 domain expression of personality disorders and his evolutionary model and its personality derivatives are illustrated.

Chapter 2 provides a summary of the MCMI-III scale composition. Characteristic features and a look inside the instrument are provided. The rigorous three-step strategy of test development and validation—theoretical–substantive, internal–structural, and external–criterion—is presented.

The MCMI-III format includes hand scoring or computer-assisted scoring available through National Computer Systems. Chapter 3 provides general guidelines for administrative and hand-scoring procedures. Although computer scoring is a more practical and effective method, the hand-scoring procedures are recommended for the first-time user to gain familiarity with the instrument.

Chapters 4, 5, and 6 discuss the procedures for interpreting the validity indicators and Modifying indices, clinical personality patterns, and clinical syndromes. Rules governing scale interpretation are relatively straightforward and are discussed in the context of Millon's criterion-referenced base-rate anchors. Personality disorders and clinical/severe syndromes are examined in chapters 5 and 6 to include relevant research and *DSM-IV/III-R* criteria for each scale. Mental status descriptions and brief treatment capsules of the personality disorders are included to provide the reader with a diagnostic profile relative to the clinical setting.

Although the MCMI-III is an accurate assessment tool, Millon cautions that it should not be used in isolation when formulating an Axis I or Axis II diagnosis. Chapter 7 explores an assessment strategy that includes the use of the mental status examination and *DSM-IV* multi-axial classifications for added diagnostic precision. In addition, this chapter reviews the framework of the psychological report and discusses the necessary elements included in its format. A notional interpretive report is discussed and analyzed. Finally, each chapter concludes with individual exercises to review one's understanding of the materials presented.

Appendix A provides a sample MCMI-III computer-scored comprehensive profile report distributed through National Computer Systems. Appendix B offers the reader several case vignettes to practice interpreting the MCMI-III. Appendix C contains the answers for all of the chapter exercises.

The first clinical diagnosis to be made is often an intense time for the beginning clinician. These chapters are designed to provide the reader with a basic, straightforward approach to the MCMI-III—a fundamental course, as it were, through which the complex, winding paths of psychological diagnosis can be more easily explored.

A Beginner's Guide to the
MCMI-III

Understanding Millon's Theory | 1

How do we define personality? We use the word rather freely, though many of us would be hard-pressed to define its meaning. Since the time of Hippocrates, theorists have attempted to describe the salient features of the individual—how people are put together, what makes them tick, why they break down. Their perspectives are as varied as the nature of personality itself, which leads to the question, Why do people behave in the ways they do? The answer remains elusive. It is with an appreciation of these historical perspectives that Millon formulated his typology and presented a schema for classifying personality patterns. Let us now discuss Millon's integrated concept of personality.

In addressing the nature of personality, Millon reminds us that although the question is easily posed, it is difficult to answer:

> Personality is seen today as a complex pattern of deeply embedded psychological characteristics that are largely nonconscious and not easily altered, expressing themselves automatically in almost every facet of functioning. Intrinsic and pervasive, these traits emerge from a complicated matrix of biological dispositions and experiential learnings, and ultimately comprise the individual's distinctive pattern of perceiving, feeling, thinking, coping, and behaving. (Millon & Davis, 1996, p. 4)

Looking at the key concepts in this definition, we can say that personality is a pattern of innate characteristics that take shape through an intricate pattern of genetic and environmental influences. The characteristics are firmly fixed, cannot easily be changed, and are manifested uniquely in everything we think, feel, and do, almost without our awareness.

Millon and Davis (1996, p. 8) wrote, "the essence of personality lies in its implicit holism"—that is, the notion that our thoughts, feelings, and behaviors are interconnected, all subject to an underlying purpose. Viewing personality through a holistic lens, Millon has explored the central questions pondered by theorists back to the time of early Greek thinkers—the "what, how, and why" of personality. His recently developed theory of an evolutionary system, which establishes a series of prototypes and a wide range of personality subtypes, serves to integrate the multiple domains of personality. Let us turn first to his earlier perspectives, the foundation for the beginnings of his evolutionary system.

Early Biosocial Learning Theory

As the individual grows and develops, behavior is shaped into habitual patterns of interaction with others. These habitual patterns become

---

THE MEANING OF PERSONALITY

"Know thyself," read the inscription over the portal of the sixth-century BC Greek temple of Apollo at Delphi. But what exactly do we know when we know ourselves? Does our outward behavior reflect who we are? Shakespeare tells us, "All the world's a stage." Is it on this stage where we come to know ourselves? What constitutes self? What is the essence of human nature? Such questions, the core of personality, consumed the minds of some of the greatest thinkers: Plato, Socrates, and Aristotle. Personality is derived from the Latin word *persona*, a mask worn by actors in Greek and Roman drama. Do the masks we wear, then, reveal who we really are? Given that each individual is a unique character, it is ultimately our role on the stage of life that defines who we are.

repetitive and consistent, and it is the collective grouping of these patterns that Millon refers to as personality patterns. This conception of personality—embracing both biological and environmental influences—forms the basis of Millon's early theory, known as the biosocial learning system.

As Millon and Everly (1985, p. 9) defined it, "Biological factors set the foundation that undergirds personality development, whereas environmental factors act to shape the form of their expression." A major theme of the biosocial learning theory asserts that personality and psychopathology develop as a result of the interplay of organismic and environmental forces. Biological factors, as well as neural maturation, are shaped through environmental influences. Individuals with similar biological potentials, however, perceive the environment differently, undergo distinct neurological growth, and develop varying personality styles. We question, at times, why people who grow up under similar conditions sometimes become very different personalities or why two children raised in the same family grow up very differently. Even though individuals may have similar biological temperaments or biological raw material, as Millon terms it, everyone perceives, matures, and interacts with the environment differently. Biological maturation is, for the most part, a consequence of favorable environmental experiences, and our development is facilitated or limited by the nature of the interaction between these processes.

THE THREE POLARITIES

Millon's exhaustive review of the works by earlier theoreticians concluded that amid the diversity of the varied theories, a similar threefold group of dimensions were used in part or whole by theorists as the cornerstone of personality construction. It is these concepts of a tripartite structure of polarities (active–passive, pleasure–pain, and subject–object) that govern all of mental life to which he returned (Millon, 1969). These polarities, considered the essence of mental life, are central to Millon's theory.

According to Millon (1981, p. 58), the vast range of behaviors in which an individual engages may be grouped in terms of whether an individual takes the initiative in shaping the environment (active) or whether behavior is largely reactive to the events (passive). Through an active or passive posture, an individual takes a stance toward life—actively seeking goal-directed behaviors or passively allowing events to take their course. Among all objects and things in the environment, there are two that transcend all others with regard to their impact on us—reinforcement from self or other. Finally, individual motivations are ultimately aimed in one of two directions, pleasure or pain—toward events that are positively reinforcing and away from those that are aversive.

THE PRINCIPLE OF REINFORCEMENT

In formulating his earlier biosocial theory, Millon developed a structure that integrated these polarities with the notion of reinforcement. The individual's biological disposition is modified through learned experiences. Learning is acquired in several fashions—through a close association with another, through observation of another, and by reinforcement of one's behaviors. Our personality is shaped through learning that can be adaptive, in which case normal, healthy development occurs, or maladaptive, in which an unhealthy, abnormal personality takes shape.

How does maladaptive learning occur? For some, it is a case of insufficient learning, whereas for others, maladaptive behaviors can provide positive and negative reinforcement, albeit in the short term. An applicant who fabricates a job resume, for example, may be rewarded with the position, though he may ultimately discover that he does not possess the necessary skills required and may eventually grow uncomfortable in that position. Or the child who lies about stealing money may initially avoid the consequences of punishment; however, learning responsibility for one's actions becomes thwarted. Abnormal personality, then, is shaped by these repetitively reinforced maladaptive behaviors.

Millon and Everly (1985, p. 29) suggested that the process of reinforcement can be considered from two interacting perspectives: sources through which reinforcement is sought and instrumental behaviors used to seek reinforcement. The source dimension addresses these three questions: Where does the individual seek reinforcement? From which sources does an individual gain satisfaction (positive reinforcement) and avoid emotional pain (negative reinforcement)? Are they found within the self or are they sought from others? Within this dimension, Millon initially defined four types of patterns that describe the "styles" of reinforcement. They are the independent, dependent, ambivalent, and detached. A fifth type of pattern, the discordant, was later added. Complex strategies based on and reflected in the kinds of reinforcements an individual has learned are subsequently developed. Millon refers to these complex strategies of instrumental behavior as personality "coping patterns" from which distinctions in personality are derived.

The instrumental dimension addresses the question, How does the individual seek reinforcement? This dimension reflects the characteristic behavior adopted by the individual to maximize rewards and minimize pain. The individual responds either actively or passively. The

WHAT IS LEARNING?

Learning can be defined as experiential knowledge uniquely attained by each individual. We may say that the function of learning underlies the "nurture" side of the nature–nurture coalescence. Behaviorists consider learning as outward changes in observable behavior, whereas from the cognitive perspective, it is viewed as an inward change of cognitions. Millon's (1969; Millon & Everly, 1985) earlier writings suggest that most learning relevant to personality development may be categorized under three headings: contiguous, vicarious, and instrumental. The simplest form is contiguous learning, in which environmental associations are formed. Vicarious learning, on the other hand, is acquired through observation, with direct consequences on our actions. Instrumental learning, arguably the most effective form of learning, is based on negative and positive reinforcement. As Millon and Everly (1985) asserted, it would seem reasonable that all three types of learning combine to shape the formation of the healthy, normal individual, as well as the abnormal, unhealthy individual.

active pursuit describes individuals who exhibit active, goal-directed behaviors, whereas passive behavior is reactive, with individuals seemingly content to wait for others to provide their reinforcement.

ORIGINAL FRAMEWORK

Using the three polarities and principles of reinforcement as a basis, Millon initially derived eight coping patterns, which formed a 4×2 matrix (source dimensions × instrumental behavior dimensions) and became the basis for the MCMI Clinical Personality scales. The matrix was subsequently adapted to a 5×2 matrix, to include the discordant style and reflect the classified personality disorders of *DSM-III-R*. This matrix formed the basis for the MCMI-II Clinical Personality scales. The initial matrix included eight cells (eight basic styles of personality), to which three severe patterns were later added, for a total of 11 theory-based patterns (Millon, 1981). Inclusion of the discordant instrumental coping style, which contained the masochistic and sadistic personalities, increased the patterns to a total of 13. Table 1-1 provides an overview

TABLE 1-1

Theory-Based Framework for Personality Pathology

Pathology Domain	Self–Other			Pain–Pleasure	
Reinforcement source	Other + Self −	Self + Other −	Self ↔ Other	Pain ↔ Pleasure	Pleasure- Pain ±
Instrumental coping style/ interpersonal pattern	Dependent	Independent	Ambivalent	Discordant	Detached
Passive variant	Dependent	Narcissistic	Compulsive	Self-defeating (masochistic)	Schizoid
Active variant	Histrionic	Antisocial	Passive–aggressive	Aggressive (sadistic)	Avoidant
Dysfunctional variant	Borderline	Paranoid	Borderline or Paranoid		Schizotypal

Source: Manual for the MCMI-II, Second ed., by T. Millon, 1987, Minneapolis, MN: National Computer Systems. Copyright 1997 Dicandrian, Inc. Reprinted with permission.

of Millon's early theoretical framework of personality pathology. Let us now take a closer look at the dimensions that make up his framework.

Grasping the Matrix

Essentially, Millon's typology as described in the matrix explores the nature of the relationship an individual is likely to form. The first dimension relates to the sources from which the individual gains pleasure and avoids pain. Does the individual turn inwardly to self or outwardly to others for support? Those who seek reinforcement dependently tend to look to others for satisfaction. They depend on others for safety and security and conform to the other's set of expectations. Other individuals, who have learned to depend on themselves, reflect the independent pattern. This pattern measures satisfaction in terms of self-reliance according to one's own values. Unlike the definitive preferences made by the dependent and independent personality styles, the ambivalent is uncertain about where to find gratification. The ambivalent personality is conflicted and vacillates between submissive and autonomous behaviors. The discordant personality style seeks satisfaction through the substitution of pain for pleasure. The last style, the detached, refers to those individuals who experience few rewards from self or others because of a lack of motivation or an inability to seek reinforcement.

The second dimension found in the matrix reflects the individual coping behavior used to maximize rewards and to minimize pain. Essentially, an individual either takes an active posture toward life, actively seeking goal-directed behavior and avoiding discomfort, or is passive, allowing events to take their course without any personal control. The active variant characterizes individuals, who are proactive, whereas the passive variant describes those who are reactive.

Finally, Millon categorizes the schizotypal, borderline, and paranoid as structurally defective pathologies, representing more extreme variants of the clinical personality patterns. In Millon's evolutionary model, these severe patterns are classified under structural pathology. Now that we have a firm grasp of Millon's early theoretical formulations, let us proceed to his more recent developments.

Evolutionary Theory

With a focus on the principles of evolution, Millon (1990) reconceptualized his theoretical framework of personality. The shift from the biosocial perspective to an evolutionary perspective explored the deeper layers of human functioning. Sharing key elements with the evolutionary model, the earlier biosocial learning theory focused on the developmental dimensions of the individual; recent formulations are grounded in evolutionary laws of nature from which personality patterns are derived.

THE PROCESS

Individuals go through four "stages" of neuropsychological development (sensory–attachment, sensorimotor–autonomy, pubertal–gender identity, intracortical integration), coinciding with four stage-specific "tasks" (developing trust of others, acquiring adaptive confidence, assimilating sexual roles, and balancing reason and emotion) in the maturation process. These stages and tasks correspond to four phases (existence, adaptation, replication, and abstraction) of evolution. Applying the three polarities (active–passive, self–other, pain–pleasure), Millon constructed his evolutionary-based classification of personality disorders. Millon's four components of the evolutionary model are presented in Table 1-2.

In the theory of evolutionary development, Millon (1999) notes three requisites necessary in the progression of the evolutionary

TABLE 1-2

Four Components of the Evolutionary Model

Evolutionary Phase	Survival Functions	Neuropsychological Stage	Developmental Task
Existence	Life enhancement (pleasure) Life preservation (pain)	Sensory-attachment	Developing trust of others
Adaptation	Ecological modification (active) Ecological accommodation (passive)	Sensorimotor-autonomy	Acquiring adaptive confidence
Replication	Progeny nurturance (other) Individual propagation (self)	Pubertal-gender identity	Assimilating sexual roles
Abstraction	Intellective-reasoning (thinking) Affective resonance (feeling)	Intracortical integration	Balancing reason and emotion

Source: Disorders of Personality DSM-IV and Beyond (2nd ed.) by T. Millon and Davis, 1996, New York. Copyright 1996 John Wiley & Sons, Inc. Reprinted with permission.

process—that is, each organism must survive, it must adapt to the environment, and it must reproduce. Commonalities in adaptive styles exist among the evolved species; however, each species' capacity for adapting to the environment differs in style and success. "Psychological fitness derives from the relation of the entire configuration of personal characteristics to the environments in which the person functions" (Millon, 1999, p. 96). The neurological stages, which coincide with an individual's particular "tasks," take place during specific evolutionary phases and affects adaptive or maladaptive functioning in relation to the environment. "Disorders of personality, so formulated, would represent particular styles of maladaptive functioning that can be traced to deficiencies, imbalances, or conflicts in a species' capacity to relate to the environments it faces" (Millon & Davis, 1996, p. 71). The four phases of evolutionary principles, it can be said, frame one's human expression. Let us look at these phases individually to appreciate their holistic significance in reference to personality development.

PHASES OF EVOLUTIONARY THEORY

The mechanisms derived from the first phase, existence, relate to an individual's orientation toward life—enhancement and preservation. During the first years of life, the child is wholly dependent on the caregiver. How the child attaches to the caregiver sets the stage for later development. Is the child's quality of life during the first 18 months enhanced or is the toddler's orientation simply toward preservation from stimuli that decrease the quality or possibly threaten existence itself? Are a child's aims toward enhancing pleasure and avoiding pain realized? Failure to develop feelings of trust in others at the sensory–attachment phase may leave the toddler conflicted between the signals of pleasure and pain. Understimulation, at this stage, may result in apathy, depression, and deficits in social connectivity. As a consequence, some individuals are apt to reverse pain for pleasure (e.g., the sadistic personality), whereas others (e.g., the schizoid personality) form deficits in these aims (Millon & Davis, 1996).

The second evolutionary stage, adaptation, addresses how the child adapts to the environment—how existence is maintained. This phase refers to *how* the child continues to exist, with the goal being the acquisition of adaptive confidence. During the sensorimotor–autonomy phase, sometimes known as the "terrible twos," the world becomes the child's new frontier, ready to be discovered and explored. Less dependent on the caregiver, then, the child develops an individual orientation to the world. Does the orientation attempt to actively modify the child's environment or passively develop a tendency toward accommodating it? During this phase, the child develops an independent, active disposition or reinforces the dependency that was critical for survival in the earlier stage.

The third phase, replication, relates to the time-limited dimension of nature. More specifically, this phase relates to the replicatory strategies of living organisms. To explain these strategies, Millon borrows from population biology. Millon and Davis (1996, p. 98) wrote, "These strategies relate to what biologists have referred to as an r- or self-propagating strategy, at one polar extreme, and a K- or other-nurturing strategy at the second extreme." A self-propagating strategy represents a pattern that produces multiple offspring, though provides minimal effort in the survival of their progeny; whereas an other-nurturing strategy typifies those who produce few progeny though provide considerable effort to ensure their survival. Assimilation of sexual roles is the developmental task during this pubertal stage, as gender roles emerge and are shaped through interaction with others. An individual's orientation toward self or other denotes this gender identity phase of development. Some personalities emerge, however, with conflicted strategies during this phase, as seen in the compulsive and negativistic personalities (Millon, 1997).

Finally, the fourth phase, abstraction, parallels the intracortical–integration phase of neuropsychological development. It is in this stage that reason and emotion find balance. This stage of abstraction transcends concrete thought, representing events and processes symbolically. Experiences internalized are infinite in number, lifting the individual from the concrete present to symbolically explore the past and future. Unbalanced integration at this stage may result in a lack of self-differentiation and direction in one's life, and as Millon and Davis (1996, p. 106) have noted, "may have wide-ranging consequences for the personality system if they fail to cohere as integrated structures, as in the more severe personality disorders (e.g., borderline and schizotypal)" (p. 106). Table 1-3 illustrates the personality disorder derivatives of the evolutionary model.

Functional and Structural Domains

Millon (1997, p. 18) posed the question, "In what domains should personality disorders be ascribed and therefore assessed?" His evolutionary theory stresses the overall multioperational construct embodied in one's personality. He systematically integrates functional processes and structural attributes across data levels (behavioral, phenomenological intrapsychic, and biophysical) that diagnostic criteria represent. Eight functional and structural domains of the personality have been formulated, embracing all relevant domains of the ecosystem. In developing an 8×14 functional/structural domain (Table 1-4) to describe criteria of the personality disorders, Millon fully captures the essence of each personality style and also allows for comparison and contrast of all personality disorders across each domain.

The functional domain represents how an individual relates to others behaviorally and interpersonally, the characteristic nature of thought processing, and defense mechanisms used. The structural domain includes the individual's perception of self, internalized representations of significant others, organization of the personality system, and how the individual displays emotion. Millon (1997, p. 19) added, "Each domain is a legitimate, but highly contextualized part of a single integrated whole, one that is absolutely necessary if the functional-structural integrity of the organism is to be maintained." Millon's expression of personality disorders across functional and structural domains (Table 1-4) provides critical points of reference for a cohesive understanding of the clinical personality patterns and severe personality pathology.

TABLE 1-3

The Evolutionary Model and Its Personality Disorder Derivatives

	Existential Aim		Replication Strategy		
	Life Enhancement	Life Preservation	Reproductive Propagation	Self–Other	Reproductive Nurturance
	Pleasure–Pain			Self–Other	
Deficiency, imbalance, conflict	Pleasure (low) Pain (low or high)	Pleasure–pain Reversal	Self (low) Other (high)	Self (high) Other (low)	Self–other Reversal
			Personality Disorders		
Adaptation Mode					
Passive: accommodation	Schizoid (low pleasure, low pain) Depressive (high pain, low pleasure)	Masochistic	Dependent	Narcissistic	Compulsive
Active: modification	Avoidant	Sadistic	Histrionic	Antisocial	Negativistic
Structural pathology	Schizotypal	Borderline, paranoid	Borderline	Paranoid	Borderline, paranoid

Source: Millon Clinical Multiaxial Inventory-III Manual, Second Edition, by T. Millon, 1987, Minneapolis, MN: National Computer Systems. Copyright 1997 Dicandrian, Inc. Reprinted with permission.

TABLE 1-4

Expression of Personality Disorders Across the Functional and Structural Domains of Personality: Overview

Disorder	Functional Processes				Structural Attributes			
	Expressive Acts	Interpersonal Conduct	Cognitive Style	Regulatory Mechanisms	Self-Image	Object Representations	Morphologic Organization	Mood/Temperament
Schizoid	Impassive	Unengaged	Impoverished	Intellectualization	Complacent	Meager	Undifferentiated	Apathetic
Avoidant	Fretful	Aversive	Distracted	Fantasy	Alienated	Vexatious	Fragile	Anguished
Depressive	Disconsolate	Defenseless	Pessimistic	Asceticism	Worthless	Forsaken	Depleted	Melancholic
Dependent	Incompetent	Submissive	Naive	Introjection	Inept	Immature	Inchoate	Pacific
Histrionic	Dramatic	Attention-seeking	Flighty	Dissociation	Gregarious	Shallow	Disjointed	Fickle
Narcissistic	Haughty	Exploitive	Expansive	Rationalization	Admirable	Contrived	Spurious	Insouciant
Antisocial	Impulsive	Irresponsible	Deviant	Acting out	Autonomous	Debased	Unruly	Callous
Sadistic	Precipitate	Abrasive	Dogmatic	Isolation	Combative	Pernicious	Eruptive	Hostile
Compulsive	Disciplined	Respectful	Constricted	Reaction formation	Conscientious	Concealed	Compartmentalized	Solemn
Negativistic	Resentful	Contrary	Skeptical	Displacement	Discontented	Vacillating	Divergent	Irritable
Masochistic	Abstinent	Deferential	Diffident	Exaggeration	Undeserving	Discredited	Inverted	Dysphoric
Schizotypal	Eccentric	Secretive	Autistic	Undoing	Estranged	Chaotic	Fragmented	Distraught or insentient
Borderline	Spasmodic	Paradoxical	Capricious	Regression	Uncertain	Incompatible	Split	Labile
Paranoid	Defensive	Provocative	Suspicious	Projection	Inviolable	Unalterable	Inelastic	Irascible

Source: Millon Clinical Multiaxial Inventory-III Manual, Second Edition, by T. Millon, 1987, Minneapolis, MN: National Computer Systems. Copyright 1997 Dicandrian, Inc. Reprinted with permission.

Defining Dysfunction

How do we determine if a personality is dysfunctional? This is a relatively complex question because the differentiation between normal and abnormal personality functioning is difficult at times to see, even for the trained eye. The *DSM-IV* classification system is a helpful guide, classifying the various categories of disorders, though it has its limitations. The judgment of the clinician (based on quantitative and qualitative measures) ultimately is the truest means of making this distinction.

According to the *DSM-IV* (American Psychiatric Association, 1994, p. 630), "the essential feature of a personality disorder is an enduring pattern of inner experience and behavior that deviates markedly from the expectations of the individual's culture and manifested in at least two of the following areas: cognition, affectivity, interpersonal functioning, or impulse control." Millon proposed that pathology results from similar forces as those involved in the development of normal functioning; important differences in the character, timing, and intensity of these influences will lead some individuals to acquire pathological traits and others to develop adaptive traits. Central to our understanding, Millon recognizes that normality and pathology are relative concepts, each representing arbitrary points on a continuum. To help clarify the differences between normality and pathology, Millon (1981) presents three interdependent criteria that characterize a pathological condition.

ADAPTIVE INFLEXIBILITY

This feature refers to an inappropriately rigid strategy that an individual uses in relation to the environment—interpersonally, socially, and cognitively. The individual is unable to adapt effectively to life's circumstances and arranges the environment specifically to avoid events perceived as stressful. As a consequence, the individual's opportunities for learning new, more adaptive behaviors are narrowed, with life situations becoming even more rigidly defined (Millon, 1981).

The behaviors and cognitions of the *compulsive-disordered personality* depict this feature. The rigidity, constriction, and controlled behavior prevent the compulsive individual from trying new and creative responses in reaction to the stressful demands of life. The compulsive individual becomes "trapped," vacillating between conformity on one hand and autonomy on the other. In the face of life's stressors, the compulsive individual persists in using repetitive behaviors, preventing the possibilities for effective, practicable solutions.

TENUOUS STABILITY

Some individuals experience a fragility or lack of resilience under conditions of subjective stress. Faced with recurrent failures and an inability to develop new strategies, these individuals are likely to revert to former pathological ways of coping. They are extremely susceptible to new difficulties and disruptions because of their past vulnerability to events. A scarcity of effective coping mechanisms contributes to an individual's continued instability (Millon, 1981).

The overall instability of the *borderline-disordered personality* illustrates this feature well. The borderline individual's emotional state is often intense and unstable and marked by drastic mood swings. Vulnerable to separation anxiety, borderline individuals become increasingly unpredictable when fears of abandonment surface. During episodes of instability, the borderline progressively reinforces the instability by exhibiting intense clinging behavior.

VICIOUS CIRCLES

Although rigidity and inflexibility distinguish normal from pathological patterns, there is also the resultant tendency to foster vicious circles. Modifying one's environment to meet one's needs is normal behavior; however, as Millon (1981, p. 9) noted, "Maneuvers such as protective constriction, cognitive distortion, and behavioral overgeneralization restrict opportunities for new learning, misconstrue essentially benign events, and provoke reactions from others that reactivate earlier problems."

The persistent pessimism of the *depressive-disordered personality* embodies this feature. The depressive individual usually views and relates to the world through distorted negative self-evaluations, and being so perceived, the distorted view of self is "verified." Setting into motion a string of self-defeating sequences, a feedback loop is created, which reinforces original cognitive maneuvers, strengthening and perpetuating an already depressed mood.

As mentioned, Millon depicts a key feature of individual personality as having enduring and pervasive characteristics that are not easily altered. "Clinical signs in *personality disorders* (PD) reflect the operation of a pattern of deeply embedded and pervasive characteristics of functioning, that is, a system of traits that systematically 'support' one another, and color and manifest themselves automatically in all facets of the individual's everyday life" (Millon, 1999, p. 112).

THE STORY OF PROFESSOR PNIN

In the novel *Pnin*, Vladimir Nabokov (1957/1985) illustrated dysfunctional behavior as found in the compulsive pattern—a pattern that can reflect normal, healthy characteristics. Through the title character Pnin, compulsive-disordered behavior is demonstrated to be a self-destructive and maladaptive pattern.

The compulsive individual is a conscientious, efficient, and perfectionistic personality. Every detail is meticulously planned, and every decision is heavily weighed. The story opens with Professor Timofey Pnin traveling by train to Cremona to give a lecture in a language he has never mastered. Excessively compulsive, he maps out every detail of his planned trip, to include preparing a verbatim text for the lecture. Almost comically, though tragic, the conductor tells him the train no longer stops at Cremona, as it inexorably moves down the track. The train schedule he has had for five years is outdated. Eventually, he finds an alternate means of transportation—a bus—to reach his destination for the purpose of delivering a lecture. Misstep begets misstep, as he realizes he does not have the claim ticket to retrieve his Gladstone bag that contained his black suit for the lecture, as well as his other papers. Content to retrieve the bag on his return trip, he boards the bus and is relieved that he could arrive for the lecture on time. In the end, his meticulous planning is, however, ineffectual. After seating himself on the bus, he reaches for his lecture that was safely tucked into his coat pocket, only to discover it was not the text of his Cremona lecture but instead his student's paper. Maddened, he hastily alights the bus and finds himself in the park of Whitchurch, where his defenses finally break down. He is struck with a panic attack—again. In the pangs of his attack, he reverts to his circumscribed reasoning, which has "worked well" since childhood to maintain control. With restricted reasoning, he wonders if this time it could possibly be pneumonia. Sweating profusely, he rationalizes that he is having a heart attack by recalling similar symptoms from his past. Tragically, with illogical, constrained thinking, he comforts himself in his mistaken self-diagnosis. In Pnin's world, others were deficient, and it was his self-imposed task to set them right. This conscientious and meticulous person, however, even though doing everything "perfectly," discovers he brought the wrong text to the lecture. His preoccupation with perfectionism ultimately becomes his undoing.

In Summary

We began this chapter by exploring the elusive nature of personality. An appreciation of Millon's typology, we found, leads us in the direction of a clearer understanding of what personality means. We have examined Millon's early conceptions formulated in the biosocial learning theory—a theory that endorses the interplay of both organismic and environmental forces in personality development. His earlier formulations relied heavily on the principle of reinforcement, as well as the three polarities that govern all of mental life: active–passive, self–other, and pleasure–pain.

Over a decade ago, Millon began reconceptualizing his original theory to go beyond the traditional boundaries in psychology. The path he chose was to fundamentally shift from psychology as we know it to an expression that falls somewhat beyond the periphery of its boundaries. He formulated personality in terms of the evolutionary laws of nature. Conceptualizing personality as an integrated system, Millon provides an 8×14 domain matrix through which he expresses personality disorders. With a grasp of his typology, clearer distinctions can be made in understanding the nature of personality, allowing for finer differentiation between normal and abnormal behavior. Let us turn now to the instrument in which his theoretical constructs are applied—the MCMI-III.

Test Yourself Exercises 1

Fill in the Blanks.

Please note: Answers for all chapter exercises are in appendix C.

1. A major theme of Millon's biosocial learning theory is that personality and psychopathology develop as a result of _____ and _____ forces.
2. The tripartite structure used by Millon that governs all of mental life include _____, _____, and _____.
3. According to the biosocial learning theory, _____ may be viewed as complex forms of instrumental behavior, reflecting the kinds of reinforcements an individual has acquired.
4. Most basic learning relevant to personality development may be categorized under three headings: _____, _____, and _____.
5. List the four phases of Millon's evolutionary theory: _____, _____, _____, and _____.

6. The fourth phase of Millon's evolutionary theory parallels the _____ _____ stage of neuropsychological development.
7. Millon views the schizotypal, borderline, and paranoid as structurally _____ personality pathologies.
8. According to the *DSM-IV*, the essential feature of a personality disorder is _____ _____.
9. An individual who adopts a rigid stance in relation to the environment and is unable to adapt effectively describes _____ _____, a criterion that helps to distinguish between normal and abnormal behavior.
10. Professor Pnin could be diagnosed as having _____ _____ disorder.

Quick Quiz

Mark True or False.
_____ 1. Personality is seen currently as a complex pattern of deeply embedded psychological characteristics.
_____ 2. Individual motivations are ultimately aimed in one of two directions—either pleasure or pain.
_____ 3. Compulsive traits can reflect normal, healthy characteristics.
_____ 4. The independent coping style is oriented almost exclusively toward receiving support and nurturance from others.
_____ 5. Effects of stimulus impoverishment at the sensory–attachment stage include apathy and depression.
_____ 6. Millon notes three requisites necessary in the progression of the evolutionary process: that each organism must survive, it must adapt to the environment, and it must reproduce.
_____ 7. Adaptive biological maturation for the most part is contingent on favorable environmental experiences.
_____ 8. The masochistic personality is included under the discordant instrumental style.
_____ 9. Characteristics of one's personality can be easily altered.
_____ 10. The sadistic personality is apt to reverse pleasure and pain.

MCMI-III Composition 2

T he Millon Clinical Multiaxial Inventory-III (MCMI-III) is a proven objective personality assessment instrument and is increasingly becoming a valuable tool among clinical professionals. Clinicians use it for its brevity, theoretical basing, structural characteristics, and three-stage validation framework, and also for its close alignment with the *DSM-IV* (American Psychiatric Association, 1994) classification system. It provides a clear and accurate measure for diagnosing or evaluating personality disorders and pathological syndromes within the psychiatric population. Diagnostic instruments are normally strengthened when they are systematically linked to a comprehensive theory, and herein lies the strength of the MCMI-III. Like a classic musical composition, the MCMI-III is finely orchestrated. Let us take a closer look at its characteristic features.

Characteristic Features of the MCMI-III

The MCMI-III inventory is considerably shorter than other objective personality instruments. Its concise 175-item, true–false self-report format is sufficient to thoroughly assess a full span of clinical patterns and syndromes, yet brief enough (completion time approximately half an hour) to reduce apprehension experienced by particularly anxious and depressed examinees. The MCMI-III is easy to administer and comes in several formats. The test can be administered on paper or taken electronically. A standard form available from National Computer Systems (NCS) is typically used to administer the test. NCS also will compute the scores and provide a clinically detailed, computer-generated narrative report arranged in a multiaxial format. This report includes response tendencies, clinical syndromes, and personality pathology descriptions, with Axis I and Axis II diagnostic recommendations, psychosocial–environmental Axis IV considerations, noteworthy response items, and treatment implications. NCS also makes available telescoring, computerized scoring–interpretation programs, software packages, multilanguage formats, and audiocassettes.

The inventory contains 24 clinical scales arranged into four distinct groups: Clinical Personality Patterns, Severe Personality Pathology, Clinical Syndromes, and Severe Clinical Syndromes (see Exhibit 2-1). In addition, one Validity index and three Modifying indices detect response biases. Items and scale content of the MCMI-III are intricately woven into Millon's evolutionary theory and closely parallel *DSM-IV* criteria. In addition to its theoretical grounding, the close diagnostic consonance with the *DSM-IV* may arguably be its greatest strength. Each of its Axis II scales is an operational measure of Millon's evolutionary model. Using criterion referencing, Millon created anchor base rates (BR) for the scales that are representative of actual clinical prevalence rates of a particular attribute in the psychiatric population. Let us begin with an overview of the scales' construction.

Primary Diagnostic Uses of the MCMI-III

- Mental hospitals
- Outpatient clinics
- Forensic setting
- Substance abuse evaluation
- Correctional institutions
- Marital counseling
- Clinical and experimental research
- Treatment planning and psychotherapy

EXHIBIT 2-1

The MCMI-III Scales

Modifying indices:	
Validity index	(Scale V)
Disclosure	(Scale X)
Desirability	(Scale Y)
Debasement	(Scale Z)
Clinical personality patterns:	
Schizoid	(Scale 1)
Avoidant	(Scale 2A)
Depressive	(Scale 2B)
Dependent	(Scale 3)
Histrionic	(Scale 4)
Narcissistic	(Scale 5)
Antisocial	(Scale 6A)
Sadistic (aggressive)	(Scale 6B)
Compulsive	(Scale 7)
Negativistic (passive–aggressive)	(Scale 8A)
Masochistic (self-defeating)	(Scale 8B)
Severe personality pathology:	
Schizotypal	(Scale S)
Borderline	(Scale C)
Paranoid	(Scale P)
Clinical syndromes:	
Anxiety disorder	(Scale A)
Somatoform disorder	(Scale H)
Bipolar: manic disorder	(Scale N)
Dysthymic disorder	(Scale D)
Alcohol dependence	(Scale B)
Drug dependence	(Scale T)
Posttraumatic stress disorder	(Scale R)
Severe clinical syndromes:	
Thought disorder	(Scale SS)
Major depression	(Scale CC)
Delusional disorder	(Scale PP)

Three-Stage Validation Framework

"The desirability of internally consistent scales is illustrated in the history of psychological assessment inventories" (Millon, 1997, p. 51). Adopting a theory-based strategy, Millon used Loevinger's (1957) three-stage process model of validity. As a result, the MCMI-III construction rigorously underwent a three-stage validation approach: (a) theoretical–substantive, (b) internal–structural, and (c) external–criterion (Millon, 1997). This three-stage process guided the development of the MCMI-III, and throughout construction every effort was made to maximize the MCMI-III's diagnostic concordance with the *DSM-IV*. Therefore, its clinical utility in identifying examinees that have particular personality disorders makes it a foremost objective instrument among clinicians.

Theoretical–Substantive Validity

The first validation stage establishes a large item pool that reflects the theoretical constructs. The question the test constructor addresses at this stage is, How well do the test items conform to the given theory? The pool of items was generated to conform both to Millon's theoretical framework and specific *DSM-IV* criteria. To enhance correspondence with the *DSM-IV*, new items were created beyond the 175 MCMI-II items. Self-report items were scrutinized by expert judgment and combined into a 325 true–false research form. The items were selected for their consistency with the theoretical design, as well as their ability to be easily understood by the layperson.

Internal–Structural Reliability

This stage examines the association between selected items and scales, evaluating the scales with respect to the constructs defined by Millon's theory. The research form was constructed with data collected from 1079 research participants in 26 U.S. states and Canada. The participants were undifferentiated but representative of psychiatric populations. After the participants were excluded for various reasons (e.g., under the age 18, excessive missing responses, and a greater than 1 score on the Validity index), the final sample was determined. Two additional rules determining invalidity were later implemented. Those who scored below BR 60 on Scales 1-8B and/or had a raw score below 34 or above 178 on the Disclosure index (Scale X) were excluded. Following exclusions, the total sample numbered 998 participants. These participants were then divided into two groups: 600 were assigned to the development sample and 398 to the cross-validation sample (Millon, 1997). Items with unexpectedly high or low endorsement rates were eliminated, and items that were substantively validated were then readministered to participant populations. The items were assigned to their respective construct scales, forming the design of the preliminary MCMI-III scales.

Males made up 48.8% of the sample, and females 51.2%. The majority of participants were White (86.3%), followed by Black (8.7%), Hispanic (2.8%), Native American (1%), Asian (.3%), and other participants (.8%). The age ranged from 18 to 88, with the largest group of 33.2% between the ages of 26 to 35. Approximately 82% completed a high school education, with almost 20% having received a college degree or beyond. The outpatient population was almost 50%, and inpatient mental health participants totaled approximately 27%, with correctional inmates making up 8.5%. The demographics of the cross-validation sample approximated those of the development sample, varying by only a few percentage points in certain areas (Millon, 1997).

Millon's procedure was iterative—that is, a process in which all of the statistics were reevaluated simultaneously, adding and removing items from their selective scales on the basis of statistical (internal and external) and substantive (*DSM-IV* and Millon's recent theory) criteria (Millon, 1997). Two basic issues are addressed at this point in the process: internal consistency and the stability of the test over time. The reported item intercorrelations were limited to the cross-validation sample ($N = 398$).

Internal Consistency

These measures are generally obtained through the use of Cronbach's alpha, with relatively high alphas, though not extremely high, being the preferred measuring gauge. Internal consistency (alpha) coefficients for the clinical scales range from .66 for Scale 7 (Compulsive) to .90 for Scale CC (Major Depression). Alpha coefficients exceed .80 for 20 of the scales (Millon, 1997). Retzlaff (1998, p. 668) noted, "the internal consistency reliabilities of the MCMI-III scales are the highest in the industry."

Test–Retest Stability

Eighty-seven participants took the MCMI-II-R a second time within 5 to 14 days of the initial administration. Test–retest reliabilities were very high, ranging from .82 on Scale Z (Debasement index) to .96 on Scale H (Somatoform disorder). The median stability coefficient was .91, suggesting the results are stable over a short period of time (Millon, 1997).

UNDERSTANDING RELIABILITY AND VALIDITY

With reference to reliability, the test constructor wants to determine that the test is consistent. A test is reliable if it produces the same scores consistently by the same individuals when retaking the test, or with different sets of equivalent items, or under variable testing conditions. For example, consider a stopwatch. A stopwatch that yields the same timed results in race after race, we can say, is a reliable measure; by this we mean, it yields the same results with repeated uses. Our first question then asks, How consistent a measure do we have?

Next, the test constructor must ensure that the sample items in the test accurately and thoroughly represent the domain to be presented. In other words, does the test actually measure—and how well does it measure—what it is designed to measure? We can say, for example, that a thermometer can provide reliable readings as the mercury rises or falls with relation to the temperature. If, however, the temperature markings are not properly labeled along the sides of the instrument, the thermometer cannot provide an accurate temperature reading, in which case it is not a valid measure. Validity, then, answers the question, "Does the test accurately measure what it is supposed to measure?"

External–Criterion Validity

The external–criterion stage contains items that have withstood the rigors of the earlier phases. As Millon (1997, p. 67) noted, "[this] stage of validation is intended to ensure that an instrument's scales have value in the real world." During this stage, the validity of the MCMI-III scale scores was assessed by calculating correlations between base-rate scores for each scale against other instruments with similar constructs and by using a hit rate analysis against clinician's ratings of psychiatric patients. Such data are fully illustrated in the *MCMI-III Manual* (1997); notable correlations follow.

External Correlations

Correlations measured between the MCMI-III and collateral instruments were found to be high and appropriate (Retzlaff, 1998). Measuring the Beck Depression Inventory (BDI) against the scales, correlations of .56 were obtained on the Depressive and Borderline scales, and .53 on the Masochistic and Schizoid scales. The Major Depression and Dysthymia scales correlated highest, with .74 and .71 respectively. Likewise, the MMPI-2 Depression scale posits a strong correlation with the MCMI-III Major Depression (.71) and Dysthymia (.68) scales. MCMI-III Axis II disorders, however, correlated fairly low to the MMPI-2, with the strongest correlation evidenced between the MMPI-2 Depression scale and MCMI-III Depressive scale (.59). Other instruments used (the General Behavior Inventory, Symptom Checklist-90-Revised, Michigan Alcohol Screening Test, Impact of Events Scale, and the State-Trait Anxiety Inventory) resulted in relatively high correlations when measured against the respective MCMI-III scales (Millon, 1997).

Clinician Ratings

Sixty-seven clinicians acquainted with the MCMI instruments and Millon's evolutionary theory participated in the MCMI-III diagnostic validity study. All had substantial direct contact sessions with the patients they evaluated. Diagnostic efficiency was calculated in terms of first highest personalities and their correspondence to the MCMI-III results as judged by clinicians. The positive predictive power (PPP) statistic represents the percentage of patients having a particular MCMI-III personality scale as the highest in their profile and who were judged by clinicians as having the same disorder as a primary diagnosis (Millon, 1997).

In determining the PPP of the Axis I scales, the question posed is, "To what extent does the BR 85 cutoff rate correctly predict the patient's most prominent syndrome?" Positive predictive power statistics for Axis I range from 33% for Delusional Disorder to 93% for Drug Dependence. Anxiety and Dysthymia achieved positive predictive powers of 75% and 81%, respectively (Millon, 1997).

The diagnostic efficiency for Axis II scales is relatively strong, with the exception of the Depressive, Negativistic, and Masochistic scales, obtaining PPPs of 49%, 39%, and 30%, respectively. Millon (1997) has noted that the relatively low PPP results on these scales may be influenced by the narrow treatment the *DSM-IV* has afforded these constructs. The highest PPPs were obtained on the Dependent (81%) and Compulsive (79%) scales (Millon, 1997).

The Use of Base Rates

Millon recognized the problems encountered with norm-referencing and standardized the MCMI-III using criterion-based referencing. Rather than anchoring cutoff scores to an invariable statistic, criterion referencing directly anchors base-rate cutoff scores to the actual prevalence rates of characteristics measured in the psychiatric population. A BR score, we can say, corresponds to a fixed verisimilitude, or closeness, to the construct that indicates the probability that the individual actually has the diagnosed disorder. Millon's approach, therefore, is much more efficient than the widely used norm-referencing and is preferable because it is truer and more representative of actual clinical prevalence rates.

WHY USE BASE-RATE SCORING?

Millon (1997) originally adopted base-rate scoring specifically to overcome two problems intrinsic to linear T score distributions when used with a personality instrument. First, when computing linear T scores, the same T score elevation (e.g., a score of T 70) represents different percentile values of the population for different scales. In other words, a T score of 70 obtained on one scale is associated with a different percentile rank than the same T score on another scale.

Second, the prevalence rates of the attribute being measured are not taken into account. Linear T scores basically reflect a comparison of the examinee to the standardized population. For example, the linear T score, with the mean set at 50 and a standard deviation of 10, sets a cutoff score of $70T$ (two standard deviations above the mean). It defines approximately 2% of the population, which, in reality, rarely corresponds to the actual prevalence rate of a particular disorder in a particular population. The use of uniform T scores, however, has to some degree addressed these problematic features of the linear T scores.

Base rates reflect the target prevalence rates of particular character-istics measured in the psychiatric population. The prevalence rates for the scales were determined by calculating the number of times clini-cians' ratings indicated the presence or prominence of the characteristic traits represented in the MCMI-III clinical scales in the clinical popula-tion. Researched base-rate anchor-point cutoff scores were adjusted to epidemiological prevalence rate studies of the characteristics measured, forming the basis for the development of the base-rate transformation scores. Specific cutoffs along a continuum were developed, designating the presence of traits or disorders, and prominent or present syndromes, as measured within the psychiatric population. Exhibit 2-2 illustrates the base-rate anchor points used by Millon.

Base-rate scoring measures the severity of a disorder on a contin-uum, indicating the prevalence rates of the particular condition. Anchor cutoffs were set at critical points. BR 60 was set as the median score obtained by psychiatric patients; BR 75 was set for the definite presence, though not the primary problem, of the patients; and BR 85 was set as the point at which the condition was judged as the predominant problem.

Elevations on the clinical scales are clinically significant when ele-vated at the base-rate 75 level and beyond. For the personality disorders (Scales 1 through P), BR 75 indicates the probability that the examinee has the particular trait, and BR 85 and beyond suggests the presence of a disorder. For the clinical syndromes (Scales A through PP), BR 75 indicates the presence of a syndrome, and BR 85 the prominence of a syndrome. Within each scale, Millon developed a weighting system to identify the items that are most central to the definition of his personal-ity construct. A weighting of 2 is given to the central or prototypical items, and a weighting of 1 is given to those that are more peripheral to the defined construct. Because the MCMI-III's construction sought consonance with the official nosology of the *DSM-IV*, prototypical items directly reflect *DSM-IV* diagnostic criteria. Let us consider an example.

EXHIBIT 2-2

MCMI-III Base-Rate Anchor Prevalence Points

BR 60: *Median score for the psychiatric population*
BR 75: *Presence of a particular characteristic measured*
Indicates the presence of a trait
Indicates the presence of a syndrome
BR 85: *Predominant characteristic measured as primary problem*
Indicates the presence of a disorder
Indicates the prominence of a syndrome

A male examinee, for instance, who endorses six prototypical items (17, 38, 53, 101, 113, and 139)—that is, marks six keyed items in the true direction on the Antisocial scale (6A), obtains a raw score of 12. This raw score transforms into a base rate of 75.

In this case, a BR 75 on Scale 6A is clinically significant and suggests a high probability of the presence of an antisocial personality trait. Additional clinically significant elevations may likely be found on the Alcohol Dependence scale (Scale B) or Drug Dependence scale (Scale T) on Axis I, because of a strong covariation between antisocial and substance abuse disorders. (Additional discussion on scale interpretation is presented in chapters 5 and 6.) Suffice it to say, elevations obtained by the examinee between BR 75 to 84 inclusive indicate the likelihood of the presence of a trait or syndrome, and elevations of BR 85 and beyond indicate the presence of a disorder or prominence of a syndrome.

MCMI-III Scales: A Brief Overview

The inventory contains 27 scales and a Validity index. Its 24 clinical scales are arranged into four distinct groups: Clinical Personality Patterns, Severe Personality Pathology, Clinical Syndromes, and Severe Clinical Syndromes. The three scales of the Modifying indices and the Validity index (three items) measure response biases. In addition, the MCMI-III item pool contains six areas called *noteworthy responses* (critical items). They provide supplemental information for the clinical scales. Now let us take a moment to acquaint ourselves with a brief description of each scale.

VALIDITY INDEX

The Validity index (Scale V) contains three items and detects random or deviant responding. The items, such as, "I have not seen a car in the last ten years"—(item 157; Millon, 1997)—depict highly improbable occurrences among the normal population. If two or more—items 65, 110, and 157—are marked true, the test is invalidated.

MODIFYING INDICES

The Modifying indices component comprises three scales: Disclosure, Desirability, and Debasement. Although the majority of examinees are truthful and candid in their responses, some examinees will attempt to influence the results of the instrument. If an examinee is not truthful, the clinician must determine whether such records are intentionally contaminated (e.g., random responding) or unintentionally contaminated (e.g., inability to comprehend the questions). For accurate interpretation of the MCMI-III, the examiner must be assured that the examinee responds to the inventory in an honest and candid manner. Millon developed these scales for that purpose.

Disclosure Index (Scale X)

The Disclosure index detects whether an examinee's response style is open and candid or secretive and reticent. Its score is derived from the composite raw score of the Clinical Personality Patterns (Scales 1–8B). The Disclosure index includes an adjustment factor to be used if the response style deviates from the midrange adjusted raw scores values.

Desirability Index (Scale Y)

The Desirability index measures the degree to which an examinee is inclined to adopt a favorable image, projecting an appearance of being socially acceptable and emotionally sound. Scale Y contains 21 items.

Debasement Index (Scale Z)

The Debasement index measures the opposite tendency measured by Scale Y: an attempt to appear emotionally disturbed by deprecating and devaluing oneself. Scale Z contains 33 items.

Clinical Personality Patterns Scales

The MCMI-III Clinical Personality Patterns scales parallel Axis II personality disorders of the *DSM-IV*, except for four scales. The Sadistic and Masochistic (Self-Defeating) scales, included in the *DSM-III-R*, were not extended to the *DSM-IV* classification; and the Depressive and Negativistic (Passive–Aggressive) scales are appended in *DSM-IV* as criteria sets requiring further study. The following brief summaries highlight the essential features of each Clinical Personality Patterns scale.

SCHIZOID (SCALE 1)

Schizoid personalities are marked by a pervasive pattern of social detachment and emotional withdrawal. They are typically indifferent to the needs of others and lack social support systems. Scale 1 contains 16 items.

AVOIDANT (SCALE 2A)

As the Avoidant scale implies, this scale measures a strong tendency to avoid others, primarily as a result of fears of anticipated rejection. An anxious pattern of social inhibition is present. Scale 2A contains 16 items.

DEPRESSIVE (SCALE 2B)

Key features of the depressive personality include pervasive and enduring feelings of pessimism, gloom, and unhappiness. This scale is appended in the *DSM-IV* as criteria sets requiring further study. Scale 2B contains 15 items.

DEPENDENT (SCALE 3)

Individuals who demonstrate a submissive clinging to others for guidance, nurturance, and security, while foregoing their own autonomy, are high scorers on the Dependent scale. Scale 3 contains 16 items.

HISTRIONIC (SCALE 4)

Essential features of the Histrionic scale include a manipulative pattern of attention-seeking, through gregarious and socially engaging behaviors. Scale 4 contains 17 items.

NARCISSISTIC (SCALE 5)

Individuals who display a self-centered disposition that is coupled with a need for admiration score high on the Narcissistic scale. An overvaluation of self-worth produces an arrogant and assuming demeanor. Scale 5 contains 24 items.

ANTISOCIAL (SCALE 6A)

A pervasive disregard for values and standards of society, coupled with a callous indifference to the feelings and rights of others, are characteristics of high scorers on the Antisocial scale. Scale 6A contains 17 items.

SADISTIC (SCALE 6B)

Alternately known as the aggressive personality, the Sadistic scale is perceived more broadly than simply sexual sadism and is marked by underlying feelings of hostility. Such individuals are highly combative and abusive in interrelationships. This pattern has not been extended into the *DSM-IV* classification. Scale 6B contains 20 items.

COMPULSIVE (SCALE 7)

A conscientious, accommodating pattern, highly suggestive of perfectionism, describes high scores on the Compulsive scale. Elevations on this scale, however, should not be confused with the obsessive–compulsive disorder classified on Axis I in the *DSM-IV*. Scale 7 contains 17 items.

NEGATIVISTIC (SCALE 8A)

Alternately known as the passive–aggressive personality, an elevation on the Negativistic scale commonly displays an underlying resentfulness through indirect or passive behaviors. This personality pattern is classified in the *DSM-IV* classification as criteria sets requiring further study. Scale 8A contains 16 items.

MASOCHISTIC (SCALE 8B)

The masochistic personality is marked by a sacrificial demeanor, content to serve the needs of others. Devaluation of self is pervasive, exhibiting martyr-like behaviors. Alternately classified in the *DSM-III-R* as self-defeating, this personality was not extended into the *DSM-IV*. Scale 8B contains 15 items.

Severe Personality Pathology Scales

The MCMI-III includes three Severe Personality Pathology scales: Schizotypal, Borderline, and Paranoid. They are classified as personality disorders in the *DSM-IV*. Millon's theory proposes that the severity of these scales indicates a marked difference from the basic personality patterns in both degree and kind.

SCHIZOTYPAL (SCALE S)

Cognitive confusion, perceptual distortion, and interpersonal detachment are characteristics representative of schizotypal disorder. Mild forms of schizophrenia may be evidenced as elevations increasingly rise. Scale S contains 16 items.

BORDERLINE (SCALE C)

The essential features marking the borderline disorder are a pervasive pattern of unstable interpersonal relationships and labile emotions. Underlying this instability, two precipitants may coexist: a confused self-image and an overwhelming fear of abandonment. Scale C contains 16 items.

PARANOID (SCALE P)

The key aspects of the paranoid personality disorder are suspiciousness and mistrust of others. Fear of losing independence and being controlled by others mark this pattern. Scale P contains 17 items.

Clinical Syndromes Scales

MCMI-III clinical syndromes represent disorders of moderate severity that are classified in the *DSM-IV* as Axis I syndromes. Millon suggests that these syndromes are best understood as disorders embedded in an individual's basic personality pattern and should be assessed in that context. Though relatively distinct and transient in nature, elevated scores serve to accentuate the basic personality disorder.

KEEP IN MIND

Millon (1997) noted that MCMI-III normative data and transformation scores are based entirely on clinical samples and are designed for use only with those individuals evidencing problematic and interpersonal symptoms.

ANXIETY DISORDER (SCALE A)

Feelings of anxiety, tension, and apprehension are measured by the Anxiety Disorder scale. Somatic symptoms and phobic reactions may be present when scores are elevated. Scale A contains 14 items.

SOMATOFORM DISORDER (SCALE H)

The Somatoform Disorder scale identifies individuals manifesting physical symptoms, with no apparent evidence stemming from a physiological basis. The *DSM-IV* distinguishes among seven types of somatoform disorders, of which hypochondriasis and somatization disorder are classifications. Scale H contains 12 items.

BIPOLAR: MANIC DISORDER (SCALE N)

Bipolar: Manic Disorder Syndrome is characterized by persistent, elevated, expansive, and irritable mood during a distinct episode. Descriptively, most scale items of the MCMI-III depict a hypomanic episode. Scale N contains 13 items.

DYSTHYMIC DISORDER (SCALE D)

Depressed mood for at least two years characterizes the Dysthymic Disorder Syndrome. Symptoms include insomnia, loss of appetite, low self-esteem, apathy, fatigue, and poor concentration. Scale D contains 14 items.

ALCOHOL DEPENDENCE (SCALE B)

Problems associated with alcohol are likely present as elevations increase. High elevations on the Alcohol Dependence scale usually signal problems in family and work settings. Scale B contains 15 items.

DRUG DEPENDENCE (SCALE T)

Similar to the Alcohol Dependence scale, high elevations on the Drug Dependence scale suggest a history of drug dependence. As with Scale B, this scale contains indirect, subtle items. Scale T contains 14 items.

POST-TRAUMATIC STRESS DISORDER (SCALE R)

The Post-Traumatic Stress Disorder scale was added to the MCMI-III. The scale measures the display of defined symptoms of anxious arousal for at least one month after experiencing a traumatic event that is outside the range of natural experience (e.g., combat, rape, etc.). The characteristic symptoms are specified in the *DSM-IV*. Scale R contains 16 items.

Severe Clinical Syndromes Scales

The three severe Clinical Syndromes scales—Thought Disorder, Major Depression, and Delusional Disorder—reflect syndromes of marked severity and are categorized by Millon as a distinct group. As with the Clinical Syndromes, Severe Syndromes accentuate and intensify features underlying basic personality patterns (Millon, 1997).

THOUGHT DISORDER (SCALE SS)

Schizophrenia or other major psychoses are indicated with high elevations on the Thought Disorder scale. Fragmented thinking, blunted affect, disorganized behavior, and withdrawn–seclusion are most notable characteristics. Scale SS contains 17 items.

MAJOR DEPRESSION (SCALE CC)

High elevations on the Major Depression scale suggest an inability to adequately function in a normal environment. A marked affective disorder, characterized by depressed mood most of the day, suicidal ideation, and an overwhelming sense of hopelessness, is likely present in high scorers. Scale CC contains 17 items.

DELUSIONAL DISORDER (SCALE PP)

Central characteristics of the Delusion Disorder scale include nonbizarre and logical delusions in individuals who are acutely paranoid. Disturbed thinking and ideas of reference may be present. Scale PP contains 13 items.

Noteworthy Responses: Additional Information Fields

Although not distinct scales, noteworthy responses are supplemental categories that can support hypotheses derived from elevations of particular scales. Each noteworthy response category contains a set of critical items used to identify select problem areas. For example, item 4, "I feel weak and tired much of the time," is listed under health preoccupation. Items marked true are considered relevant to a particular noteworthy response category. Millon classifies six supplemental categories of responses that identify problem areas for consideration: health preoccupation, interpersonal alienation, emotional dyscontrol, self-destructive potential, childhood abuse, and eating disorder. The items included in each category are found in appendix E of the *MCMI-III Manual, Second Edition* (1997).

In Summary

This chapter presents an overview of the MCMI-III scale composition. Note that its brief 175-item format and straightforward approach provides the clinician with a valuable means of efficient and effectual objective assessment. The MCMI-III is systematically organized into six sections, with close alignment to the *DSM-IV* classifications. Its base-rate anchoring provides a truer representation of the prevalence of disorders in the target population than norm-referencing. Millon operationalized his theory through a three-stage validity framework, ensuring the MCMI-III's reliability and validity. Based on this validation process, Millon verified that the MCMI-III scales are indeed true to his theoretical constructs. Now that we have an overview of the MCMI-III, we will discuss the general guidelines for administering and scoring this instrument.

Test Yourself Exercises 2

Fill in the Blanks.

1. The MCMI-III contains _____ clinical scales, _____ Modifying indices, and _____ Validity index.
2. The _____ index detects whether an examinee is open and candid in responding to the MCMI-III.
3. The _____ personality is marked by a pervasive pattern of social detachment and emotional withdrawal.
4. Individuals who exhibit physical symptoms with no apparent evidence stemming from a physiological basis most likely have an elevated _____ scale.

5. High elevations on Scale _____ suggest a possible diagnosis of schizophrenia.
6. Base rate _____ defines the median score for the psychiatric population.
7. The three sequential components of Millon's test development and validation framework are _____, _____, and _____.
8. Measures of internal consistency are generally obtained using _____ alpha.
9. The use of the MCMI-III should be limited to the _____ population.
10. _____ is preferable to the more widely used norm-referencing because it is more representative of actual clinical prevalence rate of the attribute being measured.

Quick Quiz

Mark True or False.

_____ 1. The MCMI-III provides an accurate measure in diagnosing personality disorders and pathological syndromes within the psychiatric population.
_____ 2. In the MCMI-III, nonprototypic items receive a weighting of 2.
_____ 3. The diagnostic consonance, which the MCMI-III shares with the *DSM-IV* classification system, may arguably be its greatest strength.
_____ 4. The Validity index comprises three items: 65, 110, and 157.
_____ 5. The MCMI-III contains seven supplemental fields of information known as noteworthy responses.
_____ 6. The MCMI-III construction was based on a representative, but undifferentiated, sample of psychiatric populations.
_____ 7. Millon standardized the MCMI-III by using the norm-referencing approach.
_____ 8. BR 75 indicates the presence of a trait or syndrome.
_____ 9. Reliability addresses the question, Does a test actually measure what it is designed to measure?
_____ 10. The MCMI-III uses two types of reliability measures: internal consistency and test–retest.

Scale Identification

Write in the corresponding MCMI-III scale number/letter(s) for each of the following:

_____	Debasement	_____	Delusional Disorder
_____	Major Depression	_____	Anxiety Disorder
_____	Desirability	_____	Sadistic
_____	Dependent	_____	Depressive
_____	Thought Disorder	_____	Schizotypal
_____	Schizoid	_____	Disclosure
_____	Borderline	_____	Avoidant
_____	Narcissistic	_____	Masochistic
_____	Paranoid	_____	Alcohol Dependence
_____	Somatoform Disorder	_____	Drug Dependence
_____	Antisocial	_____	Negativistic

_____ Compulsive   _____ Histrionic

_____ Dysthymic Disorder   _____ Bipolar Manic Disorder

_____ Post-Traumatic Stress Disorder

General Guidelines for Administering and Scoring 3

T o provide meaningful data for both clinical and research uses, the MCMI-III must be properly administered and correctly scored. Test scores must accurately reflect the individual's true condition. Although the MCMI-III is a psychometrically sound and clinically useful instrument, improper administration and scoring can undermine its effectiveness. A prime responsibility of the MCMI-III examiner is to ensure that the standardized instructions and procedures are always followed carefully when administering the MCMI-III, as well as any other instrument. According to Principle 8 in *Casebook on Ethical Principles of Psychologists:*

> In the development, publication, and utilization of psychological assessment techniques, psychologists make every effort to promote the welfare and best interests of the client. They guard against misuse of assessment results. They respect the client's right to know the results, the interpretations made, and the basis for their conclusions and recommendations. Psychologists make every effort to maintain the security of tests and other assessment techniques within limits of legal mandates. They strive to ensure the appropriate use of assessment techniques by others. (American Psychological Association, 1987, p. 109)

Guidelines for Administration

An entire chapter can be devoted to a discussion of the proper procedural steps for test administration in general. However, such a review is beyond the scope of our presentation. In this section we will limit our focus to the general guidelines and procedural information for administering the MCMI-III. Before administering the MCMI-III, then, it is important for the beginning student to become acquainted with the various MCMI-III formats (available in English and Spanish), to include audiocassette recordings. If administered properly, all formats will yield comparable results. Let us begin with an overview of the general administration guidelines.

PROVIDE CLEAR AND STANDARDIZED INSTRUCTIONS

The test directions are clearly printed on the second page of the MCMI-III hand-scoring test booklet published by National Computer Systems (NCS). Remember that standardization implies uniform procedures. Sufficient time should be taken at the onset to present clear and standardized instructions to the examinee. It is my customary practice to ask the examinee to read the instructions privately before beginning the test, and, after addressing any questions, follow with a review of the printed procedures.

- Self-report inventory. As with other objective personality instruments, the MCMI-III functions as a "self-report" inventory and should never be construed as a self-administered inventory. A trained clinical professional should be available to the examinee before, during, and after the administration to respond to any concerns. However, the test items should be answered with no coaching assistance from the examiner. Although the examinee is encouraged to complete all items, undecided items by the examinee should be marked in the false direction rather than omitted. In addition, because it is a self-report inventory, the true results of the MCMI-III are contingent on the examinee's ability to respond to its items. In that light, the examiner should ensure that the examinee's condition (e.g., sedated or intoxicated) is not a cause for a distorted protocol.
- Administration location. The inventory should be administered in a well-lighted, quiet environment, one that is free from distrac-

tions. The optimal location is a quiet office removed from the activity of a busy workplace, where the examinee can be as comfortable and relaxed as possible. The logistics of the location should be identified beforehand to avoid unnecessary stressors for both the examiner and examinee at the time of testing.

- Examinee characteristics. The MCMI-III has been designed for use by adults who have at least an eighth-grade reading level. Ensure that the examinee is capable of adequately reading the questions before the actual test administration. If reading problems are suspected and determined to be limited, an audiocassette recording can be administered in place of the written format. This format can also be used for visually impaired individuals.

- Equipment. Instruct the examinee to use a number 2 black lead pencil for marking the answer form, and provide the examinee a hard surface on which to take the test, particularly when the MCMI-III is scored by computer. If a hard surface desk is not available, provide the examinee with a hard-covered textbook to place beneath the answer sheet.

- Demographic data. Before starting the test, ensure that gender and all necessary requested demographic information are accurately entered by the examinee on the answer sheet. If gender information is not specified, the instrument cannot be scored. The examiner may assist the examinee in completing the required data. To protect confidentiality, identification numbers are used in place of names on the computer-scored forms.

- Review of data information. As a general practice, it is best to review the information in the presence of the examinee immediately following the completion of the instrument. A thorough review of the answer sheet is necessary at this time not only to check for required data information but also to scan for excessive item omissions and random responding (e.g., all true/all false). If errors or excessive omissions (12 or more) are found, the materials should be returned to the examinee to allow for corrections. At this time, the examiner can also address other concerns that the examinee may have about the instrument, as well as in general terms describe the process that will follow.

- Administration time. Most people take about a half an hour to complete the instrument. Be flexible, however, and allow the examinee to work at a comfortable pace. The examinee's test-taking responses, as well as administrative time required, will vary according to the individual's state. Response times of anxious or impulsive clients may differ appreciably from depressed clients or those with limited intelligence.

TAKING AND SCORING THE TEST

As previously mentioned, the MCMI-III is available in several formats. Examinees can complete the inventory by using paper and pencil or computer. With the advances in computerization today, more mental health facilities are equipped with computerized testing equipment. In this case individuals directly enter their responses into the computer, with scores and reports automatically generated. If the MCMI-III is administered by computer, care should be taken to ensure that the examinee is comfortable with the automated testing process. A basic familiarity with computer use is recommended when this procedure is used.

If, however, conventional test-taking (paper and pencil) is preferred, examinees can mark their responses on an answer sheet. These answer sheets can then be scanned through optical mark reading or key-entered into the computer for processing. Mail-in processing is also available with the purchase of prepaid answer sheets.

The speed and accuracy of computer-assisted administration, scoring, and report preparation make it more practical and efficient than processing by hand. There are several MCMI-III processing options available from NCS to include telescoring, mail-in scoring, and individual software. All testing formats are published and distributed exclusively by NCS.

HAND-SCORING PROCEDURE

Hand-scoring the MCMI-III can be complex and tedious. Diligence should be used to avoid unnecessary transformation, recording, and calculation errors. The hand-scoring materials provided by NCS must be used when hand-scoring the MCMI-III. The following materials are required for hand-scoring the MCMI-III and are included in the hand-scoring starter kits:

- Answer sheet
- *Hand-Scoring User's Guide*
- Answer keys
- Hand-scoring worksheet
- Profile form
- *MCMI-III Manual, Second Edition*, 1997, NCS

The MCMI-III hand-scoring worksheet (Exhibit 3-1) is functionally designed to assist the clinician in scoring the results. The examiner's review of the completed answer sheet should be thorough, rechecking all necessary information. The first-time user should become familiar with the systematic layout of the hand-scoring worksheet.

When hand-scoring is used, the examiner should exercise diligence to ensure against scoring errors. Hand-scoring can be a complex procedure. The more common errors the scorer can make include

- Use of incorrect templates
- Use of incorrect BR scores when adjusting scores
- Use of incorrect transformation tables
- Miscalculation

Although computerized administration and scoring are available, it is suggested that a first-time user hand-score at least one protocol, not only to gain familiarity with the instrument but also to understand the logical process involved in the scoring system. The first-time user is provided the following general scoring guidelines. Note that these guidelines are general in nature and not a substitute for the complete scoring procedures that are published and distributed by NCS.

INITIAL VALIDITY CHECK

The examiner should be aware that excessive omissions and double-marked responses (12 or more) will invalidate the instrument. Note, also, the responses to the three validity items: 65, 110, and 157. If no more than one response is marked true and no excessive number of omissions/double-marked items or random responding is detected, the profile can be scored.

- If scored by optical scanning, thoroughly check the answer sheet to determine that it is acceptable for optical scanning (e.g., no markings outside the response circles, no perforations). After visual review, the answer sheet is ready to be mailed to NCS for scoring and interpretation.
- If scored by hand, the MCMI-III hand-scoring worksheet is functionally designed to assist the examiner in providing an accurate record. The scorer is instructed to follow the hand-scoring worksheet's layout and directions exactly throughout the course of hand-scoring.

EXHIBIT 3-1

MCMI-III Hand-Scoring Worksheet

MCMI-III™
Millon™ Clinical
Multiaxial Inventory-III
by Theodore Millon, PhD, DSc, with Carrie Millon, PhD, and Roger Davis, PhD

Copyright © 1990, 1994 DICANDRIEN, INC. All rights reserved. Published and distributed exclusively by NATIONAL COMPUTER SYSTEMS, INC., P. O. Box 1416, Minneapolis, MN 55440.
Printed in the United States of America.
"Millon" and "MCMI-III" are trademarks of DICANDRIEN, INC.

Hand-Scoring Worksheet

NAME _____

AGE _____ RACE _____ GENDER _____ DATE TESTED ___/___/___

SETTING _____

DURATION OF AXIS I EPISODE _____

RAW X SCORE CALCULATION

6 – 2:

6 – 3:   _____ X .6667   =
         Raw 5

6 – 4:   Sum of the Results = _____

         Rounded off = _____
                          Raw X

RESULTS OF INDIVIDUAL STEPS

_____ Raw 1

_____ Raw 2A

_____ Raw 2B

_____ Raw 3

_____ Raw 4

_____

_____ Raw 6A

_____ Raw 6B

_____ Raw 7

_____ Raw 8A

_____ Raw 8B

NCS ®

Product Number
33010

C D E

Source: MCMI-III Hand-Scoring Worksheet by T. Millon, 1990, Minneapolis, MN: National Computer Systems. Copyright 1990, 1994 Dicandrian, Inc. Reprinted with permission.

MCMI–III Hand-Scoring Worksheet

V Validity ☐

ADJUSTMENT VALUES	Disclosure 1–8B Adjustment	Disclosure S–PP Adjustment	A/D 2B, 8B, C Adjustment	A/D 2A, S Adjustment	SS Impatient Adjustment	CC Impatient Adjustment	PP Impatient Adjustment	Denial/ Complaint Adjustment

MODIFYING INDICES	Raw Score	BR From Table	Adjusted BRs	Adjusted BRs	Adjusted BRs	Adjusted BRs	Adjusted BR	Adjusted BR	Adjusted BR	Adjusted BRs	Final BR Score
X Disclosure											
Y Desirability											
Z Debasement											

CLINICAL PERSONALITY PATTERNS	Raw Score	BR From Table	Adjusted BRs	Adjusted BRs	Adjusted BRs	Adjusted BRs	Adjusted BR	Adjusted BR	Adjusted BR	Adjusted BRs	Final BR Score
1 Schizoid											
2A Avoidant											
2B Depressive											
3 Dependent											
4 Histrionic											
5 Narcissistic											
6A Antisocial											
6B Sadistic (Aggressive)											
7 Compulsive											
8A Negativistic (Passive-Aggressive)											
8B Masochistic (Self-Defeating)											

SEVERE PERSONALITY PATHOLOGY	Raw Score	BR From Table	Adjusted BRs	Adjusted BRs	Adjusted BRs	Adjusted BRs	Adjusted BR	Adjusted BR	Adjusted BR	Adjusted BRs	Final BR Score
S Schizotypal											
C Borderline											
P Paranoid											

CLINICAL SYNDROMES	Raw Score	BR From Table	Adjusted BRs	Adjusted BRs	Adjusted BRs	Adjusted BRs	Adjusted BR	Adjusted BR	Adjusted BR	Adjusted BRs	Final BR Score
A Anxiety											
H Somatoform											
N Bipolar: Manic											
D Dysthymia											
B Alcohol Dependence											
T Drug Dependence											
R Post-Traumatic Stress Disorder											

SEVERE CLINICAL PATHOLOGY	Raw Score	BR From Table	Adjusted BRs	Adjusted BRs	Adjusted BRs	Adjusted BRs	Adjusted BR	Adjusted BR	Adjusted BR	Adjusted BRs	Final BR Score
SS Thought Disorder											
CC Major Depression											
PP Delusional Disorder											

Determining Raw Scores

Arrange the answer keys in the same order as the scales appear on the worksheet, ensuring that the correct template is used for each of the 26 scales. Note that there is no template for Scale X or for the Validity index (Scale V). Score the darkened circles of each scale, paying attention to the weighted values of each item. All items on Scale Y and Scale Z only receive a weighting of 1, and the rest of the scales (except Scale X) have weightings of 1 and 2. The obtained raw scores with the exception of Scale X are entered and then transformed into base-rate scores.

Scale X Validity Determination

The composite raw score of the 11 Clinical Personality Patterns (Scales 1 through 8B) determines the Disclosure index (Scale X) value. Note that the raw score of Scale 5 is multiplied by .6667. (Scale 5 is weighted by two thirds because of its length.) Profile validity requires the range of Scale X to fall between raw score 34 and raw score 178 inclusive. If raw score Scale X is less than 34 or greater than 178, the profile is invalid and scoring should be discontinued. Note: If the composite raw score of Scales 1 to 8B is not a whole number, rounding the number is necessary. If the decimal number is greater than or equal to 5, round the number up. If the decimal number is less than 5, round the number down.

Base-Rate Transformation Score

Base-rate transformation for Scale X is provided in a separate table. Note that it is the only transformation table that is applicable to both genders. See *MCMI-III Manual, Second Edition* (1997, appendix C-3), For all other scales—1 through PP and Scales Y and Z—use base-rate transformation tables (appendices C-1 and C-2). Be sure to use the correct male/female base-rate transformation tables.

Also, when entering successive base-rate scores on the MCMI-III hand-scoring worksheet, make sure entries are made in proper columns. Cumulative totals are used as each additional adjustment is made.

Base-Rate Adjustments

Millon addressed the effects of response bias, as well as the client's representative state of emotional distress, by developing base-rate adjustments. Four adjustments are used if corrections are necessary. The disclosure adjustment, derived from the obtained raw score of Scale X, is applied to Scales 1 through PP to counter problematic response styles. The anxiety/depression adjustment is applied to Scales 2A, 2B, 8B, S, and C to balance the effects of distortion experienced in acute emotional states. The inpatient adjustment is applied to the severe clinical syndrome scales (SS, CC, and PP) to offset the denial of symptom severity in recently hospitalized patients. The denial/complaint adjustment is applied to Scales 4, 5, or 7 to compensate for psychological defensiveness. These adjustments are fully discussed in appendix D of the *MCMI-III Manual, Second Edition* (1997). Let us briefly examine them.

DISCLOSURE ADJUSTMENT

Problematic responding occurs if Scale X raw score is less than 61 (underreporting) or greater than 123 (overreporting), and adjustment is necessary. Disclosure adjustments (20 to –20) to the scales are made in base-rate values. Locate the correct adjustments, then add/subtract the disclosure adjustment value to/from Scales 1 through PP if an adjustment is required. Note: Use Table 1, "Disclosure Adjustment Values" (*MCMI-III Manual, Second Edition*, 1997, NCS, appendix D, p. 178).

ANXIETY–DEPRESSION (A/D) ADJUSTMENT

The anxiety–depression adjustment is determined by the examinee's base-rate scores on Scale A (Anxiety) and Scale D (Dysthymia) and corrects for acute emotional states. The scales (2A, 2B, 8B, S, and C) most often affected by psychic turmoil are clearly identified on the hand-scoring worksheet. If BR scores for Scale A and/or Scale D are BR 75 or above, Scales 2A, 2B, 8B, S, and C are adjusted (decreased).

The degree of the A/D adjustment is contingent on the setting (non–inpatient or inpatient), as well as the duration of the client's Axis I status. Note: Use Tables 2, 3, and 4, "A/D Adjustment Values" (see *MCMI-III Manual, Second Edition*, NCS, appendix D, pp. 177–180).

INPATIENT (AXIS I DURATION) ADJUSTMENT

The inpatient/Axis I duration adjustment is designed to offset the tendency of recently hospitalized patients to underrate the level of their emotional condition. This correction factor, if applicable, will increase (2 to 10 BR) an examinee's base-rate scores on the Severe Clinical Syndromes scale (SS, CC, PP). Inpatient Axis I duration status and setting determine the adjustment to be applied. If an examinee is not an inpatient or if the examinee is an inpatient whose Axis I presenting problem is present for longer than four weeks, no adjustment is necessary. Note: Use Table 5, "Inpatient/Axis I Duration Status" (see *MCMI-III Manual, Second Edition*, 1997, NCS, appendix D, pp. 179–180).

DENIAL/COMPLAINT ADJUSTMENT

The denial/complaint adjustment compensates for psychological defensiveness among examinees whose highest scale obtained on the Clinical Personality Patterns (Scales 1–8B) is Histrionic (Scale 4), Narcissistic (Scale 5), or Compulsive (Scale 7). If one of these three scales (4, 5, or 7) is the highest elevation obtained among the 11 Personality Patterns scales, 8 BR points are added to only that scale. Note: Use "Denial/Complaint Adjustment" (see *MCMI-III Manual, Second Edition*, 1997, NCS, appendix D, p. 180).

Final BR Score

The final BR scores are the scores that determine scale interpretation. After all necessary adjustments are made, the final base-rate scores must fall between BR 0 and BR 115. Any adjusted scores less than BR 0 should be changed to BR 0; any scores greater than BR 115 should be changed to BR 115. If the final BR scores for each of the Clinical Personality Patterns (Scales 1–8B) are all less than BR 60, the result is a flat profile, and it is thus uninterpretable. That is to say, if no elevations on Scales 1 through 8B are above 59, no clear personality pattern emerges, and no subsequent interpretation should be made. Before interpretation, the final base-rate scores are transferred to the corresponding scales on the profile form.

Profiling

A profile is a chart that graphically depicts the configuration of the base-rate scores obtained by the examinee. Profiling is a simple process that merely requires the plotting of each scale's base-rate score by marking an "X" in the appropriate score location on the hand-scoring profile form. Profiling provides a useful visual representation of the configural relationship among the scale scores. (See Exhibit 3-2.)

Coding

Relevant information for interpreting the MCMI-III protocols is configural in nature. It is, therefore, helpful to index the scale elevations in relation to each other. The process of coding facilitates this procedure by recording the most essential information about a profile in concise form. The rules for coding are found on pages 114 and 115 in the *MCMI-III Manual, Second Edition* (1997). The 24 clinical scales of the MCMI-III are divided into four distinct sections and coded as distinct segments. The first two sections comprise the personality code; the second two sections comprise the syndrome code. Note that the 24 clinical scales are automatically coded on computer-scored profiles.

In Summary

In this chapter, general guidelines were included for administering and scoring the MCMI-III. Although hand-scoring is tedious, it is important for the individual who is learning the instrument to have a basic understanding of the process. Once familiarization with the instrument is acquired, computerized scoring will likely become the preferred choice for scoring the MCMI-III. In addition to accurately scoring the instrument, computer-processed protocols also include a comprehensive report of the results, though a final caveat is in order: Learn well the basic

EXHIBIT 3-2

MCMI-III Hand-Scoring Profile

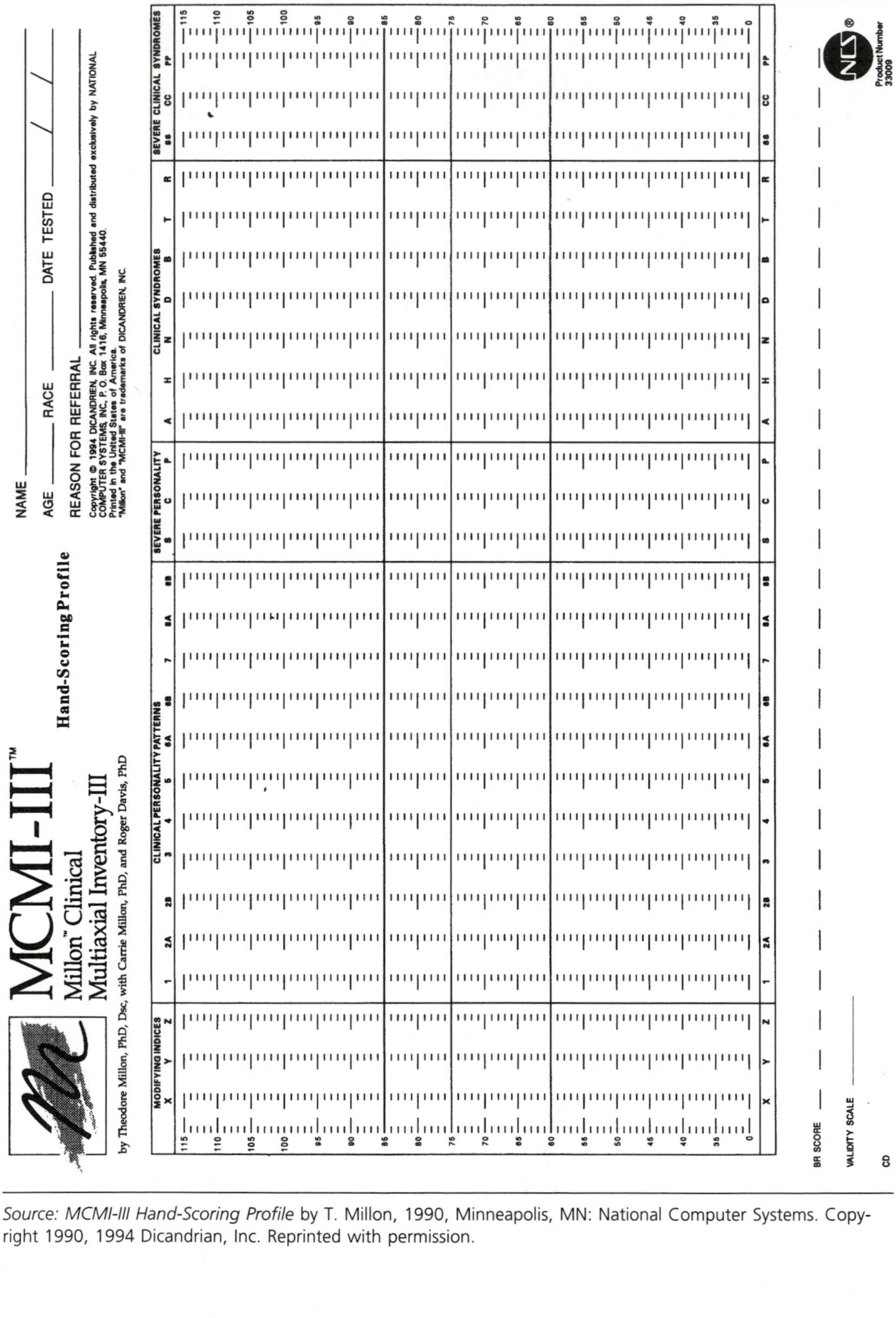

Source: MCMI-III Hand-Scoring Profile by T. Millon, 1990, Minneapolis, MN: National Computer Systems. Copyright 1990, 1994 Dicandrian, Inc. Reprinted with permission.

techniques of interpretation, so that a fuller and richer understanding of the computerized results can be gained. We now turn to the key area of scale interpretation.

Test Yourself Exercises 3

Fill in the Blanks.
1. Clients being administered the MCMI-III should have at least a(n) _____ grade reading level.
2. If the Validity index score totals 2 or 3, the protocol is _____, and the clinician should _____ scoring.
3. Items on Scales Y and Z have weighting values of _____.
4. The _____ scale is the total of the summed raw scores of the 11 Clinical Personality Patterns scales.
5. There is no MCMI-III scoring template for Scale _____.
6. The A/D adjustment is applied to the following scales:
   a. _____   b. _____
   c. _____   d. _____
   e. _____
7. If no A/D adjustment is necessary, a value of _____ is entered in the A/D adjustment box.
8. Scales that make up the denial/complaint adjustment are Scale _____, Scale _____, and Scale _____.
9. If all of the final BR scores for Scales 1 through 8B are less than BR 60, the result is a _____ profile.
10. _____ is the process of plotting each scale's BR score.

Quick Quiz

Mark True or False.
_____ 1. A prime responsibility of the examiner is to ensure that the standardized instructions and procedures are followed carefully when administering the MCMI-III.
_____ 2. The MCMI-III test instructions are clearly printed on the third page of the MCMI-III hand-scoring test booklet.
_____ 3. Virtually anyone who is familiar with the MCMI-III can administer the instrument.
_____ 4. Most people complete the MCMI-III administration in about 1½ hours.
_____ 5. Among the more common errors made when hand-scoring the MCMI-III is using the incorrect gender tables when transforming scores.

_____ 6. The process of coding records the most essential information about a profile in concise form.

_____ 7. The denial/compliant adjustment compensates for psychological defensiveness.

_____ 8. The value of Scale X is derived from the composite raw score of Scales 1 through P.

_____ 9. The inpatient adjustment is designed to balance the tendency of recently hospitalized examinees' denial of their emotional states.

_____ 10. If scores for Scales A and D are both less than BR 75, no A/D adjustment is necessary.

BR Exercise

Transform the following raw scores into final base-rate scores.
(Client is an outpatient female. Validity index = 0).
(1) Calculate Scale X raw score and convert raw scores to BR scores.
(2) Code the profile.

Transform the following raw scores into final base-rate scores.
(Client is an outpatient female. Validity index = 0.)
1. Calculate Scale X raw score and convert raw scores to BR scores.
2. Code the profile.

Scale Y	18	Scale S	4
Scale Z	8	Scale C	8
Scale 1	10	Scale P	12
Scale 2A	13	Scale A	6
Scale 2B	9	Scale H	10
Scale 3	9	Scale N	9
Scale 4	9	Scale D	12
Scale 5	1	Scale B	11
Scale 6A	4	Scale T	9
Scale 6B	10	Scale R	8
Scale 7	23	Scale SS	7
Scale 8A	15	Scale CC	7
Scale 8B	5	Scale PP	4

Interpretation: Validity and the Modifying Indices 4

E nglish novelist Samuel Butler wrote, "I do not mind lying, but I hate inaccuracy." Examinees taking self-report inventories sometimes "twist the truth," rendering accurate profile interpretation difficult. Self-report inventories are occasionally distorted by the examinee, and the MCMI-III is no exception. Motivations vary when taking a test, and some examinees can portray an entirely different picture of themselves than what actually exists. Examinees may deliberately respond in a deceptive way to avoid self-disclosure, whereas others may simply distort the results in an attempt to present a favorable or unfavorable image of themselves.

Fortunately, though, deliberate bias in test-taking is not prevalent, with most examinees approaching the self-report inventory in an open and candid fashion. This chapter discusses the interpretation of an examinee's response styles with regard to obtained scores on the Validity index and Modifying indices of the MCMI-III. Although this chapter is relatively brief in relation to the following interpretive chapters, it is critically valuable. The validity or invalidity of a protocol relies on the candor of the examinee, and that candor ultimately determines whether the protocol is interpreted or simply discarded. Before we discuss interpretation, let us begin with a look at how setting and client's attitude can affect the assessment process.

Setting

Why is the setting in which the MCMI-III is administered an important consideration? Beyond the customary understanding of setting (e.g., inpatient psychiatric), our understanding of setting is expanded to include the context in which the assessment takes place—that is, the reason for conducting the evaluation (e.g., inpatient/outpatient, child custody, fitness for duty evaluation, and Social Security Disability [SSD] determination). Some settings influence a greater probability that the examinee's responses will be slanted. For instance, a parent being evaluated by the courts to determine custodial rights may take great pains to appear in a favorable light by presenting an overly psychologically sound image, whereas a person applying for SSD determination may wish to present the opposite impression and exaggerate the degree of symptoms. The setting, as well as the client's motives, may provide varied impressions.

Psychiatric settings can present a different array of questions when determining the accuracy of response data. Are the inpatients mentally alert, or are they confused and disoriented? Have they been recently medicated? Are they cooperative? Knowledge and observation regarding the mental bearing of the inpatient are critical and must be considered when gauging the appropriateness of the examinee's condition at the time of testing. The clinician should be attentive to the specific context, particularly when evaluating the inpatient population.

Client Attitude

Now that we have considered the notion of setting, let us take a moment to understand how the client's attitude affects the assessment.

Being alert to the client's attitude toward assessment can provide additional evaluative data, furnishing important clues in determining the interpretive validity of the profile. Although the Modifying indices provide the clinician with quantitative data about the client's test behavior, qualitative data—such as observed anxiety, resistance, inattentiveness, and so forth—can reinforce or contradict the clinician's inferences. Examinees, for the most part, approach the testing situation in an open and honest manner, and their protocols are usually not problematic. Some, however, do not, and it is particularly in these situations that vigilance on the part of the clinician is necessary when evaluating the possibility of distortion.

Measuring Response Styles

The MCMI-III contains four indices to identify distortions in response style: the Validity index, Disclosure index, Desirability index, and Debasement index. Each index provides a distinct function to identify the type of response style. Scores obtained on the Validity index and Disclosure index, as addressed in chapter 3, affect profile validity; scores on the Desirability and Debasement indices can be adjusted to reflect response biases. Clinical and syndrome scales affected by elevations on the Desirability and Debasement indices are subsequently adjusted to counter these response biases. Let us investigate their significance.

VALIDITY INDEX

The Validity index is the easiest means to detect response bias. Items 65, 110, and 157 (Millon, 1997) that make up the Validity index express highly improbable occurrences for the normal population. Profile validity is in question if any one of the items is endorsed in the true direction; however, if two or more items are endorsed in the keyed direction, the profile is invalid. For example:

> Item 65. "I flew across the Atlantic 30 times last year."
> Item 110. "I was on the front cover of several magazines last year."
> Item 157. "I have not seen a car in the last ten years."
> (Millon, 1997, pp. 164–166)

If one item is endorsed, the likelihood of random or deviant responding can be determined by examining the remaining response patterns. Note, however, that the Validity index items are keyed in the true direction, and an "all false" response pattern would yield a score of 0 on this index. "Despite its brevity, the Validity index is highly sensitive to careless, confused, or random responding" (Millon, 1997, p. 118).

DISCLOSURE INDEX (SCALE X)

The Disclosure index measures the candidness of an individual (Exhibit 4-1). As mentioned in the previous chapter, this index is derived from the composite raw score of the 11 Clinical Personality Patterns (Scales

Hypotheses Associated With Scale X Scores

Raw Disclosure Scores		
< RS 34	Invalid Profile	RS 178 >
RS 34 → RS 60	Tendency toward defensiveness	
RS 61 → RS 123	Average disclosure	
RS 124 → RS 178	Tendency toward guileless self-revelation	

Approximate Base-Rate Disclosure Scores		
BR 0 → BR 34	Tendency toward defensiveness	
BR 35 → BR 74	Average disclosure	
BR 75 → BR 100	Tendency toward guileless self-revelation	

1–8B). The frequency of base-rate scores for Scale X in the total normative sample was 14.1% for the BR 0 to 34 range, 57.8% for the BR 35 to 74 range, 16.3% for the BR 75 to 84 range, and 11.8% for BR 85 to 115 range (Millon, 1997, p. 62).

Recall that a raw score of less than 34 or greater than 178 renders the profile invalid. Even though the score may fall within the acceptable validity range (RS 34 to RS 178), scores at both extremes are suggestive of a distinct response style. Degrees of an examinee's disclosure level are considered in relation to its position on the continuum.

Elevated scores approaching raw score 178 are suggestive of an individual who may be overly frank and wholly self-revealing. Depressed scores approaching raw score 34, on the other hand, are suggestive of secretiveness and reticence in revealing information indicating a guarded, cautious, and careful individual.

DESIRABILITY INDEX (SCALE Y)

The Desirability index measures the individual's partiality to appear in a favorable light. For instance, a positively keyed response to item 172, "People tell me that I'm a very proper and moral person" (Millon, 1997), may indicate a tendency to portray a favorable self-image. The frequency of base-rate scores for Scale Y in the total normative sample was 15.7% for the BR 0 to 34 range, 58.9% for the BR 35 to 74 range, 16.5% for the BR 75 to 84 range, and 9.0% for BR 85 to 115 range (Millon, 1997, p. 62).

Clinically significant elevations on this scale suggest a propensity toward denying one's problems and the tendency to appear psychologically healthy. Generally, BR scores equal to or greater than 75 suggest an inclination to place oneself in a favorable or virtuous light. As the BR score elevations increase, the likelihood of suppressing existing psychological difficulties increases. Extremely elevated scores on the Desirability index, however, do not invalidate a profile. See Exhibit 4-2 for possible hypotheses of significantly elevated Scale Y scores.

DEBASEMENT INDEX (SCALE Z)

The Debasement index detects the opposite propensities measured by the Desirability index: the tendency to present oneself in an unfavorable light. For instance, a positively keyed response to item 15, "Things that are going well today won't last very long" (Millon, 1997), may indicate a tendency to portray an unfavorable self-image. Generally, elevated scores equal to or greater than BR 75 suggest a tendency to deprecate and devalue oneself, as well as exaggerate one's degree of symptoms. Diligence is necessary in determining whether an extremely elevated score is an attempt to "fake-bad" or indicates the true presence of serious pathology. As with Scale Y, extremely elevated scores do not invalidate the profile. The frequency of base-rate scores for Scale Z in the total normative sample was 15.9% for the BR 0 to 34 range, 53.6% for the BR 35 to 74 range, 16.6% for the BR 75 to 84 range, and 13.9% for BR 85 to 115 range (Millon, 1997, p. 62). See Exhibit 4-3 for possible hypotheses of significantly elevated Scale Z scores.

Configural Considerations

As with other scales, Millon recommends a configural interpretation when interpreting the Modifying indices. This approach helps the clini-

EXHIBIT 4-2	
Hypotheses Associated With Desirability Index BR Score (Scale Y)	
BR 75 → BR 84	Tendency to present in a favorable light Attempt to seem morally virtuous Inclination to appear psychologically healthy
BR ≥ 85	Probable denial of psychological difficulties Possible faulty psychological insight Potentially a fake-good response set

EXHIBIT 4-3

Hypotheses Associated With Debasement Index BR Score (Scale Z)

BR 75 → BR 84	Inclined to devalue and deprecate oneself Exaggeration of psychological symptoms Possible indication of anxiety or depression
BR ≥ 85	Possible indication of extreme emotional turmoil Perhaps a "cry for help" Potentially a fake-bad response set

cian evaluate the interpretive integrity of the scale results for the remaining personality and syndrome scales.

Some configurations are relatively easy to interpret, such as a low base-rate score on Scale X, with a low Scale Y and an elevated Scale Z, suggesting moderately exaggerated emotional discomfort. Closer examination, though, is required in more complex configurations. In the second edition of the *MCMI-III Manual*, Millon (1997) cited an example in which the client may score a low Scale X, and Scales Y and Z are highly elevated. In this situation, the client endorses antithetical items, raising concerns regarding the validity of the profile. Millon noted that agitated depressives may occasionally obtain this configuration.

With more complex configurations, closer scrutiny of the entire profile may be required. Studies reviewed by Choca and Van Denburg (1997), for example, cite research suggesting that defensive fake-good response sets tend to yield a compulsive or a blended narcissistic–compulsive profile; whereas fake-bad response sets typically have multiple clinical and syndrome elevations above BR 85, including the severe personality patterns. Close examination of the clinical scales is advisable, particularly when a complex configuration is produced on the Modifying indices.

Deviant Response Styles

Recall from chapter 3 that certain response sets will immediately invalidate a protocol, though occur infrequently. Deviant response styles (e.g., all true, all false, and random responding) contaminate the protocol. These response patterns are easily detected when reviewing the answer sheet. Although all true and all false patterns may be easily detected, the invalidity of a random profile may be more difficult to determine.

There are a number of reasons for excessive omissions and double-marked items, regardless of the examinee's intent. Although a profile can be determined valid, a large number of omissions and double-markings will cause the scale elevations to be lowered and scale interpretation to be questioned. For example, if a large number of the omitted items were keyed to Scale B (Alcohol Dependence), not only would Scale B result in a distorted interpretation but other scales would also be affected because of scale overlap.

Case Review

To get an idea of how the question of validity is practically incorporated, we turn to several case examples.

A FAKE-BAD PROFILE?

Behavioral Description

Scott P. is a 45-year-old single, White, unemployed male, who was evaluated to determine eligibility for Social Security benefits. Post-tramatic stress disorder (PTSD) symptoms that included disturbing and recurrent nightmares and flashbacks to Vietnam were reported. He was treated for alcohol addiction in 1994 and 1995, arrested multiple times for various substance-abuse related crimes, and reported attempting suicide the previous summer.

Interpretive Remarks

The extreme elevations on Scale X and Scale Z, coupled with a lowered Desirability-scaled score and multiple clinically significant elevations above BR 85, suggest that the examinee is attempting to look psychologically impaired (Figure 4-1). Although this configuration of Modifying indices with significant base-rate elevations on the clinical and syndrome scales are suggestive of a fake-bad profile, the possibility that the client may be seriously disturbed should not be dismissed without further supporting evidence.

Personality Code: 8B8A2B2A**36B8A//SCP*–//
Syndrome Code: ADRBT**H*//CCPP**SS*//

FIGURE 4-1

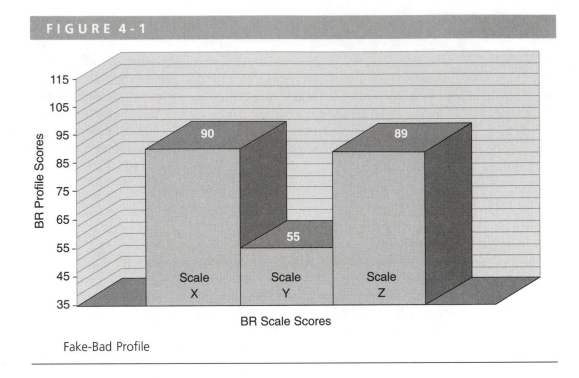

Fake-Bad Profile

A FAKE-GOOD PROFILE?

Behavioral Description

Vivian P. is a 23-year-old married, African American female recently employed as a clerk. She was evaluated to determine her suitability to regain parental rights of her two minor children. The children were both removed by Family Services following a positive test result for cocaine in her younger daughter's system at the time of birth. Vivian P. reported one incident of heroin overdose and one conviction for shoplifting. As part of her sentence, Vivian P. was remanded to County Services for drug rehabilitation. At the time of the evaluation, she was separated from her husband and reported no drug usage.

Interpretive Remarks

The high elevation obtained on Scale Y, coupled with low elevations on Scale X and Scale Z, is suggestive of a tendency toward faking-good (Figure 4-2). Research suggests such profiles have accompanying elevations on the Dependent, Narcissistic, or Compulsive scales and typically have no elevations on the Severe Personality Pathology or Clinical Syndromes scales (Millon, 1997). Only two scales reached significant elevations: Scale 3 (BR 80) and Scale 4 (BR 75). The highest elevation obtained on Axis I was Scale T (BR 70). Distinguishing a

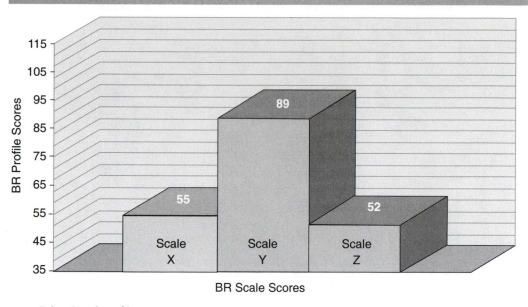

Fake-Good Profile

fake-good profile from a valid healthy profile, however, is not necessarily easy, and further evaluative information is often essential.

Personality Code: -**34*//-*–//
Syndrome Code: -*–//-*–//

A CRY FOR HELP?

Behavioral Description

James M. is a 52-year-old single, White male with a history of developmental disability. He was evaluated to determine his current level of functioning. He has lived at a nursing home for the past 10 years and is employed at this facility in the housekeeping department. At times, he is prone to periodic mood shifts, resulting in irritable and eccentric behavior. Intellectually, James M. functions in the mild range of mental retardation.

Interpretive Remarks

The high elevations obtained on Scale X and Scale Z, coupled with the endorsement of severe pathology, are suggestive of a "cry for help" (Figure 4-3). Similar elevations on the Modifying indices, as we have noted, are also obtained on the fake-bad profile. Four scales surpassed the BR 85 range on Axis II. All scales, with the exception of Scales T,

FIGURE 4-3

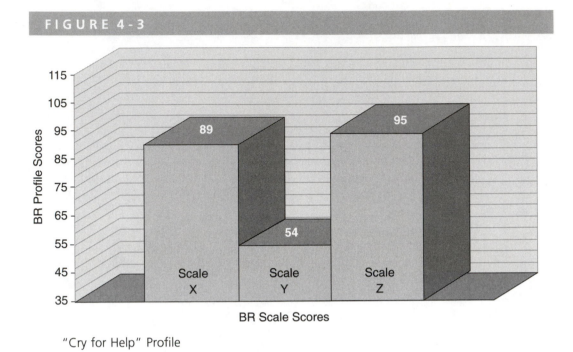

"Cry for Help" Profile

R, and CC, were elevated beyond BR 75 on Axis I. The number and degree of symptoms endorsed may suggest a cry for help and thus a need for attention. Because many of the syndrome scales are clinically elevated, a closer examination of the profile configuration may be required to determine the degree of psychological impairment and emotional distress experienced.

Personality Code: 32A8B5**8A1*//P*–//
Symptom Code: AH**DBN*//SS**PP*//

In Summary

As we have seen, evaluating questionable profiles is a complex process, yet it is the foundation for an accurate assessment. We have learned that certain rules exist where a profile can immediately be discarded as invalid; other profiles are not as clear-cut. Often, questionable inventories will arise, and the alert clinician should take care to examine these in relation to supporting data.

We have looked at how the Modifying indices identify problematic response sets and how their adjustments help to counter the examinee's test biases. These scales literally "set the stage" for clinical interpretation of the remaining scales. In chapter 5 we will discuss the next step in evaluating a profile—interpretation of the Clinical Personality Patterns and Severe Personality Pathology scales.

Test Yourself Exercises 4

Fill in the Blanks.

1. The _____ index measures whether an examinee's style is open and candid or secretive and reticent in responding to the MCMI-III items.
2. The _____ index measures the degree to which an examinee is inclined to adopt a favorable image on the MCMI-III.
3. The _____ index measures the client's attempt to deprecate and devalue him- or herself by presenting extensive emotional difficulties on the MCMI-III.
4. The context in which the assessment takes place is referred to as the _____.
5. Deviant response styles can include _____, _____, and _____ responding.
6. A significant number of omitted or double-marked items will cause the scale elevations to be _____.
7. Choca and Van Denburg suggested that defensive fake-good indices tend to yield a _____ personality profile or a blended _____ personality profile.
8. The acceptable range of validity for the Disclosure index is raw score _____ to raw score, _____ inclusive.
9. On the Desirability index the likelihood of suppressing psychological difficulties increases as the scale score _____.
10. An extremely elevated score on the Debasement index may be an attempt to _____.

Match Column A With Column B

A	B
1. Fake-good	____ Scale X = RS 34
2. Fake-bad	____ Scale X = BR 89, Scale Y = BR 89, Scale Z = BR 89
3. Valid	____ Scale X = RS 33, Scale Y = BR 47, Scale Z = BR 63
4. Invalid	____ Scale X = BR 95, Scale Y = BR 20, Scale Z = BR 95
5. "Cry for help"	____ Scale X = BR 65, Scale Y = BR 65, Scale Z = BR 65
6. Unusual self-disclosure	____ Scale Y = BR 94
7. Tendency toward self-deprecation	____ Scale X = BR 95; Scale Z = 95
8. Symptom denial	____ Scale Z = BR 83
9. Defensiveness	____ Scale X = BR 48, Scale Y = BR 89, Scale Z = BR 52, Scale 5 = BR 88, Scale 7 = BR 83
10. Symptom exaggeration	____ Scale X =BR 89, Scale Y = BR 30, Scale Z = BR 91, Scale C = BR 102, Scale P = BR 91, Scale CC = BR 90, Scale PP = BR 94

Interpretation: Clinical and Severe Patterns (Axis II) 5

N ow that we have a basic understanding of the Modifying indices, it is time to consider the interpretation of the clinical scales. Our focus in this chapter will be on the interpretation of the eleven Clinical Personality Patterns scales (1–8B) and the three Severe Personality Pathology scales (S, C, and P). We begin by examining the initial guidelines for interpretation.

Guidelines for Interpretation

The following guidelines outline the basic procedures for interpreting Scales 1 through P. Base-rate scores measure the pervasiveness and severity of a psychological characteristic on a continuum. The MCMI-III was constructed with a clear set of base-rate cutoff scores against which an individual can be evaluated. These base-rate cutoff scores serve to assist the clinician in defining an individual's personality pattern and should be used as markers, rather than rigid benchmarks. For the Axis II scales (1–P), BR 75 indicates the presence of a trait, and BR 85 the presence of a disorder. (See Exhibit 5-1.) Following is a procedural overview to begin the discussion of interpreting personality disorders:

- Ensure that the profile is valid. These criteria were presented in chapter 4.
- When multiple scales are significantly elevated, the Severe Personality Pathology scales always receive priority when interpreting the profile configuration.
- The MCMI-III measures diagnostic levels of pathology along a continuum. Base-rate score cutoffs define the severity of a particular pattern being measured—that is, as scale scores increase, the likelihood of the presence of the particular trait or disorder increases.
- The thresholds along a continuum indicate the presence of traits (cutoff score of BR 75) or disorders (cutoff score of BR 85 and above). However, BR 75 and BR 85 threshold scores should serve more as practical guides, rather than strict cutoff points.
- Begin Axis II scale interpretation of the significantly elevated Severe Personality Pathology scales; then examine the significant elevations on the Clinical Personality Patterns scales. Elevations (BR 75 and above) on the Severe Personality Pathology scales represent more dysfunctional variants of the Clinical Personality Patterns scales.
- As the number of significantly elevated scales increases above BR 75, the extent of existing pathology becomes greater.
- Where multiple scales are significantly elevated, consider the common overlapping features shared by the elevated scales.
- As a general rule, when multiple scales are elevated at or above BR 75 on Axis II scales, typically only the highest two or three are given interpretive weight.

SCALE INTERPRETATION

After the clinician is satisfied that the MCMI-III results are valid, interpretation begins with an inspection of the Severe Personality Pathology scales (Schizotypal, Borderline, and Paranoid). Review these scales in relation to the Clinical Personality Patterns scales. Severe personality pathology scales represent extreme variants of the Clinical Personality

EXHIBIT 5-1

MCMI-III Base-Rate Scale Interpretation (Axis II)

Clinical Personality Patterns Scales	
BR 75 → BR 84	Indicates the presence of a clinically significant personality trait
BR ≥ 85	Indicates the presence of a clinically significant personality disorder
Severe Personality Pathology Scales	
BR 75 → BR 84	Suggests a moderately severe level of personality functioning
BR ≥ 85	Suggests a more decompensated personality pattern

Patterns scales. For example, the more dysfunctional variants of the avoidant personality may blend into the schizotypal, the narcissistic into the paranoid, the dependent into the borderline, and so forth. (See Table 1-3.) When elevated to clinically significant levels, these scales receive priority in interpretation.

First, review each Severe Personality Pathology scale separately. Multiple scale elevations should be noted to determine the dominant pattern. If, for example, an individual obtains a BR 77 on the Paranoid scale, BR 50 on the Borderline scale, and BR 85 on the Schizotypal scale, the schizotypal pattern would be the dominant pattern, with significant paranoid features included in the personality description.

Next, the significantly elevated Clinical Personality Patterns scales are examined and serve to qualify the clinically elevated Severe Personality Pathology scales. If the Avoidant scale, for example, is elevated to the level of BR 80, and a BR 79 was obtained on the Schizotypal scale, the interpretation would emphasize the schizotypal personality attributes, forming a synthesis with the related avoidant features.

BASIC LEVEL OF INTERPRETATION

Formulating a diagnosis solely on the individually elevated MCMI-III scales is the most basic level of interpretation. This basic approach generally interprets each elevated scale in isolation, examining each scale that equals or exceeds the BR 75 and 85 levels. This approach, however, not only fails to provide an integrated understanding of the individual's personality but also may furnish an inexact diagnosis. Although circumstances (e.g., time limitations) sometimes demand the use of this method for making a diagnosis, Millon (1997) noted that it is potentially the most flawed approach. Here we are only concerned with individual elevations, basing our diagnosis solely on these elevations.

Although a basic interpretation using rigid cutoff scores of the specifically elevated scales may indeed afford useful diagnostic information, it nonetheless may fail to reveal the underlying dynamics peculiar to the individual personality being assessed. As mentioned earlier, cutoff scores are provided as practical guides, rather than strict lines of demarcation. If, for example, a male examinee obtains a BR 74 on the Schizoid scale, an additional endorsement of merely one item on the scale would place his score at BR 75. It is quite likely that schizoid traits do exist (even at the BR 74 level) and depending on the scale configuration may be factored into the individual's overall profile pattern, rather than rigidly ignored because of the prescribed BR 75 cutoff. Similarly, a BR 84 may indicate the possibility of a disorder, even though the strict interpretive guidelines of a personality disorder require a cutoff score of BR 85. To fully characterize an individual's personality and form an accurate diagnosis, Millon recommends that the clinician move beyond the basic diagnostic level by using a more integrated configural approach.

PROTOTYPICAL ELEVATION

Occasionally, though, interpretive results may produce an extreme elevation on one particular scale. In such a situation, the examinee demonstrates a rare prototypical personality pattern to the exclusion of other traits and disorders. Millon (1997) has supported interpretation of single scale elevations only when the single scale is considerably more elevated than the next higher elevation (e.g., more than 20 BR). For instance, if a female examinee obtained a BR 102 on Scale 6A, and the next highest elevation obtained is a BR 76 on Scale 4, clearly an

---

DIAGNOSIS AND TREATMENT

"Coming up with a diagnosis makes sense out of madness.
It labels the disorder, not the patient; it condenses a multitude of data into one term; it serves communication, and allows prediction of treatment response and outcome. The diagnostic assessment expresses your judgment and your conclusions about the patient." (Othmer & Othmer, 1994, p. 260)

antisocial prototype is suggested; the interpretation should, therefore, primarily reflect the antisocial characteristics defined in that prototype.

Configural Interpretation

Although single prototypical elevations do exist, they are rare. More commonly, multiple-scale elevations in the range of significance are produced. As a gauge, we use the thresholds of BR 75 and BR 85 to denote levels of severity—that is, the presence of traits and disorders, respectively. Millon (1997, p. 124) wrote, "The greater the number of scales elevated above BR 75, the greater the extent of personality pathology." Configural interpretation provides an overall integrated description and is the most effective approach in appraising the client. According to Millon (1997), configural interpretation most closely expresses an accurate characterization of an individual's personality.

Generally, within the psychiatric population, an MCMI-III assessment will yield one or more elevated scales at or above the level of clinical significance (BR 75). Although protocols will likely show several elevations within the range of significance, their specific BR elevations will determine the composite personality pattern. Scales with the highest elevations serve as the predominant personality pattern, with secondary elevations providing meaningful integration. The characteristics of these scales are then blended. Assume, for example, an individual obtains the highest elevation of BR 86 on Scale 5 (Narcissistic) and the second highest elevation of BR 78 on Scale 6B (Sadistic). The predominant pattern, likely diagnosed as a narcissistic personality disorder with sadistic personality traits, will reflect the self-centered grandiosity exhibited by the narcissist. Although this personality pattern conveys an air of being "special," it also blends a conspicuous lack of empathy for others. The lack of empathy will be integrated because of the elevation on the sadistic traits. Perhaps this individual's relationships with others will incorporate the aggressiveness characterized by the sadistic personality and possibly even derive pleasure from humiliating others. The blend of the two scales, then, will likely produce a predominantly egotistical individual, who relates to others through an abusive and aggressive manner.

DIFFERING SECONDARY ELEVATIONS

Differing secondary scale elevations, however, can make for quite varied personality descriptions, as the following examples illustrate. Consider the protocols of two clients, each of whom obtains highest base-rate score elevations on the Histrionic scale but who differ on secondary-scale elevations. Having obtained elevated scores on the Histrionic scale, both clients are expected to have a great need for acceptance and approval and will likely display a high degree of emotionality and social gregariousness to gain the necessary attention they seek. Note the behavioral distinctions between the histrionic–negativistic (Client number 1) and the histrionic–dependent (Client number 2) patterns in the following descriptions:

> Client number 1: Histrionic–negativistic: In the search for attention and approval, oppositional traits may surface, adopting a negativistic attitude of disdain toward others. This histrionic personality more likely will seek to be the center of attraction and gain attention through banter, derision, or repartee.

> Client number 2: Histrionic–dependent: In the search for attention and approval, the dependent is persistent in efforts to gain harmony and will sacrifice self-values to this end. This personality may likely adopt an accommodating style, and efforts to gain attention may likely include dramatic clinging behaviors.

Both personalities present with dramatic characteristics found in the histrionic personality. However, a varying secondary pattern alters the overall personality picture of each. Although the search for emotional support exists in both personalities, notice that the attention required from others is secured in different ways.

Essentially, the overall effect of secondary and tertiary scales depends on the prominence of BR scale elevations. For instance, if Client number 1 obtained BR 90 on the Histrionic scale with BR 75 on the Negativistic scale, the negativistic traits may minimally influence the histrionic pattern, and the profile would likely reflect characteristics more prevalent of the histrionic personality. Alternately, if Client number 2 likewise scored BR 90 on the Histrionic scale but in addition scored BR 88 on the Dependent scale, equal integration of both personality patterns appears warranted.

SIMILAR ELEVATIONS AND OVERLAPPING CRITERIA

At times, two or three scales have clinically significant elevations at or near the same levels. This situation makes configural interpretation a bit more difficult. In creating a blend of the Clinical Personality Patterns scales, for example, the question arises, To which personality scale is priority given? In such cases, Millon (1997) recommends an integration of functional and structural attributes (refer back to Table 1-4) of the elevated scales. If the Dependent and Histrionic scales are both elevated similarly, which characteristics should receive priority? Millon (1997) has suggested using the following two discriminators—MCMI-III item data and using additional information—to resolve this question. We should,

- Focus on the prototypical items. Recall that items are weighted in values of 2 (prototypical) or 1 (nonprototypical). Prototypical items can be given preference in determining the blend of characteristic features.
- Verify additional clinical data. Information gathered during the clinical interview and from other instruments can assist the clinician in a blending of the features.

Where scales are relatively close in BR score, also examine overlapping criteria. Scales that are clinically elevated often share overlapping features, such as impulsivity common to both the borderline and antisocial personality disorders. When interpreting multiple scales, look for synergy among the scales. If both the Histrionic and Dependent scales, for example, are equally elevated to levels of clinical significance, it is important to note that a common criterion shared by both personalities involves a need for affection from others. Such criteria, then, can form the basis of the blended personality pattern. The differential diagnosis listed in the *DSM-IV* can be helpful in determining the overlapping features.

Understanding the Scales

A thorough understanding of each personality pattern is necessary before formulating a configural interpretation. The clinical accuracy of configural interpretation rests on the meaningful integration of each scale elevation. Knowledge of the dynamics and structure of each MCMI-III Axis II scale is required to make in-depth inferences about the client. Millon's expression of personality disorders captures the functional and structural essence of each personality pattern. These patterns are expressed on a continuum and integrated across domains, reflecting deeper underlying features intrinsic to one's functioning.

An integrative approach to assessment is diagnostically sound. A comprehensive assessment of personality disorders includes both functional and structural domains embodied within the behavioral, phenomenological, intrapsychic, and biophysical levels. Millon (1997, pp. 20–21) wrote,

> Functional characteristics represent dynamic processes that transpire within the intrapsychic world and between the individual and his or her psychosocial environment. . . . In contrast to functional characteristics, structural attributes represent a deeply embedded and relatively enduring template of imprinted memories, attitudes, needs, fears, conflicts, and so on, that guide experience and transform the nature of ongoing life events.

Consistent with configural interpretation, Millon espouses the blending and integrating of personality descriptions for each domain. Because of the MCMI-III's consonance with the *DSM*, awareness of its classification criteria for each personality leads to a clearer understanding of MCMI-III personality patterns and pathologies. Comprehending the congruence between *DSM* criteria and MCMI-III prototypic items provides the clinician a firm foundation for developing interpretive inferences.

The following material includes researched data, mental status descriptions, treatment capsules, and corresponding *DSM-IV/DSM-III-R* classifications of the MCMI-III Clinical Personality Patterns and severe personality pathology.

CLINICAL PERSONALITY PATTERNS[1]

Millon (1994) defines personality as complex patterns of deeply embedded psychological characteristics. These patterns are largely unconscious, cannot be easily eradicated, and are expressed automatically in almost every facet of functioning. A marked inflexibility and maladaptiveness of these patterns, which deviate from the expected standards of social and occupational functioning, constitute the basis for diagnosis of a personality disorder. Although personality disorders are commonly diagnosed using *DSM-IV* criteria, the constellation of an individual's unique pattern of traits in relation to collective symptoms and personal-

---

[1] *DSM* diagnostic criteria are reprinted with permission from the *Diagnostic and Statistical Manual of Mental Disorders, Fourth Edition*. Copyright 1994 American Psychiatric Association or *Diagnostic and Statistical Manual of Mental Disorders, Third Edition Revised*. Copyright 1987 American Psychiatric Association. As noted, the mental status descriptions reprinted and adapted with permission from E. Othmer and S. C. Othmer, *The Clinical Interview, Using the DSM-IV, Volume 1: Fundamentals*. Copyright 1994 American Psychiatric Association or Millon, A. (Director), Millon T. (Narration), *Millon training on personality disorders* [Video]. Copyright 1993 Theodore Millon.

ity must be systematically examined to achieve the necessary degree of accuracy in making a diagnosis. We begin by examining each of the personality patterns that make up the Axis II scales of the MCMI-III.

SCHIZOID PERSONALITY DISORDER

Schizoid personality disorder is a pattern of social and interpersonal detachment with restricted emotional expression. Schizoid individuals are described as withdrawn, aloof, distant, and listless. They are noted by their lack of desire and incapacity to experience pleasure or pain (Millon, 1994). A primary characteristic is the individual's indifference to social relationships in which emotional warmth is noticeably lacking. Akhtar (1987) described the outer world of the schizoid individual as vague, aloof, and self-sufficient and the internal world as sensitive and emotionally needy. These individuals often appear bland and describe themselves as empty. Clark (1996) suggested that one aspect of the emptiness may be defensive in nature, a means to protect the self. Deficits in areas of psychosocial functioning are prominent, with an insensibility to criticism or praise. West, Rose, and Sheldon-Keller's (1995) investigation of avoidant characteristics in the schizoid individual revealed that the schizoid individual's inability to feel secure in an attached relationship prevents impending anxiety that a closeness would bring. Thought-processing is vague, ambiguous, and lacking in focus, though no formal thought disorder is observable. Cull, Chick, and Wolff (1984) studied histories of 23 men and concluded that the childhood labeling of Asperger's syndrome, known as autistic psychopathology, corresponds to the diagnosis of schizoid personality disorder in adult life.

R$_x$ CAPSULE: SCHIZOID

Provide a supportive, nonthreatening, therapeutic setting. Stimulate the emotional capacity for pleasurable pursuits of the schizoid-disordered patient. Reinforce prosocial interactional behaviors with role-playing. If stimulants are used to increase the schizoid's energy level, they should be used judiciously. Group therapy may provide an arena in which the individual can learn constructive interactional behaviors. Simple problem-solving approaches can be effective to address the patient's current worries and concerns.

Mental Status Description

The schizoid individual is characterized by edgy body movements, lack of facial expressions, and frozen gestures. Speech is goal-directed but lacks detailed elaboration. The tone of voice rarely ever changes, not even when the individual talks about the most intimate or traumatic events in his or her life. Neither the death of a mother nor the loss of a friend seems to affect such an individual. This lack of responsiveness underscores the individual's main impairment: affective withdrawal.

The more intelligent patients with this personality disorder sometimes complain about their lack of interest and motivation. They may even name this state "depression," but they usually do not report associated sadness, guilt, or anguish. Patients with schizoid personality disorder do not hallucinate or display delusional thinking. They may have some ideas of reference and a feeling that others do not care for them, but if they did, it would burden rather than please such individuals. Their memory is usually intact. They see themselves as less animated than others, but do not consider this lack of interest a disturbance. Their judgment concerning future plans is usually adequate; they rarely overestimate their potential unless they develop a schizophreniform disorder. Only if they are threatened with losing their jobs or spouses (male patients with schizoid personality rarely marry) will they possibly consult a therapist. Then they usually report vegetative symptoms and depressed mood for which they seek treatment (Othmer & Othmer, 1994, pp. 410–411).

Corresponding DSM-IV Diagnostic Criteria (Schizoid)

A pervasive pattern of detachment from social relationships and a restricted range of expression of emotions in interpersonal settings, beginning by early adulthood and present in a variety of contexts, as indicated by four (or more) of the following:

1. Neither desires nor enjoys close relationships, including being part of a family;
2. Almost always chooses solitary activities;
3. Has little, if any, interest in having sexual experiences with another person;
4. Takes pleasure in few, if any, activities;
5. Lacks close friends or confidants other than first-degree relatives;
6. Appears indifferent to the praise or criticism of others;
7. Shows emotional coldness, detachment, or flattened affectivity.

AVOIDANT PERSONALITY DISORDER

Avoidant personality disorder is a pattern of withdrawal, self-inadequacy, and hypersensitivity to criticism. The socially inhibitive behavior may appear similar to that of the schizoid individual. Unlike the pronounced emotional detachment of the schizoid personality, however, the social withdrawal of the individual with an avoidant disorder stems from an underlying fear of rejection. Although avoidant personalities want to participate in social interaction, they are reticent to do so because of their pervasive feelings of inadequacy. If uncertain of another's acceptance, they avoid any significant interpersonal contact. Avoidant features, primarily fear of embarrassment, were found significantly more often among social phobics than individuals with panic disorders (Jansen, Arntz, Merckelbach, & Mersch, 1994). Studies by Brown, Heimberg, and Juster (1995) of patients seeking treatment for interpersonal performance anxiety suggest that avoidant personality disorder is a more severe form of social phobia. The avoidant personality fears embarrassment and tends to socially withdraw. Those with this personality are unwilling to become involved with people unless they are certain of being liked.

Mental Status Description

Avoidant personalities initially show withdrawal, and this feature dominates their mental status. They are monosyllabic, vague, and circumstantial. Initially, they may appear suspicious and paranoid or anxious and phobic but void of clear-cut symptoms of *DSM-IV* clinical disorders. After they feel comfortable with the clinician and develop trust, they may reveal their sensitivity to being misunderstood and be easily hurt

---

R x CAPSULE: AVOIDANT

Counter the avoidant-disordered patient's tendency to perpetuate a pattern of social withdrawal by reducing fears and thoughts of criticism and disapproval. Teach appropriate interactional skills. Increase self-esteem and encourage gratifying activities. After a supportive relationship is firmly established, clarify and cognitively reorient self-defeating perceptions. Assertiveness-training can engender positive and effective coping techniques. Group therapy can help overcome social anxiety and feelings of embarrassment.

by criticism or disapproval. They may then discuss their fear of rejection and inappropriate behavior (Othmer & Othmer, 1994, p. 433).

Corresponding DSM-IV Diagnostic Criteria (Avoidant)

A pervasive pattern of social inhibition, feelings of inadequacy, and hypersensitivity to negative evaluation, beginning by early adulthood and present in a variety of contexts, as indicated by four (or more) of the following:

1. Avoids occupational activities that involve significant inter-personal contact, because of fears of criticism, disapproval, or rejection;
2. Is unwilling to get involved with people unless certain of being liked;
3. Shows restraint within intimate relationships because of the fear of being shamed or ridiculed;
4. Is preoccupied with being criticized or rejected in social situations;
5. Is inhibited in new interpersonal situations because of feelings of inadequacy;
6. Views self as socially inept, personally unappealing, or inferior to others;
7. Is unusually reluctant to take personal risks or to engage in any new activities because they may prove embarrassing.

DEPRESSIVE PERSONALITY DISORDER

The depressive personality disorder is a pattern characterized by long-standing negative self-thoughts and rueful emotional states. Unlike dysthymia, where episodic patterns of depression are characterized by duration, the depressive pattern uniquely suggests a sustained and continuous condition (Millon, 1994). Empirical studies reveal that only a modest relationship may exist between depressive personality disorder and dysthymic disorder, with dysthymia representing more severe symptom manifestation and depressive disorder lying on the mild end of the continuum of depressive conditions (Klein & Shih, 1998). Negative reactivity, remorsefulness, and self-denial were among characteristics identified as differing substantially in research participants categorized as formerly depressed and participants who were never depressed (Hartlage, Arduino, & Alloy, 1998). Depressive individuals appear to be "sad" much of the time, if not throughout their lives. Overall, depressive personalities take an extremely pessimistic view of life and feel burdened by the nonpleasurable lives they lead. Ironically, Craig (1999) has noted that these personalities often do not consider themselves depressed.

Mental Status Description

The depressive personality is characteristically depressed over a long period of the individual's life. The feature most notable is that the disorder is so sustained and continuous over periods of years. In evidence are the individual's dysphoric mood, glumness, cheerlessness, the sense of hopelessnes, and the rather pessimistic outlook that they have with regard to the future. An important element to identify is the depressive's proneness to feelings of guilt and a sense of worthlessness. The depressive is not unlike those who may be diagnosed with dysthymic disorder or a minor depression, but the continuous, ever-present quality is what is most notable about these individuals (T. Millon, 1993).

Corresponding DSM-IV *Research Criteria (Depressive)*

A pervasive pattern of depressive cognitions and behaviors beginning by early adulthood and present in a variety of contexts, as indicated by five (or more) of the following:

1. Usual mood is dominated by dejection, gloominess, cheerlessness, joylessness, unhappiness;
2. Self-concept centers around beliefs of inadequacy, worthlessness, and low self-esteem;

R x C A P S U L E : D E P R E S S I V E

Initially adopt a supportive stance and positive outlook for the depressive-disordered patient. Encourage constructive social interaction to alleviate the pervasive sense of hopelessness experienced. Antidepressant medication may be used at the onset to relieve psychic pain, as well as predispose the client for constructive ongoing therapy. Challenge the individual's negative cognitions about self and the world with logical fact. Group therapy can provide a shared, supportive setting through which appropriate interpersonal behaviors can be learned and positive feedback given.

---

3. Is critical, blaming, and derogatory toward self;
4. Is brooding and given to worry;
5. Is negativistic, critical, and judgmental toward others;
6. Is pessimistic;
7. Is prone to feeling guilty or remorseful.

DEPENDENT PERSONALITY DISORDER

The dependent personality disorder is characterized by submissive and clinging behavior in search of nurturance and security. Individuals with dependent personality disorder primarily are passive, nonassertive, and compliant. These personality patterns willingly submit to the wishes of others to maintain their protective benefits. Along with their inability to make their own decisions and their fear of being alone, their need for dependency fosters dominant–submissive relationships. As Millon (1981) notes, many dependent individuals search for a "magic helper" on whom they can rely.

Overholser (1996) examined interpersonal problems of psychiatric inpatients diagnosed with dependent personality disorder and concluded that measures of social functioning were related to negative and disruptive behaviors. Interpersonal dependency was strongly related to depressive symptoms and attitudes, with high scorers on the dependent personality scale likely meeting the criteria for histrionic personality disorder and borderline personality disorder (Overholser, 1996). Comparing dependent personality disorder with other personality disorders, Loranger's (1996) epidemiologic investigation suggested that dependent styles were more likely to have major depression and bipolar disorder than those diagnosed with other *DSM-IV*, Axis II personality disorders.

R$_x$ CAPSULE: DEPENDENT

Focus on the feelings and thoughts of inadequacy of the dependent-disordered patient with efforts directed at countering an extreme reliance on others. Cognitive–behavioral techniques can be used to strengthen a weak and needy self-image. Guard against nurturing the characteristic submissive behavioral patterns within the therapeutic relationship. Group sessions may be pursued as a means of learning and practicing independent skills and strengthening self-confidence.

Mental Status Description

The mental status is colored by the associated disorders that bring dependent individuals into therapy in the first place. The overriding features, however, are their dependency, submissiveness, anxiousness, and their need to please. They try to give the clinician answers that they think the clinician will like. Their affect strikes the clinician often as anxious and depressed, with some obsessive features.

The thought content mirrors themes of low self-esteem, desertion, and anxiety of doing the wrong thing. Patients with dependent personality disorder are oriented to their surroundings and have good memories, but they fail to appreciate the degree of their lack of initiative and its effect on their lives. Their judgment is hampered by their dependency (Othmer & Othmer, 1994, p. 435).

Corresponding DSM-IV *Diagnostic Criteria (Dependent)*

A pervasive and excessive need to be taken care of that leads to submissive and clinging behavior and fears of separation, beginning by early adulthood and present in a variety of contexts, as indicated by five (or more) of the following:

1. Has difficulty making everyday decisions without an excessive amount of advice and reassurance from others;
2. Needs others to assume responsibility for most major areas of his or her life;
3. Has difficulty expressing disagreement with others because of fear of loss of support or approval. (Note: This does not include realistic fears of retribution.);
4. Has difficulty initiating projects or doing things on his or her own (because of a lack of self-confidence in judgment or abilities rather than a lack of motivation or energy);
5. Goes to excessive lengths to obtain nurturance and support from others, to the point of volunteering to do things that are unpleasant;
6. Feels uncomfortable or helpless when alone because of exaggerated fears of being unable to care for him- or herself;
7. Urgently seeks another relationship as a source of care and support when a close relationship ends;
8. Is unrealistically preoccupied with fears of being left to take care of him- or herself.

HISTRIONIC PERSONALITY DISORDER

Histrionic personality disorder is a pattern of seductive manipulation, excessive emotionality, and attention-seeking behaviors. The ingeniously artful and clever social behavior often displayed makes the histrionic appear confident and self-assured, but beneath this guise lies fear of genuine autonomy and a need for repeated signs of acceptance and approval (Millon, 1997). Histrionic individuals necessarily need the attention of others, and this dependency differs from the protection and guidance required by other inadequate individuals (Choca & Van Denburg, 1996). Shapiro (1965) described the histrionic individual's cognition as "impressionistic," being global, diffuse, and lacking in sharpness. Lionells (1984) pointed out that the excessive emotion that is found among histrionics is essentially aggressive and is displayed as a protest against disruption of a relationship. Anger, she contended, may be expressed as a tantrum or tirade, or take the form of a chronic complainer and whiner. Although they may appear outwardly captivating and gregarious, the dramatic behaviors exhibited by individuals with histrionic personality often elicit a lack of sincerity and are most often displayed to gain attention. A theatrical play-acting quality is often conspicuous in hysterical behavior (Shapiro, 1965).

Mental Status Description

The mental status of patients with histrionic personality is dominated by a display of emotionality: vivid facial expressions, dramatic gestures, and a highly modulated voice. They can, however, be interrupted and redirected to a different topic, which they will take up in the same dramatic fashion. Their distractibility differs from mania, because there is no push of speech or flight of ideas. The constant drama gives the clinician the impression that they do not truly experience intense feelings. Their strong show of emotions is for the clinician's benefit, not a catharsis for them. In spite of excessive facial expressions and abundant

---

R x CAPSULE: HISTRIONIC

Temper the attention-seeking behaviors of the histrionic-disordered patient within relationships. Decrease manipulative behaviors and rapidly shifting superficial expressions of emotion. Concentrate on developing insight into the nature of repetitive relationship difficulties. Promote stable and adaptive autonomous prosocial behaviors. Cognitive techniques can focus on strengthening self-image and decreasing reliance on others. Group therapy can provide a supportive arena to reinforce appropriate prosocial behaviors and offer insightful feedback.

gesturing, they appear uninvolved in their stories. The term *la belle indifference* has been coined for this internal emotional distance (Othmer & Othmer, 1994, p. 427).

Corresponding DSM-IV *Diagnostic Criteria (Histrionic)*

A pervasive pattern of excessive emotionality and attention-seeking, beginning by early adulthood and present in a variety of contexts, as indicated by five (or more) of the following:

1. Is uncomfortable in situations in which he or she is not the center of attention;
2. Interaction with others is often characterized by inappropriate sexually seductive or provocative behavior;
3. Displays rapidly shifting and shallow expression of emotions;
4. Consistently uses physical appearance to draw attention to self;
5. Has a style of speech that is excessively impressionistic and lacking in detail;
6. Shows self-dramatization, theatricality, and exaggerated expression of emotion;
7. Is suggestible (e.g., easily influenced by others or circumstances);
8. Considers relationships more intimate than they actually are.

HISTRIONIC, NARCISSISTIC, AND COMPULSIVE SCALES: NORMALITY OR PATHOLOGY

In the second edition of the *MCMI-III Manual*, Millon (1997) noted that research conducted with all versions of the MCMI instruments revealed that elevations on the Histrionic, Narcissistic, and Compulsive scales may at times reflect personality strengths rather than personality pathology. Essentially, the nature of these personality patterns tends to minimize problems and deny difficulties. As Millon (1997) wrote,

> At modest levels of magnitude, these constructs [histrionic, narcissistic, compulsive] include normal, if not adaptive traits, while other personalities are maladaptive even at modest levels of expression. Thus, when an individual without significant personality pathology completes the instrument, the absence of pathology will tend to elevate these scales.

Millon (1997) suggested that the "shape" of these scale constructs is curvilinear—that is, high or low elevations of each of the three scales may be maladaptive, whereas moderate levels may suggest a healthy personality pattern.

When interpreting the BR scores of the Histrionic, Narcissistic, and Compulsive scales, Millon (1997) offered the following guidelines:

- Presence of pathology, rather than strength, is indicated as the base score increases in elevation;
- Presence of significant Axis I pathology supports the presence of a personality disorder;
- Presence of personality pathology can also be judged by the elevations of the three Severe Personality Pathology scales.

NARCISSISTIC PERSONALITY DISORDER

Narcissistic personality disorder is a pattern of self-centered grandiosity, constant need for attention/admiration, and a conspicuous lack of empathy toward others. Individuals with narcissistic personality disorder consistently convey an air of being "special." They determinedly seek adulation for their exploits, take great pleasure in their achievements, and display a confident air of arrogance. Relationships are exploitative, with minimal displays of empathy for the other person. In describing the concept of narcissism, Horney (1939) suggested that its essential meaning is described as self-inflation, a love and admiration of one's values for which no adequate foundation exists. In a study of narcissistic individuals, Rhodewalt, Madrian, and Cheney (1998) found that individuals with greater narcissism displayed more positive mood variability, mood intensity, and self-esteem instability than did individuals with less narcissism. They also suggested that positive interactions are viewed as self-affirming for the individual with high levels of narcissism, whereas negative reactions are perceived as threatening. The external behavioral display of superiority and arrogance may likely conceal extreme feelings of inferiority. Individuals with high levels of narcissism are incapable of loving either themselves or anyone else (Horney, 1939).

Mental Status Description

The narcissistic personality is most noted for self-centeredness. The tendency is to think of oneself as being the most important figure in the social community, and in addition, benignly arrogant, though without being hostile. They simply assume they are special and deserve special attention. They generally anticipate that they are entitled to special rights and attentions. If things are going well for the narcissistic individuals, they are competent and optimistic about life and feel very

R_x CAPSULE: NARCISSISTIC

By acknowledging the self-importance of the narcissistic-disordered patient at the onset of the therapeutic relationship, a helpful bond may be established. Be cognizant of a fragile self-image. Once rapport has been established, gradually confront the individual's false sense of entitlement and overvaluation of self. Cognitively moderate the unrestrained image of self, and increase a sensitive awareness toward others. Tactfully convey the impact that devaluing behavior has on others. Instill realistic self-attitudes and promote positive, interactional behaviors.

good about themselves; but the disparity between their actual achievements and their self-image leads to an awareness of their failure, and they begin feeling empty, shallow, and somewhat depressed. The arrogance, entitlement, and exploitiveness are most notable in the narcissistic disorder (T. Millon, 1993).

Corresponding DSM-IV *Diagnostic Criteria (Narcissistic)*

A pervasive pattern of grandiosity (in fantasy or behavior), need for admiration, and lack of empathy, beginning by early adulthood and present in a variety of contexts, is indicated by five (or more) of the following:

1. Has a grandiose sense of self-importance (e.g., exaggerates achievements and talents; expects to be recognized as superior without commensurate achievements);
2. Is preoccupied with fantasies of unlimited success, power, brilliance, beauty, or ideal love;
3. Believes that he or she is "special" and unique and can only be understood by, or should associate with, other special or high-status people (or institutions);
4. Requires excessive admiration;
5. Has a sense of entitlement (e.g., unreasonable expectations of especially favorable treatment or automatic compliance with his or her expectations);
6. Is interpersonally exploitative (e.g., takes advantage of others to achieve his or her own ends);
7. Lacks empathy: Is unwilling to recognize or identify with the feelings and needs of others;

8. Is often envious of others or believes that others are envious of him or her;
9. Shows arrogant, haughty behaviors or attitudes.

ANTISOCIAL PERSONALITY DISORDER

Antisocial personality disorder is a pattern of blatant disregard for the rights of others and society in general. Antisocial personalities are usually belligerent, intimidating, domineering, and hostile in their behavior toward others. They fail to conform to societal norms, engaging in illegal/unethical activities with perceived impunity. Berman, Whyne, and McCann (1995) hypothesized that a significant correlation exists between antisocial traits and acting out. Impulsive personality traits drive the antisocial personality. Paris (1997) noted that antisocial personality disorder overlaps with borderline personality disorder in underlying impulsive traits. Fiester and Gay's (1991) review of literature indicated the existence of significant comorbidity with narcissistic personality disorder. Millon (1997) noted that insensitivity and ruthlessness are the antisocial individual's only means of avoiding abuse and victimization. Violations of the law are commonplace. A physiological basis for antisocial behavior is also suggested by various studies. Raine, Lencz, Bihrle, LaCasse, and Colletti (2000) suggested that MRI findings indicate that the antisocial personality-disordered group had an 11% reduction in prefrontal gray matter compared to controls. Reich (1997) reported that lower social economic status is correlated with a higher degree of antisocial traits. Antisocial personalities are also referred to as psychopaths and sociopaths.

Mental Status Description

Patients diagnosed as sociopathic usually try to make a quick impression through appearance and behavior. Some come close to the following stereotype: The male patient may try to look very masculine; the female individual with antisocial personality disorder may try to appear seductive and feminine.

Motor behavior, speech, and mood of the sociopathic patient reveal some common characteristics. The male patient shows an erect posture, a forceful walk, and a strong handshake with a pronounced emphasis on movements, depending on whether he wants to appear "cool" and relaxed, strong and masculine, or display an "I don't care" attitude. The female may try to reveal her upper thighs, stretch out her breasts, and swing her hips in a provocative fashion.

R x CAPSULE: ANTISOCIAL

Because the antisocial-disordered patient is often mandated to therapy, motivation to change is often absent. Understanding the world through the individual's point of view, however, can make inroads into the therapeutic process and build a relationship of trust. Attempts to "emotionally open" the individual may lead to the discovery of positive expressions of affect. Guide the patient toward an understanding of the ramifications that current offensive behavioral patterns have on self and others. Group settings, particularly those involving team tasks, may help the antisocial adopt more appropriate interpersonal problem-solving techniques.

Speech may reveal stiltedness and boisterousness, or in males there may be noted a certain hoarseness with an attempt to appear smart and impressive with foul language or words he does not quite understand. His statements are rarely clear, detailed, and informative, but instead are exaggerated, vague, and contradictory, which suggest lying.

His mood may be irritable, depressed, or elated. He may portray a special emotional state such as modesty, which the clinician will soon recognize as being pretended to get the clinician on his side and have his way. Usually, he shows a lack of emotional control when caught lying or when asked to follow rules.

The insight of persons with antisocial personality disorder may be limited. They may have a tendency to blame the environment for their failures. However, when rapport is developed, they may admit that they "screwed up" their lives with self-destructive behavior. Judgment is often poor as well. Persons with antisocial personality disorder also lack remorse, which allows them to use unethical shortcuts in the pursuit of their goals (Othmer & Othmer, 1994, pp. 418–419).

Corresponding DSM-IV *Diagnostic Criteria (Antisocial)*

A pervasive pattern of disregard for and violation of the rights of others occurring since age 15 years, as indicated by three (or more) of the following:

1. Failure to conform to social norms with respect to lawful behaviors, as indicated by repeatedly performing acts that are grounds for arrest;

2. Deceitfulness, as indicated by repeated lying, use of aliases, or conning others for personal profit or pleasure;
3. Impulsivity or failure to plan ahead;
4. Irritability and aggressiveness, as indicated by repeated physical fights or assaults;
5. Reckless disregard for safety of self or others;
6. Consistent irresponsibility, as indicated by repeated failure to sustain consistent work behavior or honor financial obligations;
7. Lack of remorse, as indicated by being indifferent to or rationalizing having hurt, mistreated, or stolen from another.

SADISTIC PERSONALITY DISORDER

The sadistic personality disorder is a pattern characterized by aggressive behaviors. The pattern can be perceived more broadly than sexual sadism (Millon, 1997). Similar in qualities to the antisocial personality, individuals with sadistic personality are highly abusive in relationships and seemingly derive pleasure from humiliating others. Choca and Van Denburg (1997) suggested that this aggressive pattern is probably a more pathological variant of the antisocial personality. In studying the case histories of serial murderers, Geberth and Turco (1997) suggested that the offenders displayed antisocial behaviors during childhood, taking on elements of sexual sadism in adulthood. Reich's (1993) study of outpatient veterans diagnosed with sadistic personality disorder suggests that such individuals had significantly more bipolar and panic disorders than did individuals with antisocial personality disorder, but shared common high prevalence levels of depression, alcohol dependence, and posttraumatic stress disorder with the group with antisocial personality disorder. Geberth and Turco (1997) illustrated a style and pattern to the killings of serial murders that involved domination, control, humiliation, and sadistic sexual violence. Dill, Anderson, Anderson, and Deuser (1997) suggested that the aggressive personality includes a generally hostile schema, which influences expectations and perceptions of social interactions. Variants of "Type A" behavior may be associated with this pattern (Millon, 1997).

Mental Status Description

The physical and mental cruelty and lack of empathy that patients with sadistic personality disorder show for their victims will impress the clinician each time they are encountered. They are capable of finding victims; usually, they choose somebody under their control, such as a child, wife, student, employee, or elderly person. If their rank does not

R_x CAPSULE: SADISTIC

Be cognizant of the sadistic-disordered patient's ability to exploit the therapeutic relationship. Alter attitudes of control and domination of others, and convey the benefits derived from a healthy relationship. Address hostile and impulsive behaviors through anger-management training. Explore positive outlets for discharge of anger and teach restraint in its expression. Instill an attitude of tolerance toward others. Use role-reversal techniques to foster an appreciation of the other's perspective by giving the sadistic personality an opportunity to "walk in the other person's shoes."

assure them superiority, they will pick on somebody physically weaker. They find pleasure in dominating, torturing, and inflicting pain on their victims. Not only are they interested in the dominance and the ensuing increase in self-esteem, but also in the pain that they can unnecessarily and deliberately cause.

Means that can enhance both dominance over and torture of others have a magical fascination for them. Therefore, they like weapons, the martial arts, and professions that allow them to use them.

Patients with sadistic personality disorder do not seek treatment to have their sadism diffused. Sometimes, the clinician may encounter sadistic features in patients who suffer from other problems, such as persecutory delusions or alcohol or substance abuse. Usually, the clinician meets them through their victim. When the clinician interviews such persons, they may make attempts to intimidate, bluff, and make the clinician suffer, too. They will use their ways to impose their will on the clinician (Othmer & Othmer, 1994, pp. 443–444).

Corresponding DSM-III-R *Diagnostic Criteria (Sadistic)*

A pervasive pattern of cruel, demeaning, and aggressive behavior, beginning by early adulthood, as indicated by the repeated occurrence of at least four of the following:

1. Has used physical cruelty or violence for the purpose of establishing dominance in a relationship (not merely to achieve some noninterpersonal goal, such as striking someone to rob him or her);

2. Humiliates or demeans people in the presence of others;
3. Has treated or disciplined someone under his or her control unusually harshly (e.g., a child, student, prisoner, or patient);
4. Is amused by, or takes pleasure in, the psychological or physical suffering of others (including animals);
5. Has lied for the purpose of harming or inflicting pain on others (not merely to achieve some other goal);
6. Gets other people to do what he or she wants by frightening them (through intimidation or even terror);
7. Restricts the autonomy of people with whom he or she has a close relationship (e.g., will not let spouse leave the house unaccompanied or permit teenage children to attend social functions);
8. Is fascinated by violence, weapons, martial arts, injury, or torture.

COMPULSIVE PERSONALITY DISORDER

The compulsive personality is characterized by a preoccupation with orderliness, perfectionism, and control. Compulsive individuals are rigid, constricted, and organized in their behaviors, as well as in their thinking. Ritualistic behavior conforms in a clear way to the description of the obsessive–compulsive activity as mechanical, effortful, and as though in the service of an external directive (Shapiro, 1965). Repeated compulsions and obsessions experienced in the Axis I obsessive–compulsive disorder, however, are not in evidence in the Axis II obsessive–compulsive personality disorder. Analyses suggest that a significant correlation exists between obsessive–compulsive traits and reaction formation (Berman et al., 1995). Individuals with compulsive disorder exhibit prudent, controlled, and perfectionistic ways that are derived from a conflict between hostility toward others and fear of social disapproval. Such individuals' ambivalence is resolved by suppressing resentment, being overconforming, and placing high demands on themselves and others (Millon, 1997). Lacking in affective experience, the compulsive style is aptly described as "driven," marked by a rigidity in all undertakings (Shapiro, 1965). The "drive" may be expressed through excessive devotion to work, duty, or obligation.

Mental Status Description

The mental status of patients with obsessive–compulsive personality disorder is overshadowed by one difficulty: making decisions. This shows in their ambivalence and the way that they keep the clinician in limbo when answering questions. Should they open up to the clini-

R_X C A P S U L E : C O M P U L S I V E

The compulsive-disordered patient will expect a rigidly structured therapeutic environment. An initial supportive approach
can moderate the patient's anxiety, however, helping to secure
a bond of trust. Explore underlying feelings of resentment and
fears of disapproval by others. Examine and identify repressed
emotions, particularly conflicts regarding expectations of self and
other. Challenge the rigid cognitive assumptions that interfere
with desired goals, and identify practical, workable solutions.
Stress-management techniques can provide useful coping alterna-
tives with regard to daily stressors.

cian or be misunderstood? They may decide not to open up, but will
wonder, is that right? Should they spend their money on a clinician
and then risk not getting a true reading of their problems? Is the
clinician the best person to talk to? Probably not. They have to find
out from the clinician what is wrong. They should ask the questions;
the clinician should provide the answers. Who is in charge? Should they
or the clinician be in charge, since the clinician is the supposed expert?

Obsessive–compulsive patients perceive themselves as being neu-
tral—a quite distorted view. The clinician senses a low-grade, chronic
anger that can flare up into tenacious, persistent, bothersome questioning that cannot be satisfied by any answer. Their anger will become
overt when their obsessive expectations are not met, when they feel
shortchanged in interviewing time, overcharged for the visit, or not
rewarded with useful answers to their questions (Othmer & Othmer,
1994, p. 438).

Corresponding DSM-IV *Diagnostic Criteria (Obsessive–Compulsive)*

A pervasive pattern of preoccupation with orderliness, perfectionism,
and mental and interpersonal control, at the expense of flexibility,
openness, and efficiency, beginning by early adulthood and present in
a variety of contexts, as indicated by four (or more) of the following:

1. Is preoccupied with details, rules, lists, order, organization,
   or schedules to the extent that the major point of the activity
   is lost;

2. Shows perfectionism that interferes with task completion (e.g., is unable to complete a project because his or her own overly strict standards are not met);
3. Is excessively devoted to work and productivity to the exclusion of leisure activities and friendships (not accounted for by obvious economic necessity);
4. Is overconscientious, scrupulous, and inflexible about matters of morality, ethics, or values (not accounted for by cultural or religious identification);
5. Is unable to discard worn-out or worthless objects even when they have no sentimental value;
6. Is reluctant to delegate tasks or to work with others unless they submit to exactly his or her way of doing things;
7. Adopts a miserly spending style toward self and others, and money is viewed as something to be hoarded for future catastrophes;
8. Shows rigidity and stubbornness.

NEGATIVISTIC PERSONALITY DISORDER

The negativistic (passive–aggressive) personality disorder is a pattern of marked vacillation between dependence and independence. Compliant at one moment, oppositional the next, individuals with negativistic personality disorder are conflicted between satisfying their own needs and complying with the desires of others. One moment they may lash out in anger, the next they are seeking contrition. Perpetual inner turmoil and anxiety are likely the result of their ambivalence. Rapid succession of mood and behavior shifts is the rule.

Fine, Overholser, and Berkoff's (1992) dimensional model proposed that passive–aggressive behavior is related to five critical elements: rigidity, resentment, resistance, reactance, and reversed reinforcement, with rigidity and resistance being the foundation on which other passive–aggressive behaviors are demonstrated. Sprock and Hunsucker (1998) also suggested a pattern of passive resistance and a reactance through procrastination as features of the passive–aggressive patients examined. An overall negative stance in life is evident through a pervasive distrust of the world. Negativistic personalities experience endless wrangles and disappointments as they vacillate between deference and defiance (Millon, 1997).

Mental Status Description

During an interview, patients with passive–aggressive personalities may not show much psychopathology. Their stories become transparent

R x C A P S U L E : N E G A T I V I S T I C

Treatment may resemble a tug-of-war because of the characteristic ambivalence of the negativistic-disordered patient. Supportive techniques can be helpful to attenuate initial anxiety, though medication may also be indicated. The therapeutic focus should be placed on the reduction of the patient's ambivalence of whether to submit to others' desires or satisfy self needs and wishes. Replace negative and contrary thinking with increased feelings of contentment. Positively rechannel anger and resentment. Strengthen feelings of self-control through assertiveness training techniques.

when they talk about social disappointments, interpersonal conflicts, and bad breaks. Typically, patients do not openly oppose demands, but accept commitments and make promises even when they know they will not keep them. They say "yes," but act "no." This characteristic leads to disappointments and rejection by colleagues, friends, and family members; and such patients will complain bitterly about being rejected without understanding how they set it off.

Their affect appears to be well-adjusted and pleasant, except when they talk about situations in which they were asked to perform. Then they show signs of resentment, irritability, or anger. If the clinician fails to identify these trigger situations, the underlying personality disorder may be missed (Othmer & Othmer, 1994, p. 441).

Corresponding DSM-IV Research Criteria (Passive–Aggressive)

A pervasive pattern of negativistic attitudes and passive resistance to demands for adequate performance, beginning by early adulthood and present in a variety of contexts, as indicated by four (or more) of the following:

1. Passively resists fulfilling routine social and occupational tasks;
2. Complains of being misunderstood and unappreciated by others;
3. Is sullen and argumentative;
4. Unreasonably criticizes and scorns authority;
5. Expresses envy and resentment toward those apparently more fortunate;

6. Voices exaggerated and persistent complaints of personal misfortune;
7. Alternates between hostile defiance and contrition.

MASOCHISTIC PERSONALITY DISORDER

The masochistic (self-defeating) personality disorder is marked by devaluation and denigration of self, eliciting a martyr-like complex. The masochistic personality displays a pattern of sacrificing oneself for the "good" of the other. Lebe (1997) suggested that although self-defeating personalities can be sensitive to others, they are unable to be sensitive to themselves. Typically acting in an unassuming and self-effacing manner, they often exaggerate their deficits and place themselves in an inferior light or abject position (Millon, 1997). Masochistic individuals suffer from low self-esteem, depression, and an inability to enjoy their successes or life experiences (Lebe, 1997). Williams and Schill (1994) found that research participants with self-defeating tendencies have difficulty trusting and depending on others in relationships and display fear and anxiety of being unloved and abandoned. Horney (1939) contended that masochistic trends can also serve a need for power and control, with underlying drives for control being projected through a sense of suffering and helplessness. Choca and Van Denburg (1997) considered the self-defeating pattern to be a more pathological variant of the negativistic personality style.

Mental Status Description

The characteristics that self-defeating individuals display are the sacrificing of their interests for others. They give up their pleasure and

---

R x CAPSULE: MASOCHISTIC

Initially establish a supportive, compassionate relationship to counter the masochistic-disordered patient's expectations of "deserved rejection." Identify self-defeating, negative thought and behavior patterns, and cognitively challenge the self-imposed role of martyr. Empower the individual to adopt prosocial, self-promoting behaviors without incorporating painful feelings of guilt or shame. Assertiveness training can help the individual learn methods to positively manage self- and other-directed abuse. Engender a positive sense of self.

professional opportunities in favor of someone else's. Their sacrifice is often unsolicited, and, therefore, a bother to others and not appreciated, which can cause rejection. Typically, they misinterpret the reason for this rejection. They believe that they have not given enough and, thus, they increase contempt rather than ameliorate rejection. Dysphoric feelings and hopelessness result.

If the clinician explores their needs and confronts them with their denial of those needs, they will indicate that their needs are egotistical and that it is repulsive to them to pursue those needs. They seem to consider it a sin to even talk about them. If the clinician points out how their self-denial contributes to their misery, they may reject the clinician as materialistic and nonunderstanding and lose interest (Othmer & Othmer, 1994, p. 448).

Corresponding DSM-III-R *Diagnostic Criteria (Self-Defeating)*

A pervasive pattern of self-defeating behavior, beginning by early adulthood and present in a variety of contexts. Such persons may often avoid or undermine pleasurable experiences, be drawn to situations or relationships in which they will suffer, and prevent others from helping them, as indicated by at least five of the following:

1. Chooses people and situations that lead to disappointment, failure, or mistreatment even when better options are clearly available;
2. Rejects or renders ineffective the attempts of others to help him or her;
3. Following positive personal events (e.g., new achievement), responds with depression, guilt, or a behavior that produces pain (e.g., an accident);
4. Incites angry or rejecting responses from others and then feels hurt, defeated, or humiliated (e.g., makes fun of spouse in public, provoking an angry retort, then feels devastated);
5. Rejects opportunities for pleasure, or is reluctant to acknowledge enjoying him- or herself (despite having adequate social skills and the capacity for pleasure);
6. Fails to accomplish tasks crucial to his or her personal objectives despite demonstrated ability to do so (e.g., helps fellow students write papers, but is unable to write his or her own);
7. Is uninterested in or rejects people who consistently treat him or her well (e.g., is unattracted to caring sexual partners);
8. Engages in excessive self-sacrifice that is unsolicited by the intended recipients of the sacrifice.

Severe Personality Pathology

Millon refers to the severe personality pathology disorders as structurally defective personalities. The three personalities—schizotypal, borderline, and paranoid—parallel, in more severe form, the 11 Clinical Personality Patterns (Millon & Davis, 1996). They can be considered more severe variants of the clinical patterns. For example, the more dysfunctional variants of the schizoid and avoidant personalities blend into the schizotypal personality and so forth. See Table 1-3 for Millon's evolutionary model and its personality disorder derivatives. As with the interpretation of the Clinical Personality Patterns, these scales should be configurally interpreted.

SCHIZOTYPAL PERSONALITY DISORDER

The schizotypal personality disorder is a pattern of prominent behavioral peculiarities and eccentricities, with an emphasis on social isolation. Individuals with schizotypal personality disorder prefer to be alone and actually experience discomfort within personal relationships. Isolation generally becomes more acute with time, as they detach from societal affairs and wander aimlessly through life. Cognitive confusion and flattened affect are usually present. Negative symptoms include social isolation and impaired functioning. Though absent of delusions and hallucinations, the oddities found in this disorder are similar to the positive symptoms of schizophrenia (Othmer & Othmer, 1994).

Battaglia and Bellodi (1992) proposed that schizotypal personality disorder is a separate, milder, and probably more common disorder than schizophrenia. Trestman and colleagues (1995) suggested that schizotypal patients may share some of the cognitive deficits observed in schizophrenia, many of which involve executive functioning. In their review of data, Jacobsberg, Hymowitz, Barasch, and Frances (1986) indicated that schizotypal personalities share additive symptoms with those with borderline personality disorder. Craig (1999, p. 27) noted, "It is believed that they are prone to developed schizophrenia if sufficiently distressed."

Mental Status Description

The mental status of patients with schizotypal personality disorder shows several characteristic features. The patients' attire may be some-

R x CAPSULE: SCHIZOTYPAL

Appropriate antipsychotic medication may be indicated if severe symptoms are present in a schizotypal-disordered patient. A caring, supportive approach that emphasizes a sense of self-worth is initially helpful. Clear and simple instructions can promote more focused thinking. Teach the individual to differentiate between fact and fantasy and help develop simple strategies for coping. Training in social skills, emphasizing social interaction, should proceed in a graduated manner. For the patient with a mild disorder, group therapy may offer a supportive milieu through which social interaction is experienced and communication skills can be practiced.

what peculiar. They may use words with an unusual meaning or in an unusual context. Their sense of humor may strike one as bizarre and their thoughts may be hard to follow. They will make an effort to communicate their thoughts and feelings to the clinician, provided they trust the clinician and believe it is worthwhile to talk to the clinician.

The patients' thought content is indeed remarkable. They may show paranoid ideation, suspiciousness, ideas of reference, and magical thinking. They may claim to have access to a fourth dimension, to have out-of-body experiences, ESP, and premonitions. The peculiarities in formulation and thought content give the impression that the patients are odd, strange, eccentric, and superstitious. Their affect changes with the thought content. They may appear aloof and cold when the clinician involves them in topics of the clinician's choosing, but become lively and even intense in their affect when they talk about their "telepathic experiences."

Their orientation, memory, and information processing are intact and their speech is coherent. Their judgment, however, is influenced by thoughts situated outside the realm of verifiable reality. They have partial insight; they know that others consider them odd, strange, and sometimes hard to understand. However, they see these others as unable to look beyond a simplistic reality and not as critics of their poor reality testing (Othmer & Othmer, 1994, pp. 413–414).

Corresponding DSM-IV *Diagnostic Criteria (Schizotypal)*

A pervasive pattern of social and interpersonal deficits marked by acute discomfort with, and reduced capacity for, close relationships, as well as by cognitive or perceptual distortions and eccentricities of behavior, beginning by early adulthood and present in a variety of contexts, as indicated by five (or more) of the following:

1. Ideas of reference (excluding delusions of reference);
2. Odd beliefs or magical thinking that influences behavior and is inconsistent with subcultural norms (e.g., superstitiousness, belief in clairvoyance, telepathy, or "sixth sense"; in children and adolescents, bizarre fantasies or preoccupations);
3. Unusual perceptual experiences, including bodily illusions;
4. Odd thinking and speech (e.g., vague, circumstantial, metaphorical, overelaborate, or stereotyped);
5. Suspiciousness or paranoid ideation;
6. Inappropriate or constricted affect;
7. Behavior or appearance that is odd, eccentric, or peculiar;
8. Lack of close friends or confidants other than first-degree relatives;
9. Excessive social anxiety that does not diminish with familiarity and tends to be associated with paranoid fears rather than negative judgments about self.

BORDERLINE PERSONALITY DISORDER

The borderline personality disorder is a pattern of disruptive, unstable, and superficial relationships, marked by intense clinging behavior. Underlying this instability is an uncertain self-image (Millon, 1997). Emotions are intense and labile. Repeated dissolution of relationships results in feelings of dejection and periods of intense depression, irritability, and anxiety. Individuals with borderline personalities are particularly vulnerable to separation or abandonment, and as a consequence incessantly seek the attachment of others. Behavior becomes unpredictable and impulsive when fears of abandonment surface.

In a review of the literature, Torgensen (1994) proposed two syndromes of a borderline personality disorder: the impulsive, characterized by instability and intensity; and the empty, consisting of behaviors that include suicidal threats, abandonment anxiety, and identity disturbances. Most etiological theories stress psychological factors in the development of borderline personality. Borderline personality disorders tend to occur in females who have experienced severe physical, emotional, or sexual abuse during childhood (Galletly, 1997). Basic instability in mood, thinking, behavior, relationships, and self-image aptly characterizes a borderline personality.

R x C A P S U L E : B O R D E R L I N E

With multiple symptoms, antidepressant, antianxiety, or antipsy-chotic agents may be indicated, at times, during treatment for the borderline-disordered patient. A supportive, though struc-tured, therapeutic setting can serve as the cornerstone of treat-ment and help attenuate underlying fears of abandonment. Pro-vide steady assurances to counter emotional lability. Gradually reframe the individual's ways of defining the environment by de-signing adaptive and autonomous strategies. Control of emotions and behaviors can be learned and rehearsed within the context of a secure and trusting therapeutic relationship. Group therapy can serve as an effective means to encourage constructive be-haviors.

Mental Status Description

The overriding feature in mental status of individuals with borderline personality disorder is the intense but labile affect. It varies from eu-phoric to depressed, from appreciative to angry and critical. The affect shows a close relationship to both the content of the patients' stories and the way they experience the clinician. The labile affect is paralleled by the description of a labile mood.

The excessive intensity of affect and mood is impressive. Unlike histrionic personality disorder, in which the affect appears more in-tensely expressed than felt, patients with borderline personality disor-der genuinely experience an intense affect and mood. The flair of phoniness is missing. Investigators have found that patients with bor-derline personality disorder show a strong relationship to patients with bipolar disorder and may be a variant.

The lability in emotions persists also in the patients' social attitude. Intense ambivalence to close friends leads to contradictory reports about their characteristics: They are either overidealized or devaluated. Since patients with borderline personality disorder have no distance from their intense feelings, they have no insight into the source of their difficulties (Othmer & Othmer, 1994, pp. 423–424).

Corresponding **DSM-IV** *Diagnostic Criteria (Borderline)*

A pervasive pattern of instability of interpersonal relationships, self-image, and affects, and marked impulsivity beginning by early adulthood and present in a variety of contexts, as indicated by five (or more) of the following:

1. Frantic efforts to avoid real or imagined abandonment. (Note: Do not include suicidal or self-mutilating behavior covered in Criterion 5.);
2. A pattern of unstable and intense interpersonal relationships characterized by alternating between extremes of idealization and devaluation;
3. Identity disturbance: markedly and persistently unstable self-image or sense of self;
4. Impulsivity in at least some areas that are potentially self-damaging (e.g., spending, sex, substance abuse, reckless driving, binge eating). (Note: Do not include suicidal or self-mutilating behavior covered in Criterion 5.);
5. Recurrent suicidal behavior, gestures, or threats, or self-mutilating behavior;
6. Affective instability as a result of a marked reactivity of mood (e.g., intense episodic dysphoria, irritability, or anxiety, usually lasting a few hours and only rarely more than a few days) and chronic feelings of emptiness;
7. Inappropriate, intense anger or difficulty controlling anger (e.g., frequent displays of temper, constant anger, recurrent physical fights);
8. Transient, stress-related paranoid ideation or severe dissociative symptoms.

PARANOID PERSONALITY DISORDER

The paranoid personality disorder is characterized by suspiciousness and an intense mistrust of others. Shapiro (1965) identified two differentiations of suspiciousness among individuals with paranoid personality: (a) the furtive, constricted, and apprehensive; and (b) the rigidly arrogant, aggressive, and megalomaniacal. Such individuals vigilantly patrol the environment with remarkably acute, intense, and active attention. Thinking is rigid and inflexible and is oftentimes distorted. Individuals with paranoid personality often misread situations because they anxiously expect to be deceived. Always perceiving and interpreting the reactions of others to be threatening, they are generally tense, hostile, argumentative, and combative.

Comparing paranoid personalities with normal controls, Turkat, Keane, and Thompson-Pope (1990) found that the paranoid research participants were more likely to respond to varied provocations with anger than did the controls. In a study of panic-disordered patients,

Reich and Braginsky (1994) found slightly more than half of the research participants studied to have paranoid personality disorder, suggesting that paranoid traits may be secondary to chronic anxiety illnesses. The ever-constant vigilance is incompatible with spontaneous and reactive emotions, severely restricting the paranoid's affective response.

Mental Status Description

Hypervigilance and suspiciousness overshadow the mental status of patients with paranoid personality disorder. Their attire may be meticulous so as not to give anyone reason for criticism or show some neglect if they are depressed. They may, then, express that they are not interested in pleasing anyone. Their speech is usually fluent and goal-directed. The content of these goals is characteristic of their disorder: checking of the clinician's intentions, expressing that they look through the clinician's maneuvers, and voicing their displeasure about the clinician's "secret plans." Their affect vacillates between anxiousness and overt hostility. Memory and orientation are intact, but their judgment is impaired by their suspiciousness. They may acknowledge their suspiciousness, but staunchly defend it as justified and not accept it as part of a personality disorder (Othmer & Othmer, 1994, p. 408).

Corresponding **DSM-IV** *Diagnostic Criteria (Paranoid)*

A pervasive distrust and suspiciousness of others, such that their motives are interpreted as malevolent, beginning by early adulthood and

---

Rₓ CAPSULE: PARANOID

Medication, if indicated, should be used judiciously, to avoid heightening suspicion in an already untrusting paranoid-disordered patient. As with the other severe patterns, building a supportive, trusting therapeutic setting is of paramount importance. Although establishing rapport with the paranoid may present a challenge to the therapist, a trusting therapeutic relationship is the key component for successful treatment. Only after such a bond is established can other therapeutic techniques be effectively used. Though various therapeutic methods may prove helpful, a supportive approach is the treatment of choice.

present in a variety of contexts, as indicated by four (or more) of the following:

1. Suspects, without sufficient basis, that others are exploiting, harming, or deceiving him or her;
2. Is preoccupied with unjustified doubts about the loyalty or trustworthiness of friends or associates;
3. Is reluctant to confide in others because of unwarranted fear that the information will be used maliciously against him or her;
4. Reads hidden demeaning or threatening meanings into benign remarks or events;
5. Persistently bears grudges (e.g., is unforgiving of insults, injuries, or slights);
6. Perceives attacks on his or her character or reputation that are not apparent to others and is quick to react angrily or to counterattack;
7. Has recurrent suspicions without justification regarding fidelity of spouse or sexual partner.

Comorbidity Among Clinical Personality Disorders

Millon's research indicates that various disorders frequently accompany or overlap with particular disorders and provide varying comorbidities of individually diagnosed personality disorders. Exhibit 5-2, adapted from *Disorders of Personality DSM-IV and Beyond* (Millon & Davis, 1996), presents Millon's research for the varying comorbidities existing among patterns of personality disorders.

The more prevalent associations among personality disorders are depicted in Exhibit 5-2 as primary covariations with more modest associations depicted as secondary covariations. For example, looking at the first disorder listed in the exhibit, the most prevalent association can be found between the schizoid and avoidant personalities. The avoidant, therefore, is labeled as a primary covariation of the schizoid personality. Associations also exist with the schizotypal, dependent, compulsive, and negativistic personalities, though with more modest levels of comorbidity. These are labeled as secondary covariations. Primary and secondary covariations are included for all the clinical personality patterns and severe personality pathology disorders.

EXHIBIT 5-2

Comorbidity Among Clinical Disorders

Disorder	Primary Covariations	Secondary Covariations
Schizoid	Avoidant	Schizotypal Dependent Compulsive Negativistic
Avoidant	Schizoid Depressive Dependent Paranoid	Masochistic Schizotypal Borderline Negativistic
Depressive	Masochistic Avoidant	Borderline Negativistic Dependent
Dependent	Masochistic Avoidant	Depressive Histrionic Negativistic Compulsive
Histrionic	Narcissistic	Dependent Antisocial Borderline Negativistic Compulsive
Narcissistic	Histrionic Antisocial	Sadistic Paranoid Negativistic
Antisocial	Narcissistic Sadistic	Borderline Histrionic Paranoid Negativistic

continued

CASE REVIEW

We will now review a case history that exhibits an individual with schizotypal personality disorder, a more serious variant of the schizoid personality disorder. The MCMI-III data is found in Exhibit 5-3.

Recurrent Depression in the Schizotypal Personality

Reason for Referral

Mr. J. is an outpatient recently discharged from a psychiatric hospital. He came to the emergency room clinic saying that "he was not able to manage his life." Mr. J. has an extensive history of psychiatric hospitalizations, as well as drug and alcohol abuse.

EXHIBIT 5-2 (Continued)

Comorbidity Among Clinical Disorders

Disorder	Primary Covariations	Secondary Covariations
Sadistic	Antisocial Negativistic	Narcissistic Paranoid Borderline
Compulsive	Schizoid Dependent	Paranoid Negativistic
Negativistic	Paranoid Borderline Sadistic	Histrionic Depressive Avoidant Masochistic Antisocial
Masochistic	Dependent Borderline Depressive	Avoidant Negativistic Compulsive Schizotypal
Schizotypal	Schizoid Avoidant Paranoid	Borderline Masochistic Dependent
Borderline	Negativistic Masochistic	Antisocial Sadistic Histrionic Depressive Avoidant Schizotypal
Paranoid	Compulsive Avoidant Sadistic Negativistic Narcissistic	Schizotypal Antisocial

Source: Disorders of Personality DSM-IV and Beyond (2nd ed.) by T. Millon and Davis, 1996, New York. Copyright 1996 John Wiley & Sons, Inc. Adapted and reprinted with permission.

Background Information

Mr. J. is a 46-year-old, White male with a GED education. Mr. J. never married. He is the youngest of four siblings. Both of his deceased parents were alcoholics, and his mother had a history of psychiatric hospitalizations. He has worked sporadically as a freight handler, though left his last job because he "felt out of place." He has been institutionalized and incarcerated for the greater part of his life. An initial placement was made

EXHIBIT 5-3

MCMI-III BR Scale Scores: Mr. J.

Category	BR Score	Scales	
			Validity Index = 1
Modifying indices	69	Disclosure	(Scale X)
	35	Desirability	(Scale Y)
	91	Debasement	(Scale Z)
Clinical personality patterns	96	Schizoid	(Scale 1)
	78	Avoidant	(Scale 2A)
	86	Depressive	(Scale 2B)
	40	Dependent	(Scale 3)
	30	Histrionic	(Scale 4)
	49	Narcissistic	(Scale 5)
	45	Antisocial	(Scale 6A)
	43	Sadistic	(Scale 6B)
	55	Compulsive	(Scale 7)
	80	Negativistic	(Scale 8A)
	71	Masochistic	(Scale 8B)
Severe personality pathology	102	Schizotypal	(Scale S)
	70	Borderline	(Scale C)
	78	Paranoid	(Scale P)
Clinical syndromes	90	Anxiety disorder	(Scale A)
	75	Somatoform disorder	(Scale H)
	64	Bipolar: manic disorder	(Scale N)
	91	Dysthymic disorder	(Scale D)
	95	Alcohol dependence	(Scale B)
	75	Drug dependence	(Scale T)
	79	Post-traumatic stress	(Scale R)
Severe clinical syndromes	80	Thought disorder	(Scale SS)
	95	Major depression	(Scale CC)
	63	Delusional disorder	(Scale PP)

in a state school at the age of 5, following founded allegations of parental sexual abuse. At the age of 16, he was incarcerated for being an accessory to rape and robbery. He indicated that he had been hospitalized "many times" for emotional problems and depression. He made multiple suicide attempts during his numerous incarcerations. He lives alone and has no friends, though expressed no feelings of loneliness. He indicated that his problems are complicated by people trying to be friendly, saying, "I shut them out. I don't want to get close to anyone."

Mental Status Examination

Mr. J. was apprehensive and guarded throughout the interview. He was shabbily dressed and carelessly groomed. He was alert and attentive. Thought processing was at times tangential and disorganized, though no delusions or hallucinations were present. He reported experiencing persistent suicidal ideation, stating, "I cannot get out of my mental prison." Oftentimes he experienced feelings of "being dead" inside. Long-term and recent memory were intact, though short-term memory displayed mild impairment. Affect was flat and blunted, though he appeared tense and apprehensive. He described his mood as depressed "all of the time." He complained of frequent insomnia. Psychomotor retardation was in evidence. Though cooperative and compliant, he appeared withdrawn throughout the entire evaluation.

> Positively Scored Schizotypal Prototypic Items: 48, 71, 76, 117, 138, 158, 162
> Noteworthy Responses: 18, 34, 44, 48, 74, 81, 92, 105, 132, 165, 167
> Personality Code: 12B**8A2A*8B+756A6B3"4//S**P*//
> Syndrome Code: B<u>DA</u>**<u>RHT</u>*//CC**SS*//

MCMI-III INTERPRETIVE REASONING

The Validity index of 1 suggests questionable validity, and the protocol should be interpreted with caution. The extensive psychiatric history and extreme elevation on Scale Z may suggest a client who is seriously disturbed and currently psychologically overburdened.

Individuals with similar patterns have pervasive deficits in social and interpersonal functioning. Behavior and appearance are strikingly peculiar. These passively detached individuals are dull, lifeless, and strange, generally detached and indifferent to their surroundings. They distance themselves from intimate relationships, alienating themselves from social interactions. They generally maintain a defeatist and fatalistic attitude. Affect is bland, and thinking is distorted, with evidence of cognitive slippage. Feelings of pessimism, hopelessness, and emptiness are accentuated by their inability to adapt to the external pressures of the environment. BR 102 on the Schizotypal scale indicates a more serious dysfunctional variant of the schizoid personality style. Detachment and isolation are pervasive, with ever-present feelings of estrangement to one's surroundings being the norm. Schizotypal personalities have few, if any, personal attachments. Impaired functioning, odd communication, and cognitive confusion are evident in this severe clinical pattern. Overall, this pattern represents a cognitively dysfunctional and socially detached individual, who manifests an emotionally flat affect and indifferent behavior. Ability to adequately function on a daily basis without assistance, however, is questionable. The *Harvard Mental Health Letter* (April, 2000) suggested that the schizotypal personality can be referred to as a "schizophrenic phenotype," an individual who may be biologically vulnerable to schizophrenia. Episodic psychotic processes may likely occur when external stressors become unmanageable.

Numerous elevations on the Clinical Syndromes scales and the Severe Clinical Syndromes scales are consistent with current psychological discomfort. Extreme elevations on Anxiety and Dysthymic scales are indicative of an overly anxious and edgy individual burdened with chronic feelings of pessimism and hopelessness. The elevated BR score of 95 on Scale CC likely indicates an inability to manage his daily affairs. The elevated SS scale suggests a possible thought disorder, and additional clinical evaluation may be warranted to rule out the possibility of psychosis. A positive response to question 34, "Lately I have gone all to pieces," may currently be suggestive of moderate deterioration. The presence of a cognitive disorder, as indicated on Scale SS, is exaggerated under stressful conditions. As noted in the *DSM-IV*, 30% to 50% of individuals diagnosed with schizotypal personality disorder are concurrently diagnosed with major depression.

Antidepressant medication may be indicated to moderate Mr. J.'s current pessimistic mood. Individuals having personality patterns, such as Mr. J.'s, may experience transient psychotic episodes when faced with unmanageable, external stressors. Individuals displaying milder signs of this disorder may not require medication. The risk of losing reality contact in an already socially disconnected individual should be given the clinician's full attention. The most effective therapeutic approach includes structured sessions that use supportive, problem-solving approaches. The caution, though, is to remain within the limits of the individual's boundaries without being too persistent and demanding. Once a supportive therapeutic alliance is developed, social-skills training can be used to enhance adaptive functioning through individual and group settings. A 12-step alcohol meeting, for example, may prove to be an appropriate group format for this client.

DIAGNOSTIC IMPRESSIONS

Axis I: 96.33 Major Depression (recurrent, severe)
Axis II: 301.22 Schizotypal Personality Disorder With Schizoid
Personality Traits

In Summary

We have seen that defining personality and pathology, even within a classification system, is at times elusive. This chapter discussed a range of Axis II personality disorders and provided guidelines for their interpretation using the MCMI-III. The line between normal and abnormal personality is one of degree more than of kind. Each personality disorder has distinct functional processes and structural attributes from which Axis I symptoms derive their meaning. Now we turn our attention to the third part of our discussion on interpretation and explore the clinical syndromes classified on Axis I of the *DSM-IV*.

Test Yourself Exercises 5

Fill in the Blanks.

1. The MCMI-III measures diagnostic levels of pathology along a _____ continuum.

2. Millon established cutoff scores of BR _____ to indicate the presence of a personality trait, and BR _____ to indicate the presence of a personality disorder.

3. _____ interpretation most clearly defines an accurate characterization of an individual's personality pattern.

4. Millon suggests interpretation of single-scale (prototypic) elevations when the scale is more than _____ above the next highest elevated scales.

5. In general, the greater the number of elevations on the MCMI-III means _____.

6. Elevations on the _____, _____, and _____ scales at times reflect personality strengths rather than pathology.

7. Configural interpretation becomes more difficult when scales are elevated to approximately _____.

8. A dependent personality displaying rigid, perfectionistic, and orderly traits may likely have a secondary elevation on the _____ scale.

9. A negativistic personality displaying ego-centered confidence and haughty traits may likely have a secondary elevation on the _____ scale.
10. An avoidant personality displaying a hyperalertness and suspicious traits may likely have a secondary elevation on the _____ scale.

Fill in the Blanks

Identify the following descriptors with the correct Clinical Personality Patterns/Severe Personality Pathology scales.

1. _____ detachment from social relationships, restricted range of emotion, incapacity for pleasure or pain.
2. _____ preoccupation with orderliness, perfectionism; "driven," constricted in behavior/thinking.
3. _____ disruptive and unstable relationships, fears of abandonment, intense clinging behavior.
4. _____ underlying hostility, combative and abusive in relationships, delights in destructive behavior.
5. _____ overly suspicious and mistrustful of others, mild delusional thinking, irritability with others.
6. _____ submissive and clinging behavior, reliant on others, passive, nonassertive, and compliant.
7. _____ pervasive disregard for societal values, callous unconcern for others' rights, self-centered egocentricity.
8. _____ guarded for fear of rejection/devaluation, withdrawal from others, approach/avoidance conflict.
9. _____ sustained feelings of pessimism and gloom, despair about the future, feelings of worthlessness and guilt.
10. _____ negative stance in life, uses forgetfulness, procrastinates.
11. _____ self-centered grandiose disposition, lack of empathy, "special" character.
12. _____ acute discomfort in personal attachments, disorganized, autistic-like thinking, eccentric behavior.
13. _____ pervasive devaluation of self, self-effacing behaviors, self-sacrificing demeanor.
14. _____ attention-seeking and dramatic behaviors, seductive and manipulative demeanor, relationships tend to be shallow.

Identify the following "class-disordered" student patterns with their corresponding Clinical Personality Patterns/Severe Personality Pathology scales.

1. _____ Matthew seems very strange. He appears confused much of the time and aimlessly wanders about. When called on by the professor, his responses are very bizarre, almost "other-worldly."
2. _____ Emily always feels uneasy when called on in class. She changed groups for a class project, because she said she didn't feel part of the group. She seems shy.

3. _____ Hannah comes to class each week and tells her classmates about her newfound boyfriends. Her responses are very impulsive, and she often winds up in a heated discussion with the professor. She became very angry when the professor hinted that she might be better off enrolling in another section.

4. _____ Ashley never seems to be able to concentrate in class. She says that much of the class work is very taxing for her. She says that she has been fatigued for the longest time and doesn't know if she'll have the energy to finish the semester.

5. _____ Daniel never misses a class and always sits in the same seat. He comes to class at least 15 minutes ahead of time—to get his favorite seat. His papers always look professionally typed, and he always receives *A*s. He seems determined to graduate *summa cum laude*.

6. _____ Tyler thinks he is really "something." He rarely comes to class because he says that "he doesn't need to." He never seems to care about others in class. You can usually find him smoking in the "no smoking" zones.

7. _____ Sarah really angered her group. The day the group presentation was due, she sheepishly announced that her section wasn't completed and couldn't do the presentation. She seemed angry with the group when the group reminded her that the project was her idea. After class she expressed her apologies and said next time she'll be ready.

8. _____ Taylor has a flare for the dramatic. She enjoys giving class presentations. She likes to flirt a lot.

9. _____ No one really knows Andrew. He rarely talks, and when he does, he seems vague about everything. He usually sits way in the back of class by himself. He never comes to the monthly class parties.

10. _____ Zachary has a strange habit. Before entering the class, he stands at the door for a few moments and looks around the classroom. He never seems to believe what anyone says and always asks, "Is that what you really mean?" He thinks the professor always refers to him in the examples used.

11. _____ Jonathan thinks he's omniscient. He always says he should be teaching the class because he knows more than the professor. He thinks he's "special."

12. _____ Alyssa always seems to be asking everyone for help with her assignments. She will go along with whatever her friends want to do. Once she makes a friendship, it seems as if it is a lifetime relationship.

13. _____ Amanda can never seem to do enough to help her classmates. She got an A in the course, but said she was just lucky and didn't deserve it.

14. _____ Nicholas always seems to be combative and mocks his group members. When one member respectfully challenged his abusive attitude, he really became angry. It seems that he enjoys humiliating others.

Match

Match personalities in column A with descriptions in column B.

A	
A	**B**

A

Histrionic–borderline
Avoidant–negativistic
Compulsive–paranoid
Schizoid–dependent
Paranoid–antisocial
Compulsive–schizoid
Schizotypal–avoidant
Depressive–dependent
Borderline–negativistic
Narcissistic–sadistic
Antisocial–narcissistic
Avoidant–masochistic

B

1. _____ Self-sacrificing demeanor; devaluation of self; socially inhibited, feelings of inadequacy; low self-esteem; hypervigilant to rejection and refusal.

2. _____ Socially inhibited; feelings of inadequacy; odd, eccentric behavior; cognitive slippage; magical thinking; fear of rejection and humiliation.

3. _____ Variable, labile, and unpredictable moods/behaviors; unstable relationships; displays underlying resentfulness; overly sensitive; resistant to the demands of others.

4. _____ Conflict between fear of autonomy and the need for attachment; socially inhibited; fear of embarrassment; resistant to occupational/social performance; resentful of others.

5. _____ Detachment in relationships; quiet submission to others; feelings of emptiness with aimless direction; feelings of weakness and inadequacy abound; uneventful life.

6. _____ Overcontrolled and rigid in thought/behavior; lack of social attachment; minimal emotional expression.

7. _____ Excessive attention-seeking behaviors; gregarious; feelings of superiority, and being "special"; disregard for others; manipulation of others.

8. _____ Fear of genuine autonomy; veneer of social gregariousness; labile emotions; demanding, clingy behavior; fear of abandonment.

9. _____ Distrustful and suspicious of others; callous, tough-minded; overly self-confident, competitive, inflated, self-esteem; aggressive behaviors.

10. _____ Long-standing negative thought patterns; rueful emotions; clingy, submissive behaviors; sense of total inadequacy.

11. _____ Rigid, disciplined; perfectionistic tendencies; distrusting of others; feelings of inadequacy; suspicious of other's motives; constricted; apprehensive.

12. _____ Strong need for admiration; self-centered; highly combative; superior attitude toward others; feelings of being "special"; delights in destructive behaviors; lacks empathy.

Interpretation: Clinical and Severe Syndromes (Axis I)

6

Personality, as we discussed earlier, is a pattern of collective temperament, behaviors, emotions, cognitions, and traits that make up distinctive qualities of an individual. By definition, it can be said that personality patterns embody particular syndromal patterns and are associated with common mental illnesses. These complex patterns are groupings of symptoms that, to a lesser or greater degree, appear at the same time in a particular diagnosis. Debate has long been held regarding whether various mental disorders derive from specific disease processes or occur at an extreme end of symptom formation. Distinct syndromes—whether biological or psychological in nature—do exist, nevertheless, and reflect particular syndromal features. Although distinctions between Axis I and Axis II are blurred at times, the syndromes can and do reflect discrete pathology.

Millon (1999, p. 118), however, emphasized that

> although each complex syndrome crops up with greater frequency among certain personalities than others, they do arise in a number of different patterns. . . . [and] this

observation points up the importance of specifying the
basic personality style or disorder from which a complex
syndrome arises. For example, somatoform syndromes
occur most commonly among patients exhibiting a basic
avoidant, dependent, histrionic, compulsive, or
negativistic personality pattern; conduct disorders are
found primarily in narcissistic, antisocial, and sadistic
patterns.

Integrating Axis I and Axis II

Clinical syndromes are extensions or distortions of the basic personality
pattern. As Millon wrote,

> Personality disorders and Axis I conditions may be seen as
> developing from the same constitutional soil and therefore as
> existing on a continuum . . . [and] personality disorders not
> only contribute to vulnerability but also likely influence the
> course of an Axis I disorder. (Millon & Davis, 1996, p. 18)

Syndromes, such as anxiety and depression, are the outgrowth of
particular personality disorders and can also be understood as defining
the nature of the particular disorder. Diagnostically, the most suitable
interpretation of the clinical syndromes is within the context of the
existing and prevailing personality patterns.

Echoing Millon's understanding, the *Harvard Mental Health Letter*
(April, 2000, p. 5) noted,

> The connection between symptom and personality needs special
> attention when it comes to treatment, because patients rarely
> see psychotherapists to have their characters improved or
> transformed. [Patients] want help for depression, anxiety,
> alcoholism, or difficulties in their work and personal
> relationships, but they tend to regard any direct attempt to
> change them fundamentally as unnecessary and intrusive. . . .
> What therapists can do (often a great deal) is help patients
> change the thinking and behavior that result from personality
> traits or limit the consequences. An understanding of
> personality may also help in choosing treatments for a patient's
> symptom (Axis I) disorders.

It may be said that personality disorders influence the course a
syndrome may take, and its manifestation is largely dependent on the
personality of the client. Although certain symptoms are common to
a particular syndrome and are expected (e.g., the "blue" feeling of the

individual with depression), the manifestation of these symptoms can be expressed in various ways. For example, assume two individuals both obtain elevations of BR 85 on Scale D (Dysthymia); the first individual is an avoidant personality; the second, a histrionic. Both obtaining clinically significant elevations on Dysthymia (Scale D) would most likely manifest depressive symptoms in different ways. Each presumably would experience common feelings of low self-esteem, inadequacy, and fatigue, though the manifestation of the syndrome is apt to differ. The avoidant personality, an expressively fretful personality, would likely exhibit a withdrawn, apathetic expression of dysthymia, whereas the histrionic personality would be more dramatic and typically display more agitated and distraught symptom patterns. As this example illustrates, various personality patterns will more than likely manifest symptoms in different ways.

Although a clinical syndrome is manifested differently through various personality patterns, we can suggest also that the expression of a symptom actually changes in relation to the nature of a particular personality pattern. Assume two individuals, for example, both obtain BR 85 elevations on the Alcohol Dependence scale. One individual also obtains BR 85 on the Dependent scale, and the other obtains BR 85 on the Antisocial scale. The dependent personality likely consumes alcohol to soothe symptoms of anxiety, loneliness, and social apprehensiveness. The antisocial personality, on the other hand, likely consumes alcohol to "get high" and simply have a good time.

Although classified as discrete entities, Axis I syndromes can and should be understood in light of the individual's larger personality pattern. Exhibit 6-1, provided by Choca and Van Denburg (1997), presents the expected primary and secondary MCMI elevations of clinical syndromes and personality patterns with which they are associated.

Guidelines for Interpretation

The course that syndromes take, as we have emphasized, are influenced by an individual's personality pattern. Throughout his work, Millon (1969, p. 103) consistently emphasized that

> symptom disorders are logical extensions of that [personality] pattern displayed under exaggerated or special conditions; regardless of how distinctive they may appear, they take on meaning and significance only in light of the patient's pre-

Expected MCMI Elevations With Different Clinical Syndromes

Problem Area	Highest Scale	Other Elevations
Anxiety	Anxiety	Avoidant, negativistic, self-defeating
Somatoform	Somatoform	Anxiety, histrionic, compulsive
Eating disorder	Borderline	Schizoid, avoidant, dependent, schizo-typal
Mania	Hypomania	Histrionic, narcissistic, antisocial, paranoid, drug abuse, psychotic delusion
Dysthymia	Dysthymia	Avoidant, negativistic
Alcohol abuse	Alcohol abuse	Negativistic, antisocial, dependent, anxiety, dysthymia, drug abuse
Drug abuse	Drug abuse	Alcohol abuse, antisocial, negativistic, narcissistic, histrionic
Schizophrenia	Avoidant	Schizotypal, schizoid, dependent, narcissistic, negativistic, self-defeating
Major depression	Dysthymia	Major depression, anxiety, avoidant, dependent, self-defeating, negativistic
Delusion	Psychotic delusion	Psychotic thinking, paranoid, narcissistic, aggressive

Source: Interpretive Guide to the Millon Clinical Multiaxial Inventory (2nd ed.). By J. P. Choca and E. Van Denburg, 1996 Copyright 1997 by American Psychological Association. Reprinted with permission.

clinical personality and should be described only with reference to that pattern.

It is then in the light of the individual's personality structure that interpretation takes place. After each Severe Clinical Syndrome is reviewed separately, interpret the significantly elevated scales. Proceed, then, to the Clinical Syndrome scales, and similarly interpret the clincially significant elevations. Base-rate score interpretation is relatively clear-cut, though as with Axis II BR cutoff scores, the base rates should be used as practical guides.

- Significantly elevated scores (BR 75 and above) on the Severe Clinical Syndromes scales represent marked severity and should be given interpretive focus.
- Base-rate scores between 75 and 84 inclusive on Axis I scales are suggestive of the presence of a clinical syndrome, and base rate 85 and above denotes the prominence of a clinical syndrome. Base-rate scores between 60 and 74 inclusive are suggestive though not sufficiently indicative of the presence of a syndrome, unless the elevation is the highest scale in this segment of the profile.

- Clarify and examine the significance of the elevated syndromes in light of the individual's personality pattern.
- As a general guideline, when multiple scales are elevated at prominent levels of significance, the highest scale generally receives Axis I diagnostic priority.
- Clinically significant elevations (BR 75 and above) on the Severe Clinical Syndromes scales may suggest a psychotic level of disturbance.

Interpretation of Scale Elevations

The interpretation of scale elevations on the Axis I scales is relatively straightforward. As with the Axis II personality patterns, the clinical syndrome scales are measured on a continuum. Base-rate interpretations of the Clinical Syndromes scales are presented in Exhibit 6-2.

The Severe Clinical Syndromes scales (SS, CC, and PP) represent disorders of marked severity. Each scale should be reviewed separately to determine the particular nature of the disorder. Base-rate interpretations of elevated scores on the Severe Clinical Syndromes scales is presented in Exhibit 6-3.

EXHIBIT 6-2

MCMI-III Base-Rate Scale Interpretation (Axis I Clinical Syndromes)

BR 60 → BR 74	Suggestive, though not sufficiently indicative, of symptom pathology—unless the clinical scale is the highest elevation in this segment of the profile
BR 75 → BR 84	Suggests the presence of a clinical syndrome
BR ≥ 85	Suggests the prominence of a clinical syndrome

EXHIBIT 6-3

MCMI-III Base-Rate Scale Interpretation (Axis I Severe Clinical Syndromes)

BR 75 → BR 84	Suggests the presence of a severe clinical syndrome
	May indicate the presence of a psychotic disturbance
BR ≥ 85	Suggests the prominence of a severe clinical syndrome
	Strong support for the presence of a psychotic disturbance

Clinical Syndromes

The following material provides a researched overview of each clinical syndrome and identifies MCMI-III prototypical items of each syndrome with concordant *DSM-IV* classifications. Highlighted portions of selected *DSM* criteria are extracted and reprinted with permission to reflect the MCMI-III syndromes used in the Axis I scales. For a complete classification of clinical syndromes and complete diagnostic criteria, the reader should refer to the *Diagnostic and Statistical Manual of Mental Disorders, Fourth Edition* (American Psychiatric Association, 1994).

ANXIETY DISORDER

The Anxiety Disorder scale contains items descriptive of generalized anxiety, to include phobias that may be simple or social in description. Generalized anxiety disorder is characterized by chronic, exaggerated worry about everyday functioning needs. Symptoms include excessive sweating, physical discomfort, nausea, insomnia, and excessive somatic complaints, with accompanying depression in some cases. Generalized anxiety disorder is necessarily differentiated from normal nonincapacitating stress responses. A review of the literature indicates that social phobia is often associated with other anxiety disorders (den Boer, 1997).

Merikangas and Angst's (1995) review of the literature identified a strong association between social phobia and other types of anxiety disorders, affective disorders, and substance abuse. The essential feature of social phobia is excessive fear of social interaction or performance in which embarrassment or humiliation may occur. Symptoms associated with the biological stress response generally occur. Lamberg (1998) suggested that individuals with social phobias are more likely to abuse alcohol than other substances.

Determining the type of anxiety suggested by a clinically significant elevation on the MCMI-III may require a thorough review of *DSM-IV* anxiety disorders in relation to the items identified by the client. Millon (1999) noted that generalized anxiety is more often diagnosed in women and frequently coexists with depression and dysthymia.

Selected **DSM-IV** Diagnostic Criteria (Generalized Anxiety Disorder)

1. Excessive anxiety and worry (apprehensive expectation), occurring more days than not for at least 6 months, about

a number of events or activities (such as work or school performance).

2. The person finds it difficult to control the worry.
3. The anxiety and worry are associated with three (or more) of the following six symptoms (with at least some symptoms present for more days than not for the past 6 months).
   (a) restlessness or feeling keyed-up or on edge;
   (b) being easily fatigued;
   (c) difficulty concentrating or mind going blank;
   (d) irritability;
   (e) muscle tension;
   (f) sleep disturbance (difficulty falling or staying asleep, or restless unsatisfying sleep).

Selected **DSM-IV** *Diagnostic Criteria (Social Phobia)*

A marked and persistent fear of one or more social or performance situations in which they are exposed to unfamiliar people or to possible scrutiny by others. Individuals fear that they will act in a way (or show anxiety symptoms) that will be humiliating or embarrassing.

SOMATOFORM DISORDER

Somatoform disorder is characterized by unexplained somatic symptoms, exhibited through vague, bodily complaints. The somatic client expresses psychological difficulties or discomforts through somatic complaints, usually nonspecific symptoms of fatigue or weakness and develops a preoccupation with ailing health. Patients with *DSM-IV* so-

THE IMPACT OF STRESS

Research suggests that specific environmental stressors are implicated in particular syndromes. Hypertension, for example, is a common disease afflicting millions of Americans linked to stress. The *Harvard Mental Health Letter* (April, 2000, p. 4) proposed that "stress may exacerbate the symptoms of any psychiatric disorder . . . [and], in the language of the diagnostic manual, Axis I disorders may result from the combined effects of Axis II disorders and the sources of stress labeled on Axis IV."

SOCIAL PHOBIA

Social phobia is defined as the avoidance of social or performance situations because of persistent, excessive fear. Epidemiological data gathered by den Boer (1997) indicated that the lifetime prevalence of social phobia in adults varied between 2% and 5%, with a female to male ratio of 2.5 to 1.2.

matization disorder are chronically impaired and seek medical care because of the severity of symptoms and the threat that the symptoms represent (Epstein, Quill, & McWhinney, 1999). Another group of somatoform patients receives the diagnosis of hypochondriasis, a disorder characterized by the exaggerated belief of having a particular disease, or multiple diseases, without medical justification. Minor physical symptoms usually become magnified and are distressing for hypochondriacs, whose "illness" also causes distress to those around them (Ben-Tovim & Esterman, 1998). Typically, somatic complaints presented can be a means of gaining attention (Millon, 1997).

Selected *DSM-IV Diagnostic Criteria (Somatization)*

1. A history of many physical complaints beginning before age 30 that occur over a period of several years and result in treatment being sought or significant impairment in social, occupational, or other important areas of functioning.
2. Each of the following criteria must have been met, with individual symptoms occurring at any time during the course of the disturbance.
   (a) four pain symptoms: a history of pain related to at least four different sites or functions (e.g., head, abdomen, back, joints, extremities, chest, rectum, during menstruation, during sexual intercourse, or during urination);
   (b) two gastrointestinal symptoms: a history of at least two gastrointestinal symptoms other than pain (e.g., nausea, bloating, vomiting other than during pregnancy, diarrhea, or intolerance of several different foods);
   (c) one sexual symptom: a history of at least one sexual or reproductive symptom other than pain (e.g., sexual indifference, erectile or ejaculatory dysfunction, irregular menses, excessive menstrual bleeding, vomiting throughout pregnancy);

(d) one pseudoneurological symptom: a history of at least one symptom or deficit suggesting a neurological condition not limited to pain (conversion symptoms, such as impaired coordination or balance, paralysis or localized weakness, difficulty swallowing or lump in throat, aphonia, urinal retention, hallucinations, loss of touch or pain sensation, double vision, blindness, deafness, seizures; dissociative symptoms such as amnesia; or loss of consciousness other than fainting).

Selected DSM-IV *Diagnostic Criteria (Hypochondriasis)*

1. Preoccupation with fears of having, or the idea that one has, a serious disease based on the person's misinterpretation of bodily symptoms.
2. The preoccupation persists despite appropriate medical evaluation and reassurance.
3. The belief in criterion 1 is not of delusional intensity (as in delusional disorder, somatic type) and is not restricted to a circumscribed concern about appearance (as in body dysmorphic disorder).
4. The preoccupation causes clinically significant distress or impairment in social, occupational, or other important areas of functioning.
5. The duration of the disturbance is at least 6 months.

BIPOLAR: MANIC DISORDER

Bipolar mania is characterized by labile emotions, with periods of exaggerated elation and heightened feelings of well-being. MCMI-III Bipolar Manic Disorder scale essentially contains item descriptions of hypomania, a milder form of mania, characterized by excitement, energetic ideas, and exaggerated production. Some items reflect severe mania and, according to Millon (1997), very high scores can suggest psychotic processes with delusions or hallucinations. Minor forms of mania include heightened feelings of well-being with increased alertness and inflated self-esteem and expansive sociability, whereas the spectrum of deeper mania crosses into overactivity, grandiose ideas, delusions, and sometimes ideas of reference (Daly, 1997).

Cassidy, Forest, Murry, and Carroll (1998), through factor analysis of the signs and symptoms of mania, identified five clinically relevant factors. Dysphoria was the first and strongest, with other factors being psychomotor acceleration, psychosis, increased hedonic function, and irritable aggression. In reviewing the literature of hypomania, Angst (1998) found elevated rates of binge eating and substance abuse among individuals with hypomania than among individuals with depression and controls. Review of the literature regarding the diagnosis and treatment of bipolarity and depression by Manning, Haykal, and Akiskal (1999) suggested that as many as one third of depressions belong to the soft bipolar spectrum (hypomanic symptoms), noting that hypomania can be easily missed during clinical evaluations.

Selected *DSM-IV* *Diagnostic Criteria* *(Hypomanic Episode)*

1. A distinct period of persistently elevated, expansive, or irritable mood, lasting throughout at least 4 days, that is clearly different from the usual nondepressed mood.
2. During the period of mood disturbance, three (or more) of the following symptoms have persisted (four if the mood is only irritable) and have been present to a significant degree:
   (a) inflated self-esteem or grandiosity;
   (b) decreased need for sleep (e.g., feels rested after only 3 hours of sleep);
   (c) more talkative than usual or pressure to keep talking;
   (d) flight of ideas or subjective experience that thoughts are racing;
   (e) distractibility (e.g., attention too easily drawn to unimportant or irrelevant external stimuli);
   (f) increase in goal-directed activity (either socially, at work or school, or sexually) or psychomotor agitation;
   (g) excessive involvement in pleasurable activities that have a high potential for painful consequences (e.g., the person engages in unrestrained buying sprees, sexual indiscretions, or foolish business investments).

BIPOLAR: MANIC SCALE HIGH SCORES

Millon notes that very high scores on the Bipolar Manic scale can signal the presence of psychotic processes, including delusions or hallucinations. Clinically significant elevations on the Severe Clinical Syndromes scales can support this conclusion.

DYSTHYMIC DISORDER

Dysthymic disorder is characterized by mild to moderate chronic depression lasting for a period of at least two years. Dysphoric mood includes periods of low energy, fatigue, lack of initiative, and a sense of futility or hopelessness. During periods of dejection, there may be tearfulness, guilt, suicidal ideation, pessimism about the future, social withdrawal, poor or voracious appetite, a marked loss of interest in pleasurable activities, and a decreased effectiveness in overall performance (Millon, 1997). The prevalence of dysthymia in the general population is common, and a review of epidemiological studies by Sansone and Sansone (1996) placed the estimate at 3%. Degrees and duration of dysphoric mood constitute the diagnosis of dysthymia, and Millon (1997) emphasized that unless the Major Depression scale is also notably elevated, there is little likelihood that psychotic depressive features will be in evidence. The *Harvard Health Letter* (March, 1999) cautioned, nevertheless, that dysthymia can have major effects on the individual, including poor moods, eating disorders, concentration problems, and other mental disorders. As with other types of depression, dysthymia appears to be more common in women (Sansone & Sansone, 1996).

Selected DSM-IV *Diagnostic Criteria (Dysthymic Disorder)*

1. Depressed mood for most of the day, for more days than not, as indicated either by subjective account or observation by others, for at least 2 years.
2. Presence, while depressed, of two (or more) of the following:
   (a) poor appetite or overeating
   (b) insomnia or hypersomnia
   (c) low energy or fatigue
   (d) low self-esteem
   (e) poor concentration or difficulty making decisions
   (f) feelings of hopelessness

ALCOHOL DEPENDENCE

The Alcohol Dependence scale contains traits and behaviors characteristic of alcoholic drinking problems. Millon (1997) maintains that high elevations likely suggest a history of alcoholism, attempts to overcome the problem, and considerable discomfort in work and home settings.

Research suggests that alcohol dependence is more serious than alcohol abuse, and Hasin and Paykin (1999) cautioned researchers about combining the two into the same category. Most researchers currently view alcoholism as the result of both biological and psychosocial factors. Data collected by Grant (1997) indicated that male users were more likely to become dependent and remain dependent, once the dependence developed, than female users. Morgenstern, Langenbucher, Labouvie, and Miller (1997) studied the prevalence rates of alcohol typology variables and comorbidity with *DSM-III-R* personality disorders. Their findings suggest that more than half of the selected population studied met criteria for at least one personality disorder, with antisocial personality disorder being the most prevalent. Clear gender differences emerged from their studies, suggesting males are more commonly diagnosed with antisocial personality disorder, whereas females are more likely to receive a diagnosis of borderline personality disorder.

(Note: The criteria for alcohol dependence is listed below under substance dependence.) Criteria for alcohol withdrawal include

1. Cessation of (or reduction in) alcohol use that has been heavy and prolonged.
2. Two (or more) of the following, developing within several hours to a few days after Criterion 1:
   (a) autonomic hyperactivity (e.g., sweating or pulse rate greater than 100);
   (b) increased hand tremor;
   (c) insomnia;
   (d) nausea or vomiting;
   (e) transient visual, tactile, or auditory hallucinations or illusions;
   (f) psychomotor agitation;
   (g) anxiety;
   (h) grand mal seizures.

DRUG DEPENDENCE

The Drug Dependence scale indicates a recent or recurrent history of drug abuse or dependence, difficulty in restraining impulses or keeping within conventional social limits, and an inability to manage the personal consequences of this behavior (Millon, 1997). Elevations on this scale generally result in elevations on additional personality scales, with antisocial personality disorder diagnosed more frequently among men with substance dependence than any other psychiatric disorder

(Thomas, Melchert, & Banken, 1999). Substances such as cocaine, amphetamines, and phencyclidine (PCP) can induce a violent state (Gorman, 1990). Dansky and colleagues (1996) reviewed the posttraumatic stress disorder (PTSD) literature, which suggests that a strong association between victimization–PTSD and substance abuse disorders exists. Almost 90% of the population seeking treatment for substance abuse disorders in their review reported an experience of sexual and/ or physical assault during their lifetime. All research has indicated that the Drug Dependence scale's ability to rule out drug abuse is excellent (Craig, 1999).

Selected DSM-IV Diagnostic Criteria (Substance Dependence)

A maladaptive pattern of substance use, leading to clinically significant impairment or distress, as manifested by three (or more) of the following, occurring at any time in the same 12-month period:

1. Tolerance, as defined by either of the following:
   (a) a need for markedly increased amounts of the substance to achieve intoxication or desired effect;
   (b) markedly diminished effect with continued use of the same amount of the substance;
2. Withdrawal, as manifested by either of the following:
   (a) the characteristic withdrawal syndrome for the substance (refer to criteria 1 and 2 of the criteria sets for withdrawal from the specific substances);
   (b) the same (or a closely related) substance is taken to relieve or avoid withdrawal symptoms;
3. The substance is often taken in larger amounts or over a longer period than was intended.
4. There is a persistent desire or unsuccessful effort to cut down or control substance use.
5. A great deal of time is spent in activities necessary to obtain the substance (e.g., visiting multiple doctors or driving long distances), use the substance (e.g., chain-smoking), or recover from its effects;
6. Important social, occupational, or recreational activities are given up or reduced because of substance use.
7. The substance use is continued despite knowledge of having a persistent or recurrent physical or psychological problem that is likely to have been caused or exacerbated by the

substance (e.g., current cocaine use despite recognition of cocaine-induced depression, or continued drinking despite recognition that an ulcer was made worse by alcohol consumption).

POST-TRAUMATIC STRESS DISORDER (PTSD)

Elevations on the Post-Traumatic Stress Disorder scale suggest exposure to a traumatic event in which the experience is life-threatening, with resultant feelings of helplessness or intense fear being encountered. The posttraumatic reaction may begin shortly after the trauma or may develop months or years afterward. In describing PTSD, three kinds of symptoms are detailed in the *Harvard Mental Health Letter* (June, 1996): (1) Victims are often edgy, irritable, easily startled, and constantly on guard; (2) intrusion, or involuntarily reexperiencing the traumatic event in the form of memories, nightmares, and flashbacks, during which it is felt that the event is recurring, and; (3) emotional constriction or numbing—a need to avoid feelings, thoughts, and situations reminiscent of the trauma, a loss of normal emotional responses, or both. In a study assessing male combat veterans diagnosed with PTSD, Southwick, Yehuda, and Giller (1993) found that the most frequent disorders for which *DSM-III-R* criteria were met included borderline, obsessive–compulsive, avoidant, and paranoid personality disorders. The *Harvard Mental Health Letter* (July, 1996) indicated that borderline personality might arise as a result of a childhood trauma, and many patients diagnosed with borderline personality also receive a diagnosis of PTSD based on adult experiences.

NONPROTOTYPICAL ITEMS ON SCALE B AND SCALE T

Nonprototypical items on the Alcohol Dependence and Drug Dependence scales are subtle and indirect in composition and may serve to identify individuals who do not readily admit to having an alcohol or drug problem. A clinical interview, in conjunction with instruments such as the Michigan Alcohol Screening Test (MAST) or the Substance Abuse Subtle Screening Inventory (SASSI), can help determine the extent of the problem.

Selected DSM-IV *Diagnostic Criteria* (*Posttraumatic Stress Disorder*)

1. The person has been exposed to a traumatic event in which both of the following were present:
   (a) the person experienced, witnessed, or was confronted with an event or events that involved actual or threatened death or serious injury, or a threat to the physical integrity of self or others;
   (b) the person's response involved intense fear, helplessness, or horror;

2. The traumatic event is persistently reexperienced in one (or more) of the following ways:
   (a) recurrent and intrusive distressing recollections of the event, including images, thoughts, or perceptions;
   (b) recurrent distressing dreams of the event;
   (c) acting or feeling as if the traumatic event were recurring (includes a sense of reliving the experience, illusions, hallucinations, and dissociative flashback episodes, including those that occur on awakening or when intoxicated);
   (d) intense psychological distress at exposure to internal or external cues that symbolize or resemble an aspect of the traumatic event;
   (e) physiological reactivity on exposure to internal or external cues that symbolize or resemble an aspect of the trauma.

3. Persistent avoidance of stimuli associated with the trauma and numbing of general responsiveness (not present before the trauma), as indicated by three (or more) of the following:
   (a) efforts to avoid thoughts, feelings, or conversations associated with the trauma;
   (b) efforts to avoid activities, places, or people that arouse recollections of the trauma;
   (c) inability to recall an important aspect of the trauma;
   (d) markedly diminished interest in significant activities;
   (e) feeling of detachment or estrangement from others;
   (f) restricted range of affect (e.g., unable to have loving feelings);
   (g) sense of a foreshortened future (e.g., does not expect to have a career, marriage, children, or a normal life span).

4. Persistent symptoms of increased arousal (not present before the trauma), as indicated by two (or more) of the following:

(a) difficulty falling or staying asleep;
(b) irritability or outbursts of anger;
(c) difficulty concentrating;
(d) hypervigilance;
(e) exaggerated startle response.
5. Duration of the disturbance is more than 1 month.
6. The disturbance causes clinically significant distress or impairment in social, occupational, or other important areas of functioning.

Severe Clinical Syndromes

Significant elevations on the Severe Clinical Syndromes scales represent marked pathology. Clinically significant elevations on these scales may alert the clinician to the possible presence of psychosis.

THOUGHT DISORDER

"Depending on the length and course of the problem, patients with elevated scores on this scale [Thought Disorder] are usually classified as 'schizophrenic' or 'schizophreniform' or having a 'brief reactive psychosis' " (Millon, 1997, p. 24). Behaviors exhibit incongruous, disorganized, and regressive patterns; thinking is fragmented or bizarre. Trevor (1997) noted that patients with thought disorder may present with complaints of poor concentration or thought blocking, such that a patient stops in a perplexed fashion while in mid-speech. Occasionally, individuals with high elevations will display inappropriate affect, hallucinations, and delusions (Millon, 1997). Schizophrenia is likely the most common form of psychotic disorder, with a lifetime prevalence of nearly 1% of the population (Turner, 1997). Leibman and Salzinger (1998) reported that 75% of the individuals with schizophrenia experience auditory hallucinations, and 81% have persecutory delusions (Andreason, 1987). Mendel (1976) proposed three symptom clusters of schizophrenia, principally related to problems with anxiety, interpersonal relationships, and historicity. Fenton, McGlashan, Victor, and Blyler (1997) concluded that suicide is the single largest cause of premature death among individuals with schizophrenia.

Selected **DSM-IV** *Diagnostic Criteria* *(Schizophrenia)*

Characteristic symptoms: Two (or more) of the following, each present for a significant portion of time during a 1-month period (or less if successfully treated):

1. Delusions.
2. Hallucinations.
3. Disorganized speech (e.g., frequent derailment or incoherence).
4. Grossly disorganized or catatonic behavior.
5. Negative symptoms (e.g., affective flattening, alogia, or avolition).

MAJOR DEPRESSION

Major depressive disorder is characterized by a diminished sense of pleasure in life; feelings of worthlessness, guilt, hopelessness; and suicidal ideation, with an inability to function for themselves for the most part in a normal environment. Marked motor retardation or agitation, somatic problems, concentration and attention difficulties, appetite and weight changes are difficulties that appear inescapable for individuals with major depression. In their review of a sample of more than 8000 noninstitutionalized respondents, Kessler and colleagues (1994) concluded that the most common psychiatric disorders found were major depression and alcohol dependence.

The nine symptoms classified in the *DSM-IV* (American Psychiatric Association, 1994) can be divided into two divisions: (a) physical or neurovegetative symptoms and (b) psychological or psychosocial symptoms. Depression may commonly be masked by varied symptoms. Bhatia and Bhatia's (1997) review of depressive comorbidity alerted the clinician to several masks of depression that include (a) the somatic mask (hypochondriacal complications); (b) cognitive mask, or so-called pseudodementia; and (3) anxiety-disorder mask, manifesting as agitation or attentional difficulties. Nesse (2000), however, emphasized that some depressions are clearly disease states caused by brain defects.

Selected **DSM-IV** *Diagnostic Criteria* *(Major Depressive Episode)*

Five (or more) of the following symptoms have been present during the same two-week period and represent a change from previous functioning; at least one of the symptoms is either depressed mood or loss of interest or pleasure. (Note: Do not include symptoms that are clearly a result of a general medical condition or mood-incongruent delusions/hallucinations.)

1. Depressed mood most of the day, nearly every day, as indicated by either subjective report (e.g., feels sad or empty) or observation made by others (e.g., appears tearful).
2. Markedly diminished interest or pleasure in all, or almost all, activities most of the day, nearly every day (as indicated by either subjective account or observation made by others).
3. Significant weight loss when not dieting or weight gain (e.g., a change of more than 5% of body weight in a month), or decrease or increase in appetite nearly every day.
4. Insomnia or hypersomnia nearly every day.
5. Psychomotor agitation or retardation nearly every day (observable by others, not merely subjective feelings of restlessness or being slowed down).
6. Fatigue or loss of energy nearly every day.
7. Feelings of worthlessness or excessive or inappropriate guilt (which may be delusional) nearly every day (not merely self-reproach or guilt about being sick).
8. Diminished ability to think or concentrate, or indecisiveness, nearly every day (either by subjective account or as observed by others).
9. Recurrent thoughts of death (not just fear of dying), recurrent suicidal ideation without a specific plan, or a suicide attempt or a specific plan for committing suicide.

DELUSIONAL DISORDER

Individuals with delusional disorder are considered acutely paranoid (Millon, 1997). Symptoms include hypervigilance, belligerence, and various delusions. Mood is generally hostile, with accompanied disturbances in thinking, usually identified as ideas of reference and thought control. With the exception of the degree of delusional bizarreness, some overlap exists with paranoid schizophrenia. The *Harvard Mental Health Letter* (Feb., 1999) noted that according to findings of evolutionary psychologists, delusional disorders may result from the pathological activity of mechanisms necessary to maintain vigilance for survival and reproduction. The *Harvard Mental Health Letter* (Jan., 1999) also suggested that of the five specific types of delusional disorders classified in the *DSM-IV*, the most common are delusions of persecution—the belief that one is under attack and often the target of a conspiracy. In a study of 4144 outpatients, of which 1.2% were diagnosed as delusional, Yamada, Nakajima, and Noguchi's (1998) results showed the most frequent type of delusion was persecutory, with females outnumbering males by a ratio of 3 to 1.

Selected **DSM-IV** *Diagnostic Criteria (Delusional Disorder)*

Nonbizarre delusions (e.g., involving situations that occur in real life, such as being followed, poisoned, infected, loved at a distance, or deceived by spouse or lover, or having a disease) of at least one month's duration.

Specific types include:

1. Erotomanic Type: Delusions that another person, usually of higher status, is in love with the individual.
2. Grandiose Type: Delusions of inflated worth, power, knowledge, identity, or special relationship to a deity or famous person.
3. Jealous Type: Delusions that the individual's sexual partner is unfaithful.
4. Persecutory Type: Delusions that the person (or someone to whom the person is close) is being malevolently treated in some way.
5. Somatic Type: Delusions that the person has some physical defect or general medical condition.
6. Mixed Type: Delusions characteristic of more than one of the previously listed types, but no one theme predominates.

CASE REVIEW

We now turn to a case history of alcoholism in the dependent personality. The MCMI-III data is found in Exhibit 6-4.

Alcoholism in the Dependent Personality

Reason for Referral

Mr. M. was evaluated to determine his current level of cognitive and emotional functioning. He is presently enrolled in an outpatient residential aftercare program. Mr. M. has an extensive history of alcohol abuse and has undergone numerous rehabilitation treatments.

Background Information

Mr. M. is a 50-year-old, married, African American with an extensive history of alcoholism. He stated that he drank alcohol most of his adult

EXHIBIT 6-4

MCMI-III BR Scale Scores: Mr. M.

Category	BR Score	Scales	
			Validity Index = 0
Modifying indices	70	Disclosure	(Scale X)
	51	Desirability	(Scale Y)
	80	Debasement	(Scale Z)
Clinical personality patterns	74	Schizoid	(Scale 1)
	71	Avoidant	(Scale 2A)
	77	Depressive	(Scale 2B)
	85	Dependent	(Scale 3)
	26	Histrionic	(Scale 4)
	42	Narcissistic	(Scale 5)
	76	Antisocial	(Scale 6A)
	68	Sadistic	(Scale 6B)
	49	Compulsive	(Scale 7)
	79	Negativistic	(Scale 8A)
	70	Masochistic	(Scale 8B)
Severe personality pathology	68	Schizotypal	(Scale S)
	71	Borderline	(Scale C)
	72	Paranoid	(Scale P)
Clinical syndromes	92	Anxiety disorder	(Scale A)
	75	Somatoform disorder	(Scale H)
	76	Bipolar: manic disorder	(Scale N)
	85	Dysthymic disorder	(Scale D)
	95	Alcohol dependence	(Scale B)
	75	Drug dependence	(Scale T)
	67	Post-traumatic stress	(Scale R)
Severe clinical syndromes	65	Thought disorder	(Scale SS)
	74	Major depression	(Scale CC)
	63	Delusional disorder	(Scale PP)

life, customarily consuming one quart of alcohol a day. He is married and has no children. His mother died of cirrhosis of the liver, and the whereabouts of his father, also alcoholic, are unknown. He has no siblings. Mr. M. has completed eight years of education and currently functions in the mildly mentally retarded range of cognitive ability. He worked as a packager for 20 years until the company closed in 1991. Presently he is unemployed. A sole hospitalization occurred in 1991 for gall bladder surgery; currently he is being treated for peptic ulcers and recurring episodes of dizziness and lightheadedness. No psychiatric admissions were reported.

Mental Status Examination

Mr. M. arrived on time for his scheduled appointment and was accompanied by his wife. He requested that his wife be present during the evaluation. When she occasionally stepped out during the examination, Mr. M. became noticeably tense and anxious. He was appropriately dressed and groomed. Gait appeared normal, with no gross motor deficits observed. He was alert and attentive. Thought processing was normal and goal-directed, with no signs of hallucinations or delusions. He reported occasional tremors, blackouts, and one seizure. Suicidal ideation was present. Immediate auditory recall was moderately impaired. Remote and recent memory was intact. Affectively, he was noticeably anxious throughout the examination; mood was described as "lousy and depressed." Speech was normal in rate, though at times pressured. Throughout the interview, Mr. M. was fully compliant and cooperative.

> Positively Scored Dependent Prototypic Items: 16, 35, 45, 108, 135, 169
> Noteworthy Responses: 4, 44, 55, 74, 83, 96, 107, 124, 163, 171
> Personality Code: 3**8A *2*B6A*12*A8*B6B+75"4//-*–//
> Syndrome Code: BAD**<u>NHT</u>*//-*–//

MCMI-III INTERPRETIVE REASONING

Mr. M. approached the MCMI-III in an open and honest manner. The Disclosure index displays no tendency to distort his responses. This valid protocol suggests a degree of self-abasement, with a moderately high elevation of BR 80 on Scale Z.

As mentioned previously, Mr. M. functions in the mildly mentally retarded range of cognitive ability, according to his performance on the WAIS-III. It is important to note that chronic alcoholism affects certain aspects of intellectual functioning, while leaving other areas, such as information and vocabulary, relatively intact. Individuals with chronic alcoholism characteristically perform poorly on speed-dependent, visual-spatial tasks, and tests requiring motor speed. In addition, individuals with extensive histories of alcoholism can develop Korsakoff's syndrome; however, Mr. M.'s performance on the neurological screening test was within normal limits.

An individual obtaining this clinical pattern of personality typically relies on others for support and security. The dependent personality is generally preoccupied with fears of being alone and customarily looks to others for assistance. These individuals are, for the most part, passive and rely on others to make their decisions. Although Mr. M. seeks nurturance and support, mixed features of antisocial and passive–aggressive traits may give rise to conflicts between deference and defiance toward his "caregiver." Submissive behavior may, at times, shift to oppositional behavior, particularly when needs are not met or when the demands of the "caregiver" become intolerable. Oftentimes, though, feelings of aggressiveness are hidden for fear of losing the security of his spouse. These individuals feel inadequate and intimidated by the expectations of the world and tend to be oversensitive to the derision of others. Although underlying conflicts may occasionally surface, evoking resentment and argumentativeness, Mr. M. willingly submits to the demands of the "caregiver" to maintain his much-needed security and support.

A clinically significant elevation of BR 95 on Scale B suggests a strong dependence on alcohol. Clinically significant elevations on Scales A and D indicate a mixed dysphoric pattern of anxiety and depressive symptoms. Anxiety and depression are frequently linked with alcohol dependence. Feelings of helplessness and hopelessness also mark this profile. "Few things in life give me pleasure" (response 148) was scored in the positively keyed direction. As Othmer and Othmer (1994) noted, the alcoholic patient is most sensitive to the loss of a support person. Grant's (1997) review of the literature indicated that male alcohol users are more likely to become dependent than female users. A pattern of chronic dysphoria, to include self-abasement, is likely a part of this individual's characterological structure. Anxious and socially apprehensive much of the time, Mr. M. most likely turns to alcohol to relieve his anxiety. Paradoxically, alcohol, on which a lifelong dependence has developed, may dutifully serve to medicate his dysphoric state, and to some extent alleviate conflictual fears of abandonment.

Because illness provides secondary gains with this personality pattern, these individuals tend to be passive participants in the healing relationship, rather than seeking active solutions to problems. In the eyes of the dependent individual, the therapist becomes another "caregiver." Detoxification may be a necessary first course of treatment, followed by referral to alcohol rehabilitation. Therapeutic goals should focus on the client's exaggerated fears of autonomy and negative thoughts of inadequacy. Care must be taken, however, not to alienate dependent individuals by challenging their feelings of attachment or moving too aggressively toward developing a more independent life-style. Cognitive–behavioral techniques may be used to bolster self-confidence and provide active solutions to life's stressors. Clients with this pattern generally tend to improve through continued supportive approaches, but the therapist must guard against nurturing the dependent's submissive patterns within the therapeutic relationship. Assert-iveness training may prove beneficial. Strengthening the dependent's self-confidence can be pursued in group therapy sessions.

DIAGNOSTIC IMPRESSIONS

Axis I: 293.83 Alcohol-induced mood disorder, with mixed features

Axis II: 301.60 Dependent personality disorder, with negativistic personality traits

In Summary

With this chapter, we conclude our three-part presentation on interpre-tation of the MCMI-III. We have learned that clinical syndromes are more clearly defined within the context of one's personality pattern. The researched descriptions of the scales discussed existing associations between syndrome and personality, and, with a review of *DSM-IV* criteria, lead to a more focused Axis I diagnosis. Having studied the fundamentals of MCMI-III interpretation, it is time to learn how these interpretive results are integrated with other information to develop a comprehensive diagnosis. Now we advance to the final chapter, which discusses the process of formulating our findings and communicating them through a psychological report.

Test Yourself Exercises 6

Fill in the Blanks.
1. Syndromes take on meaning in the context of an individual's _____ .
2. A base-rate score between _____ and _____ inclusive on the Clinical Syndromes scales suggests the presence of a clinical syndrome.
3. Somatoform disorder is characterized by _____ .

4. _____ disorder is characterized by excessive worry and tension, with accompanying complaints of physical discomfort.
5. _____ episodes are milder forms of mania characterized by excitement, energetic ideas, and exaggerated production.
6. Studies suggest that alcoholic males are commonly diagnosed with _____ personality disorder.
7. Studies suggest that _____ disorder tends to be more common in women.
8. _____ is likely the most common form of psychiatric disorder.
9. "I have completely lost my appetite and have seriously thought of doing away with myself," may be a typical response of a client with an elevated _____ scale.
10. "Many people have been spying into my life for years, and I believe I'm being plotted against," may well be the response of a client diagnosed with _____ disorder.

Match

Match Clinical–Severe Syndromes in Column A with descriptions in Column B.

A	B
Anxiety disorder	1. _____ Acutely paranoid; hypervigilance, belligerence, logical delusions; hallucinations are rare.
Somatoform disorder	
Bipolar: manic disorder	2. _____ Feelings of tension; apprehension, or phobic reactions, disorganized speech, restlessness, physiological stress symptoms.
Dysthymic disorder	
Alcohol dependence	3. _____ History of heroin addiction.
Drug dependence	
Posttraumatic stress disorder	4. _____ Persistent and unwanted reexperience of a traumatic event involving intense fear, helplessness, or horror.
Thought disorder	
Major depression	5. _____ Experiences physical symptoms with no apparent evidence of a physiological basis.
Delusional disorder	
	6. _____ Insomnia, fatigue, loss of appetite, low self-esteem, poor concentration, accompanied with feelings of discouragement and hopelessness for a period of at least two years.
	7. _____ Suggestive of schizophrenia, schizophreniform, or brief reactive psychosis.
	8. _____ Persistent, elevated, expansive, and irritable mood; no marked impairment in social–occupational functioning.
	9. _____ Marked affective disorder characterized by diminished sense of pleasure, guilt, hopelessness, suicidal ideation; pronounced inability to function in a normal environment.
	10. _____ History of alcohol abuse.

Exercise in Observation

Observe various personality syndromes exhibited by individuals (preferably dysfunctional) with whom you may come in contact. Select one or more observations and write a paragraph about each one that describes the basic features of each syndrome.

The Psychological Report: Scripting the Results | 7

W e have gained a basic understanding of scoring and interpreting the MCMI-III in the past several chapters, and now we are faced with the question, "What should we do with this information?" Once the results have been accurately scored and interpreted, the findings are communicated to the referral source. The customary means through which assessment results are conveyed is the psychological report. For certain referral questions, the MCMI-III interpretive results can adequately address the referral problem. More commonly, though, the MCMI-III results are combined with background data, the clinical interview, a battery of tests, and other pertinent information to provide a consolidated report. The elements necessary for writing a professional report will be discussed in the second section of this chapter. First, we will consider the framework for diagnosis: the clinical interview.

Assessment Strategy

The diagnostician's *raison d'être* is to identify maladaptive behaviors and underlying conditions that maintain them. The MCMI-III is a powerful assessment tool, and its major strength is its ability to reliably identify clinically disordered individuals. For maximum effectiveness, however, the MCMI-III should be used within the context of a comprehensive evaluation. By developing a comprehensive strategy in which the MCMI-III-generated hypotheses are supported through additional data, the clinician can feel more confident about the precision of the diagnosis. Millon (1997, p. 123) maintains, "As with any instrument, auxiliary knowledge and psychological theory come together to create rich and plausible interpretations of the individual's character."

The following clinical approach provides the clinician with an overall strategy for obtaining a sound, relevant, and accurate assessment. The clinical interview is a combination of complex skills, and can at times be challenging for the beginning clinician. The goal of the interview, however, is straightforward: to obtain a snapshot of the examinee at a particular point in history in reference to the presenting problem. The first step requires collecting relevant historical information about the examinee.

HISTORICAL DATA

Information collected during the initial interview is an important element of the psychological assessment. A historical account of an illness or disorder obtained from the examinee can serve to confirm the MCMI-III results. Inconsistencies, though, may occasionally arise between the examinee's actual condition and the MCMI-III results. An examinee, for instance, may report a distant hospitalization for post-traumatic stress disorder with no display of present symptoms, yet Scale

---

QUANTITATIVE AND QUALITATIVE DATA

Regarding psychological assessment, Lezak wrote,

> When interpreting test scores, it is important to keep in mind their artificial and abstract nature. Some examiners come to equate a score with the behavior it is supposed to represent. Others prize standardized, replicable tests as "harder," more scientific data at the expense of unquantified observations. Reification of test scores can lead the examiner to overlook or discount direct observations. A test score approach to psychological assessment that minimizes the importance of qualitative data can result in serious distortions in the interpretations, conclusions, and recommendations drawn from such a one-sided data base. (1983, p. 132)

R on the MCMI-III may be elevated. The clinician would be prudent to investigate the nature or recurrence of such a disorder to verify its impact. If contradictory data arises, request clarification from the examinee. The accuracy of the assessment will depend on the verifiable data collected.

Two important tools, the mental status examination and the *DSM-IV* classification system, are then used to sharpen the clinical picture. The clinician must strive to understand the examinee uniquely—that is, by uncovering particular thoughts, behaviors, feelings, and so forth, specific to the individual. Such observations make up the mental status examination. The observed symptoms are then inspected in the context of a multiaxial system and weighed against the criteria of the *DSM-IV* classification system to establish a standardized diagnosis. Now we will turn our attention to these essential diagnostic tools.

MENTAL STATUS EXAMINATION

Mental status essentially refers to an assessment of the examinee's general state of being. Its evaluation ranges from informal observation to formal examination, and its structure is helpful in that it descriptively gathers objective characteristics that define the individual. The mental status examination should contain certain criteria, and although the format may vary, the following areas should be addressed:

- General observations
- Level of daily functioning
- Interpersonal relationships
- Mood and affect
- Quality of speech
- Thought processing/thought content
- Sensorium
- Mental capacity
- Domains of memory

General Observations

Observe and document all aspects of the examinee's appearance and behavioral presentation. Observations offer useful information not evident through other means. Next provide an overview of self-care management, motor behavior activity, and odd features or distinctive mannerisms observed. Is the client appropriately dressed? Is adequate hygiene practiced or is self-neglect indicated? Is the client's body weight proportionate to height–weight standards? Are posture and gait normal? Are apraxias in evidence? Finally, the clinician should note the attitude of the examinee toward the clinician, as well as toward the overall interview process. Clues in resolving questionable validity situations can be gleaned from the examinee's attitude, as well as provide corroboration of the quantitative data obtained on the Modifying indices. Skilled observation can yield many insightful hypotheses about a client's condition.

Level of Daily Functioning

The global assessment of functioning (GAF) on Axis V cross-references this aspect. When assessing the client's level of functioning, the clinician can begin by asking the client to describe a typical day. Areas to address include occupational and work situation, or for unemployed individuals, the duration of time out of work and the circumstances surrounding the unemployment. In addition, concerns to address may include ability to pay bills; means of transportation and the frequency of going out; shopping, and meal preparation; and other pertinent information, which can better determine an examinee's current level of functioning.

Interpersonal Relationships

To supplement the MCMI-III interpretation, it is helpful to obtain a clearer understanding of the examinee's social interrelationships. Ask pertinent questions about how the client gets along and communicates with family members, neighbors, friends, coworkers, employers, and so forth. What is the client's marital status? A client's recent divorce, for example, may give rise to exaggerated elevations on the MCMI-III Anxiety or Major Depression scales. In another situation, a mature adult living with an elderly parent may suggest the presence of a dependent personality style; however, it is important to inquire whether the health of the parent requires the individual's live-in presence. Such information, then, can serve to more clearly interpret an elevated MCMI-III Scale 3.

Mood and Affect

Mood and *affect* are often used interchangeably by clinicians. However, both mood and affect, distinct elements, should be singly investigated. Mood is not immediately discernible, as is affect. Mood is defined as a mild, transitory emotion that is reported by the examinee. Affect, on the other hand, involves verbal and nonverbal observed feelings and exhibited emotions. Is the affective message appropriate to the mood described? An individual who presents as a gregarious, happy, outgoing individual may be masking an underlying depression; and the depression may go unnoticed if the examinee's mood were not investigated.

Affect has several dimensions. *Range* involves the variability of the emotional expression. Is it normal or restricted? *Amplitude* conveys the intensity of expression. Does the amplitude match the content matter expressed? *Stability* addresses the aspect of lability. Is affect relatively intact or do "shifts" in its quality exist?

Quality of Speech

Observe the characteristics of the individual's speech, such as rate and rhythm. Slow patterns may suggest depression, whereas pressured speech may indicate the presence of mania. Is perseveration in evidence, the presence of which can alert the clinician to possible neurological deficits? Is there an absence of verbalization? Note the deficits as well as the degree of the deficits.

Thought Processing–Thought Content

Many psychological disorders are characterized by maladaptive thinking. In diagnosing thought disturbances, it is helpful to make a clear distinction between the content of the disturbance, such as delusional thinking and ideas of reference, and the observed processing of thought, such as productivity (e.g., flight of ideas) and continuity of thought (e.g., thought blocking).

The quality and degree of the examinee's processing cannot wholly be determined by self-report inventory. It goes well beyond this. Additional observation is useful to enhance the picture. Are the individual's thoughts blocked in mid-sentence? Is thought processing disconnected? Are statements tangential? For instance, a significantly elevated Scale SS on the MCMI-III may suggest the presence of fragmented and bizarre thinking and that presence may be confirmed through dyadic interaction with the individual. Examining both the content and processing of one's thoughts can provide a sharper snapshot, particularly of severe clinical syndromes.

Be mindful of distortions. Elevated scores on the MCMI-III Severe Clinical Syndromes scales should alert the clinician to the presence of perceptual distortions. Observed presence of hallucinations (false perceptions taken for objective reality) or delusions (false beliefs that cannot be changed by logic or reason) can help confirm the level and degree of psychotic disturbances.

Sensorium and Mental Capacity

The term *sensorium* is sometimes referred to as consciousness. Is the examinee attentive and alert? What is the examinee's level of con-

---

SELF-DESTRUCTIVE POTENTIAL

Although the MCMI-III contains noteworthy responses referring to self-destructive potential, it is advisable that when any suicidal tendencies are suspected by the clinician they be thoroughly investigated. Gorman (1990, p. 24) noted, "Studies have shown that many patients who commit suicide see their primary physician the week or two before, but no diagnosis of depression is made."

---

sciousness? The clinician's judgment is necessary to determine the individual's ability to adequately respond to test items, as well as to select appropriate test instruments. The clinician is also well-served to understand the nature of the problem through the eyes of the examinee, particularly when discrepancies occur. Consider, also, the timeliness of testing. If an individual is sedated or intoxicated, for example, reschedule testing.

It is advisable to allow a reasonably sufficient amount of time (e.g., several weeks) when testing a client who has undergone chemical rehabilitation.

Domains of Memory

The various domains of memory should be distinguished and any deficits noted. Psychiatric disorders, such as anxiety and mood disorders, can interfere with memory function, and clues gathered from this investigation can support a particular diagnosis. To more carefully examine disturbances in memory, as well as gain a thorough understanding of the overall mental status process, the reader can consult *The Mental Status Examination in Neurology* (Strub & Black, 1985).

Multiaxial Assessment

After we develop a consistent picture of the examinee through the mental status examination, a thorough examination of the multiaxial configuration provides the clinician with a clearer understanding of the individual. However, in reference to solely using the diagnostic criteria of the *DSM-IV* (American Psychiatric Association, 1994) for

SIGNS VERSUS SYMPTOMS

Clinicians often do not distinguish between signs and symptoms. Signs are objective evidence of the existence of a disease. The paranoid personality, for example, may clearly show evidence of suspicious behavior obvious to the clinician. Symptoms, on the other hand, generally are complaints voiced by the examinee and are defined as one's subjective understanding of a disturbance, such as the reported feelings of sadness by the depressed individual. Signs are objective evidence, whereas symptoms are subjective accounts. Both are critical indicators in determining the presence of possible disease and disorders and should be differentiated.

treatment, Millon (1999, p. 111) cautioned, "Using the *DSM-IV* criteria alone as a guide to the substantive characteristics of personality and syndromes would effectively leave some systems constraints completely unobserved. . . ."

ASSESSING SYNDROMES (AXIS I)

With the exception of personality disorders and mental retardation, all disorders are reported on Axis I. Where multiple disorders are diagnosed, prominent disorders receive priority in reporting. That is, the client's reason for the visit is the focus and should be indicated by listing it first.

By using Axis I effectively, the clinician can reinforce the presence of particular elevations on the MCMI-III in relation to observations made. A clinically significant elevation on Scale A, for example, may require a search of criteria in the *DSM-IV* anxiety disorders to determine the type of anxiety disorder the elevated scale reflects. Using a diagnostic tree approach, the clinician can explore the diagnostic criteria in determining the suitability of an identified syndrome. When no diagnosis or condition is present on Axis I or Axis II, a V71.09 code can be assigned.

ASSESSING PERSONALITY DISORDERS (AXIS II)

Personality disorders and mental retardation are reported on Axis II. The significance of the MCMI-III elevations, as well as the number of elevated scales, generally determines the severity of the client's condition. In psychological diagnoses, a hierarchy of pathological conditions exists. The classes of diagnoses range from organic psychosis (e.g., Korsakoff's), to functional psychosis (e.g., schizophrenia), to personality disorders in descending order of severity.

Personality traits observed through the clinical interview can serve as a backdrop to confirm MCMI-III results. For instance, if a significantly elevated Scale P on the MCMI-III can be reinforced through the observation of paranoid content expressed by the examinee during the interview, the classification in the *DSM-IV* of paranoid personality disorder would then be more confidently applied. When disorders of personality functioning that do not meet the criteria for a specific personality disorder arise, they can be recorded as Personality Disorder Not Otherwise Specified (NOS).

BIOLOGICAL–MEDICAL FACTORS (AXIS III)

Biological factors, to include relevant general medical conditions, can surface through a review of the categories provided in the *DSM-IV*, Axis III. Mental disorders may be related to biological and contributing factors, and additional investigation may be necessary. Examinees with affective disorders, for example, may require careful medical screening; and signs, such as lethargy related to hypothyroidism, can mask depression and sometimes be overlooked. In addition, prescription drug usage can occasionally be associated with hallucinations, paranoia, and various altered states of consciousness. An investigation of the possible biological factors, which may either cause or contribute to a mental disorder, is necessary.

PSYCHOSOCIAL–ENVIRONMENTAL FACTORS (AXIS IV)

On Axis IV, the clinician reports psychosocial and environmental problems affecting the condition of the examinee. Family backgrounds, both immediate and extended, as well as marital history, can provide valuable information. To achieve an understanding of the client's situation, the clinician should explore present and past backgrounds and ask pertinent, though sometimes difficult, questions. Has the client experienced physical, psychological, or sexual abuse? Victims of abuse often have repressed memories of early childhood traumas. Inquire about the client's present and past jobs or career. Does employment give rise to positive feelings, or is it a source of environmental stress? Keep in mind the individual's educational level and academic limits, and remain within those limits. Ask about the client's relationship with the legal system. Are arrests or incarcerations contributing factors to a client's condition? Exploring relevant psychosocial and environmental factors within the interview is absolutely necessary. We must not only understand the examinee's diagnosis within this framework but also have the foresight to make the proper social agency referral when intervention is required.

GLOBAL ASSESSMENT OF FUNCTIONING (AXIS V)

The global assessment of functioning (GAF) rates the individual's social, psychological, and occupational functioning. It is essential to assess how well the person is adjusted. Is the individual functioning well, despite an emotional condition? Or is the condition debilitating? A better understanding of the individual's relative psychological adjustment level can assist in treatment planning. The GAF may include a rating for past levels of functioning, though in most cases only the current level is rated. Rate the client's psychological, social, and occupational functioning on a continuum of mental health. Scores range from 100 (superior functioning) to 1 (severely impaired). The score of 0 indicates inadequate information.

Integrate the Findings

As we have seen, the clinical interview allows the clinician to develop a fuller picture of the examinee. As a rule, the more cogent data obtained, the clearer the diagnosis becomes. An integration of the pertinent findings forms the basis for a comprehensive diagnosis and provides the essence of the psychological report.

When using the MCMI-III, the clinician should feel as comfortable as possible in making a diagnosis. A blind interpretation of the MCMI-III, without a full understanding of the individual, can render a less than optimal diagnosis. A structured clinical interview sets the stage for diagnosis and gives perspective to the identified personality disorders and syndromes.

Even if MCMI-III results are invalid, the MCMI-III can still provide valuable information. If the MCMI-III results are invalid, quantitative results certainly cannot be used to arrive at a diagnosis. However, even though quantitative results of the MCMI-III may, on occasion, be invalid, useful qualitative inferences (e.g., length of time to complete the inventory) can prove to be helpful in forming overall clinical analyses.

Communicate
the Results

Psychological report writing is a means of communication. Effective communication assumes expression of one's thoughts in such a way that the writer is readily understood. The polished reports written by skilled clinicians flow naturally and communicate precisely the results of an assessment. For the average clinician, however, report writing may be a tedious process. Simply stated, report writing is a skill that is acquired and one that requires much practice. Although accurate analysis and integration of the test data are required for exact findings, proficient writing skills are critical to effectively communicate the findings.

PREREPORT WRITING GUIDELINES

When preparing the report, consider the referral question carefully, then construct the findings accordingly. Before composing the report, determine the nature and extent of the issues, and organize a suitable course of action. The report's objective generally will define the elements that are incorporated. The goal in preparing the report is to organize the data into an orderly, functional, and cohesive whole. The following guidelines can assist us in this process:

- Define the purpose of the report. As stated previously, the report should clearly communicate the quantitative and qualitative re-

---

HOW TO WRITE WELL

"Writing is, for most, laborious and slow. The mind travels faster than the pen. . . . Write in a way that draws the reader's attention to the sense and substance of the writing, rather than to the mood and temper of the author. . . . Write in a way that comes easily and naturally to you, using words and phrases that come readily to hand. But do not assume that because you have acted naturally your product is without flaw."

—William Strunk, Jr., and E. B. White
The Elements of Style (1979, pp. 69–70)

sults of the clinician's findings. Ensure that the purpose of the report is consistent with the referral question. Read all pertinent information provided by the referral source. If the referral question cannot be adequately addressed by the results obtained from the psychological assessment, discuss the limitations with the referral source before drafting the report. Modification of the referral question may, at times, be necessary. Strive for accuracy!

- Emphasize the central problem. Clear and direct emphasis of the referral question will eliminate confusion or misunderstanding in report writing. Structure the report in response to the referral question, and support all conclusions with reliable data.
- Be mindful of the reader. Who will read the psychological evaluation? Although the clinician directs the contents of the report to the referral agency and its professionals, keep in mind that the report may eventually reach a wider audience than the clinician had originally intended. To this end, ensure that the information presented directly addresses the purpose intended. Make certain also that proper consent forms are used and ethical guidelines practiced.
- Confidentiality is critical. Regardless of the report's purpose, confidentiality and the client's rights are always of utmost importance. Advise the client, as fully as possible, regarding the purpose, process, results of the clinical assessment, and, as appropriate, the legal limits of confidentiality. The candid sharing of information, accompanied by a signed informed consent, can eliminate any possible breach of confidentiality.
- Organize thoughts and data. Before beginning the actual report writing, organize the available information into a cohesive structure. The goal of the report should clearly address the referral question through a structured analysis of the data collected— namely, to translate the raw data into a more focused picture of the client's personality. Outlining the materials, including the findings, interpretations, possible diagnoses, and suggested treatment recommendations beforehand, will provide a logical direction for report writing. With a completed outline, the clinician can more confidently begin to write the report.

THE REPORT

Keep in mind that although no one universal format for report writing exists, the psychological evaluation is a sensitive document and should be written as professionally as possible. Whatever format is selected, the report should provide the reader with a clear understanding and focus of the client with regard to the referral question. In general, the

---

REPORT GUIDELINES

The following adapted from Sattler (1982, p. 512) offers the guidance in formulating a report:

- Consider the kinds of material necessary to include in the report.
- Synthesize the test findings with behavioral observations.
- Include examples of the client's performance that can enrich the report.
- Ensure that the certainty of the statements are based on test data.

---

length of the report is not a measure of its worth. Most standardized formats, however, are approximately five pages in length. Use of the clinician's letterhead stationery is recommended.

The following selections of a notional report are arranged by section, allowing the reader to view the components described in a psychological report. (An example of an entire psychological report written by this author is provided in appendix C; also, a nine-page comprehensive MCMI-III interpretive report by Millon can be found in appendix A. See also Exhibit 7-1.)

CONFIDENTIALITY STATEMENT

Note that information obtained during the clinical assessment is released only with the client's consent, except in circumstances in which withholding such information would result in imminent danger to the client or another person. Information is customarily released to only those having a legitimate "reason to know." A reminder of this confidentiality statement may be included in block capital letters at the top of the report. For example:

> THIS INFORMATION MAY NOT BE FURTHER DISCLOSED, RELEASED, OR SHARED, EXCEPT IN ACCORDANCE WITH THE HEALTH AND DEVELOPMENTAL DISABILITIES CONFIDENTIALITY ACT OF THE STATE OF TEXAS.

DEMOGRAPHIC DATA

Demographic data refers to preliminary information that identifies the client. The format may vary according to the purpose of the report and style of the clinician. For example:

Name of Client: Mrs. D.
Date of Birth: 05/12/66
Age at Testing: 33 yr, 6 mos.

Examiner: Dan Jankowski, PsyD
Date of Testing: 11/12/99
Referral Source: Director, HRS

REASON FOR REFERRAL

State briefly and clearly the purpose for which the examinee is being evaluated and include the referral source. Referral questions should be as specific as possible to determine the exact reason for the evaluation. Include any existing problems indicated by the referral source. For example:

> Mrs. D. was referred for psychological evaluation by Mr. R., director, Human Resource Services. Information was requested about Mrs. D.'s current level of cognitive and emotional functioning to determine the source of her problematic behavior and continued inability to perform assigned tasks. For approximately the last two years in particular, Mrs. D. has habitually resisted or ignored supervisory assignments, failing to achieve minimum job expectations.

BACKGROUND INFORMATION

Background information can be obtained from a variety of sources; however, it is derived foremost from the examinee. Family members, former and current referral sources, and the examinee's social history file can also provide additional data. Pertinent information, such as current situational disposition, previous psychiatric history, and any data relevant to the presenting problem should be included. Occasionally, information may be difficult to acquire because of confidentiality limitations of the referral source or the examinee's reluctance to disclose

---

EXHIBIT 7-1

Components of a Full Psychological Report

Demographic data	→	Information identifying the client
Reason for referral	→	What is the purpose of the evaluation?
Background information	→	Pertinent psychological/social history
Behavioral observations	→	What is the client's outward demeanor?
Assessment procedures	→	Which procedures are administered?
Intelligence testing	→	What is the client's cognitive capacity?
Neuropsychological screening	→	Functional/organic differential diagnosis
Personality assessment	→	Describe behavioral/social patterns
Diagnostic impression	→	Formulate *DSM-IV* diagnosis
Treatment recommendations	→	What treatment regimen is prescribed?
Signature block	→	Authenticates the report

> **HELPFUL HINTS**
>
> The following adapted from Greg Nail (1990) provided several helpful suggestions when writing the background information section:
> - Group related pieces of information in a single paragraph.
> - Within each topic, follow chronological development.
> - Keep information under the appropriate subheadings.
> - Be consistent in form.
> - Avoid excessive use of words such as, "reportedly, according to the client, or the client stated."
> - Include only details that are relevant to one's conclusions.

information. In such cases, the clinician can merely report the information that is available. The following background information report for Mrs. D. is provided:

> Mrs. D. is a 33-year-old divorced, White female, employed as an administrative clerk. In responding to the examiner's background information questions, Mrs. D. was vague and nonspecific. For instance, when the examiner asked what was the highest level of education attained, Mrs. D. responded, "I attended the ceremony at Avian High School." When the examiner pressed further to determine whether the implication suggested a high school degree, Mrs. D. repeated the original response. Questions regarding reported untoward behavior similarly produced vague responses. With minimal referral information received from the referral source and a reluctance to share historical information by the examinee, basic background information was limited.

BEHAVIORAL OBSERVATIONS

Describe the client's overall approach to the psychological process. Elements of the mental status presented earlier in the chapter are discussed under behavioral observations. Describe the examinee's appearance and behavior. Were any unusual speech characteristics identified? Are thought processing and thought content normal? Are mood and affect consistent? Address the examinee's disposition toward the entire assessment process. Was the client cooperative, resistant, candid, manipulative, suspicious? In addition, it is helpful to include the client's perception of the nature of the presenting problem—or lack thereof. For example,

Mrs. D. arrived promptly for her 10:00 A.M. appointment. She was unaccompanied and used public transportation to the examiner's office. Mrs. D. voiced her resistance early in the session by stating, "I have no problem." She reluctantly agreed to be evaluated and disclosed minimal information during the three-hour session. She was appropriately dressed and groomed, though markedly overweight for height–weight standards. She was alert and attentive, though most responses were vague and ambiguous.

Though thought content was, at times, tangential, no evidence of a formal thought disorder was present. No delusions or hallucinations were observed. No suicidal ideation was reported. Speech was fluent and coherent, though somewhat pressured. Throughout the evaluation, Mrs. D. presented a mildly hostile affect, laden with apathetic indifference. She hesitantly described her mood as "all right." Test results indicate that memory was adequate in all domains. Vision and hearing appeared normal. She was observed to be right-handed. Of concern to the examiner were several sudden "sleep attacks" by the examinee during the onset of the evaluation. When questioned about these sudden attacks, Mrs. D. offered no logical explanation, except to say that she was unaware of the episodes. Mrs. D. was presently taking no medication and stated that she received sufficient sleep the previous night.

ASSESSMENT PROCEDURES

At this point in the report, note all the procedures administered to the client. Begin by listing the most structured and proceed to the least structured instruments. The MCMI-III, for example, is a structured objective personality instrument, whereas the Rorschach is an unstructured, projective instrument. Neither overtest nor undertest a client. Maintain focus of the referral question, and select the appropriate instruments. Ensure that the instruments selected are suitable for the age of the client, as well as the presenting problem. For example,

Millon Clinical Multiaxial Inventory-III (MCMI-III)
Wechsler Adult Intelligence Scale-III (WAIS-III)
Luria-Nebraska Neuropsychological Screening Test
Mental status examination
Rorschach inkblot test

INTELLIGENCE TESTING

Intelligence testing should be included because it can provide further supportive data. Recall from Table 1-4 that one's cognitive style comprises a specific domain of personality. For instance, the impoverished cognitive style of the schizoid individual and the expansiveness of the narcissistic individual are specific domains of personality. Certain scale scores on the intelligence tests often can be suggestive of particular personality traits. An elevated subscale score on the WAIS-III arithmetic subtest, for example, requires meticulous attention skills. Hence, some compulsive personalities may likely score high if they combine speed with attention to detail. Conversely, a low score obtained on the digit symbol-coding, which requires visual dexterity and persistence, may be suggestive of depressive personalities. Intelligence testing can support MCMI-III findings.

Although abbreviated intelligence tests are available (e.g., Wechsler Abbreviated Scale of Intelligence), the full WAIS-III should be administered whenever possible. In the results section of the report, address any significant differences among the scales. See Exhibit 7-2 for a summary of IQ scores. It is customary to list the IQ scores summary, the index scores summary, and the subtest scale scores, to include the scaled scores (SS) and percentile rankings (PR). For example,

> Mrs. D. currently functions in the low average range of cognitive ability, according to her performance on the WAIS-III (full-scale IQ 80; verbal IQ 83; performance IQ 81). With a 95% confidence level, Mrs. D.'s full-scale IQ falls between 76 to 84 on the WAIS-III, placing her in the ninth percentile of the general population. The following results represent a valid and reliable indicator of her intellectual functioning:

On verbal subtests, vocabulary and information represent relative strengths in relation to the verbal score mean. The relatively low score on similarities, however, suggests limitations in abstract concept formation and the capacity for associative thinking. Ability to adequately apply past experience to understand and adapt to social customs is also limited. Immediate and working memory are adequate.

With regard to perceptual organizational skills, tests requiring visual or nonverbal synthesis were uniformly limited. Nonverbal reasoning and sequencing skills, as measured by picture arrangement, however, demonstrate a relative strength. In relation to the relative weakness on the comprehension subtest, this pattern suggests that although Mrs. D. may be sensitive to interpersonal nuances and can grasp social cause and effect, an inadequate practical judgment regarding social customs and disregard for social convention are likely demonstrated. Perceptual organization and processing speed measures are nearly equivalent. Overall, visual-motor coordination is adequate.

NEUROPSYCHOLOGICAL SCREENING

Depending on the nature of the referral question, instruments, such as the Luria-Nebraska Neuropsychological Screening Test, can provide

EXHIBIT 7-2

Mrs. D. IQ Scoring Summary

IQ Scores Summary			Index Scores Summary	
Vertical scale IQ	83	(low average)	Verbal comprehension	89
Performance scale IQ	81	(low average)	Perceptual organization	82
Full scale IQ	80	(low average)	Working memory	82
			Processing speed	79

Subtest Scores Summary

Verbal Subtests	Age SS	PR	Performance Subtests	Age SS	PR
Vocabulary	9	37	Picture completion	7	16
Similarities	6	9	Digit symbol-coding	6	9
Arithmetic	7	16	Block design	7	16
Digit span	7	16	Matrix reasoning	7	16
Information	9	37	Picture arrangement	9	37
Comprehension	5	5	Symbol search	6	9
Letter-number sequencing	7	16	Object assembly (not administered)		

Note: Difference between VIQ and PIQ = −2 (ns, freq = 88.3%).

useful information. This brief screening test can determine in a few minutes whether a full neuropsychological battery is warranted. Its 15 questions are actual questions extracted from the Luria-Nebraska Neuropsychological Battery. For example:

> Results of the Luria-Nebraska: Neuropsychological screening fell within acceptable norms, suggesting the absence of manifest organic impairment. Further neuropsychological testing is not warranted at the present time.

PERSONALITY ASSESSMENT

At the beginning of this section in the report, it is customary to indicate the personality instruments administered and present an overview of the examinee's personality pattern. Include a description of the individual's response style. Are the results a valid estimate of the examinee's personality? Describe the examinee's personality pattern across functional and structural domains. Describe salient clinical syndromes that are indicated by the data findings. Discuss remarkable clinical issues relevant and cogent to the referral question(s). Finally, summarize the individual's current level of personality functioning. For example,

> Mrs. D. was administered the MCMI-III and the Rorschach. Although the test results of both instruments are valid, overall

response sets suggest an oppositional, guarded, and defensive style. Clinically significant elevations obtained on the MCMI-III indicate a 2A8A (avoidant–negativistic) personality pattern. This profile is characterized by pessimism, fear of rejection, and ambivalent behaviors. Vacillating behaviors—being cooperative at one time and obstructionist the next—are common to this personality pattern. Projective findings similarly indicate a pattern of defensive withdrawal. An unusually low affective ratio signals a tendency to avoid or withdraw from emotional stimuli. As a necessary defensive strategy, Mrs. D. likely exercises physical and emotional withdrawal to cope with her anticipated fears of rejection and humiliation by others. Interpersonally, Mrs. D. approaches situations in a defensive and contrary manner and is apt to view the external world as unfriendly, uncooperative, and hostile. Expecting to be slighted or embarrassed, Mrs. D. likely adopts a hypervigilant stance toward others. Similar patterns generally assume a hypercritical attitude toward those who are unsupportive.

In summary, Mrs. D.'s test results signal the presence of chronic depressive symptoms, and if left untreated, may further impair social and occupational functioning. Although her disposition was marked with depressed mood, no indication of self-destructive tendencies was in evidence. When faced with conflictual situations and unanticipated stressors, Mrs. D. tends to actively withdraw. Distancing herself from others, both physically and emotionally, is her preferred and necessary coping strategy. This seemingly futile strategy, though, effectively serves to decrease the fears and tensions that surround her.

DIAGNOSTIC IMPRESSIONS

This segment of the report is reserved for the *DSM-IV* diagnosis. Remember that the MCMI-III is constructed with close consonance to the *DSM-IV* categories. All *DSM* axes are to be listed. Diagnostic codes should be used where applicable. For example,

Axis I: 300.4   Dysthymic disorder
Axis II: 301.82 Avoidant personality disorder with negativistic personality traits
Axis III: None
Axis IV: Discord with supervisor and coworkers
Axis V: GAF = 60 (current)

SUMMARY OF THE REPORT

We bring the report together by consolidating the summarized findings and recommendations in this section. Ensure that the summary is brief, concisely recapping the information. The summary serves as a prelude to treatment recommendations. The recommendations are numbered and ranked in order of priority. Although treatment planning is beyond the scope of this book, it is, nevertheless, an important element of testing, and several brief remarks are provided.

Keep in mind that the singular purpose for most psychological evaluations is determining *if* the examinee is in need of treatment. The goal of diagnosis is to make an accurate assessment of the individual's overall emotional condition to develop a treatment plan, rendering necessary recommendations for appropriate treatment. Certain personality configural patterns dictate specific therapeutic options to be used. These should be noted. In addition, the response style provides an important gauge regarding the examinee's amenability to treatment. For example,

> Mrs. D. is a 33-year-old divorced, White female, who was evaluated to determine current ability to perform assigned duties. Mrs. D.'s full-scale IQ scores on the WAIS-III places her in the ninth percentile of the general population. She currently functions in the low average range of cognitive ability, as measured by her results on the WAIS-III (full-scale IQ 80; verbal IQ 83; performance IQ 81). Neuropsychological screening suggests the absence of manifest organic impairment.
>
> Results of the personality tests were psychometrically valid. The examinee's overall response style, however, suggests a strong degree of defensiveness with a tendency to appear morally virtuous. Test results indicate an avoidant–negativistic personality pattern. Depressed mood characterizes this individual, and withdrawal from stressful stimuli is Mrs. D.'s preferred coping strategy. Signs of hypervigilance, guardedness, and resistance are present. Often unable to adjust to the demands of the environment, individuals with similar profiles tend to be ambivalent with regard to therapeutic intervention.

TREATMENT RECOMMENDATIONS

The goal of diagnosis is to make an accurate assessment of the individual's overall emotional condition and, if necessary, to develop a treatment plan. A thorough diagnostic assessment provides the hypothesis on which treatment plans are based.

The psychological assessment, then, should furnish the referral source with sufficient information to develop a treatment plan specific to the client's subjective resources. Provide the referent a clear picture of the client's disposition within the context of the syndromes manifested. Helpful considerations include the following:

- Are the client's syndromes chronic or acute?
- What demonstrated behaviors and underlying defenses might interfere with effective treatment?

■ Has psychotic or suicidal behavior been identified?
■ Does the client possess adequate intellectual and environmental skills required for particular treatment regimens?
■ What is the client's current level of functioning?
■ Is the client amenable to treatment?

The referral source will benefit from knowing which treatment procedures may prove effective for the particular personality evaluated—in other words, which treatment is most appropriate to meet the client's needs. Research regarding appropriate treatment has proliferated in recent years. Recommending the proper treatment procedures requires the clinician to keep up-to-date with current studies.

Outcome studies, for example, can provide useful information regarding treatment effectiveness. In their study of psychiatric inpatients who were diagnosed on Axis I primarily with affective disorders (major depression and bipolar I or II disorders, and mood disorders), Piersma and Boes (1997) provided information regarding how the MCMI-III functions as a treatment evaluation instrument. Patients were administered the MCMI-III within three days of admission and were retested one to two weeks later.

Among their findings, five Clinical Personality Patterns scales (Avoidant, Depressive, Dependent, Aggressive, and Negativistic) demonstrated significant decreases between admission and subsequent testing. Three scales (Histrionic, Narcissistic, and Compulsive) demonstrated significant increases. On the Severe Pathology scales, Borderline and Paranoid scales evidenced significant decreases. All of the Clinical and Severe Syndrome scales, with the exception of Bipolar: Manic Disorder, Drug Dependence, and Delusional disorders, decreased significantly between preadmission testing and posttesting. Researching studies such as these are advocated to determine the effectiveness of prescribed treatment regimens.

Valuable guides for treatment planning are also available in a couple of recently published textbooks, such as *The Personality Disorders Treatment Planner* by Bockian and Jungsma (2001). Listing the behavioral definitions of each disorder (as classified in the *DSM-IV*), long-term treatment goals are clearly stated. The long-term goals are then easily referenced to short-term objectives and therapeutic interventions using multiple theoretical orientations.

In *Personality-Guided Therapy*, Millon (1999) provides a comprehensive understanding of the principles underlying his theory in the development of appropriate treatment strategies. The following framework outlined in Exhibit 7-3 illustrates Millon's goals of polarity-oriented personologic therapy.

EXHIBIT 7-3

Goals of Polarity-Oriented Personalogic Therapy

Modifying the Pain–Pleasure Polarity

\+ Pleasure (schizoid, avoidant, depressive
\- Pain (avoidant, depressive)
Pain ⇔ pleasure (self-defeating, sadistic)

Balancing the Passive–Active Polarity

\+ Passive – active (avoidant, histrionic, antisocial, sadistic, negativistic)
\- Passive + active (schizoid, depressive, dependent, narcissistic,
self-defeating, compulsive)

Altering the Other–Self Polarity

\- Other + self (dependent, histrionic)
\+ Other – self (narcissistic, antisocial)
Other ⇔ self (compulsive, negativistic)

Rebuilding the Personality Structure

\+ Cognitive, interpersonal cohesion (schizotypal)
\+ Affective, self-cohesion (borderline)
\- Cognitive, affective-rigidity (paranoid)

Source: Disorders of Personality DSM-IV and Beyond (2nd ed.) by T. Millon and Davis, 1996, New York. Copyright 1996 John Wiley & Sons, Inc. Reprinted with permission.

Millon bases his personologic therapeutic approach on an integrative strategy. In restructuring polarity imbalances (discussed in chapter 1) and countering self-perpetuations, appropriate strategic goals are determined and tactical modalities are presented. A holistic treatment approach employing combined techniques is presented to achieve polarity balances within the pathological personality.

Using our case study, for example, Mrs. D. obtained clinically significant elevations on the Avoidant and Negativistic scales. Examining the polarity domains, goals of treatment are directed toward modifying the pain–pleasure polarity, balancing the passive–active polarity, and altering the self–other polarity. In Mrs. D.'s case, the clinician most likely would direct efforts toward diminishing the anticipation of pain and increasing more pleasure-enhancing behaviors. Initial supportive therapy, which provides a secure environment, can be followed by cognitive–behavioral techniques. Goals should be directed toward altering cognitive perceptions, thereby reducing the anticipation of disappointment, diminishing suspicious and fearful behavior, and lessening the conflict experienced with others.

Regarding the goals of treatment, Millon and Davis (1996, p. 191) wrote,

> Depending on the pathological polarity to be modified, and the integrative treatment sequence the clinician has in mind, the goals of therapy are to overcome *pleasure deficiencies* in schizoids, avoidants, and depressives; to reestablish *interpersonally imbalanced* polarity disturbances in dependents, histrionics, narcissists, and antisocials; to undo the *intrapsychic conflicts* in sadists, compulsives, masochists, and negativists; and to reconstruct the *structural defects* in the schizotypal, borderline, and paranoid personalities.

Let us now return to Mrs. D.'s report. The following recommendations are offered:

1. A thorough physical examination is warranted to determine whether the observed sudden "sleep attacks" are functional or organic in origin.
2. At the onset of treatment, establish a supportive environment, which can help bolster Mrs. D.'s self-image and reduce, to some extent, her initial anxiety.
3. Once a relationship of trust is established, cognitive–behavioral techniques may be used to alter perceptions of negativity, pessimism, and fears of rejection.
4. Stress management training may be used to provide useful and appropriate coping solutions and enhance self-efficacy and confidence.
5. Mrs. D. approaches situations in a highly guarded, defensive manner and perceives the external environment as threatening. To effect more appropriate social behavior, staff members, particularly supervisors, may increase Mrs. D.'s overall confidence and self-esteem by providing positive reinforcement when suitable.
6. The use of antidepressant medication should be considered.

We have written a well-organized report. Now it is time to authenticate the report properly and professionally by closing with the signature block.

SIGNATURE BLOCK

The last segment of the psychological report is the signature block. It includes the clinician's name, degree, title, and license number. A complimentary close may also be included. Leave two line-spaces between the last paragraph and the complimentary close, and four line-spaces between the complimentary close and typed signature. The clinician's signature confirms the authenticity of the report's contents. Remember to always sign the report. For example,

Respectfully submitted,

Dan Jankowski, PsyD
Licensed Clinical Psychologist
#041-442-096

Exhibit 7-4 contains Mrs. D.'s MCMI-III scaled scores.

POSTREPORT GUIDELINES

Following the completion of a report, it is important to tie up loose ends to ensure accuracy, good record keeping, courtesy, and discretion regarding recommendations in the psychological report process. Consider these points:

- Proofread the report. Unless time is of the essence, put the completed report aside (e.g., an hour or a day). Following a reasonable period of time, proofread the report for its accuracy, content, and grammatical–spelling errors. In reading the report for content, check for ambiguity of terms, flaws in the arrangement of the material, and inaccuracies of interpretation. The clinician can refer to the third edition of Strunk and White's, *The Elements of Style* (1979) regarding grammatical concerns. Since virtually all computers are equipped with spell-check and grammar-check features, why would proofreading a document visually be necessary? Consider the homonyms *forward* and *foreword,* for example; only the proofreader can determine the correct contextual usage for each of these words. Proofreading always proves beneficial.
- Retain data. Retain assessment data and other related materials, particularly when follow-up consultation is necessary. Review particular state regulations regarding requirements for retention of files.
- Make a courtesy call. It is advisable to contact the referral source following the forwarding of the psychological report. Not only can assurance be made that the report has arrived, but it also can serve as an appropriate and timely opportunity to address follow-up issues that may have surfaced after the referral was made.
- Know what you say and say what you mean. Remember that the psychological report is a definitive and sensitive report, documenting the psychological disposition of a client. A prescribed diagnosis will label the client being evaluated. Ensure that a client

EXHIBIT 7-4

MCMI-III BR Scale Scores: Mrs. D.

Category	BR Score	Scales	
			Validity Index = 0
Modifying indices	53	Disclosure	(Scale X)
	89	Desirability	(Scale Y)
	56	Debasement	(Scale Z)
Clinical personality patterns	67	Schizoid	(Scale 1)
	85	Avoidant	(Scale 2A)
	69	Depressive	(Scale 2B)
	60	Dependent	(Scale 3)
	23	Histrionic	(Scale 4)
	27	Narcissistic	(Scale 5)
	64	Antisocial	(Scale 6A)
	48	Sadistic	(Scale 6B)
	20	Compulsive	(Scale 7)
	76	Negativistic	(Scale 8A)
	60	Masochistic	(Scale 8B)
Severe personality pathology	45	Schizotypal	(Scale S)
	65	Borderline	(Scale C)
	63	Paranoid	(Scale P)
Clinical syndromes	60	Anxiety disorder	(Scale A)
	51	Somatoform disorder	(Scale H)
	60	Bipolar: manic disorder	(Scale N)
	70	Dysthymic disorder	(Scale D)
	25	Alcohol dependence	(Scale B)
	25	Drug dependence	(Scale T)
	30	Post-traumatic stress	(Scale R)
Severe clinical syndromes	26	Thought disorder	(Scale SS)
	60	Major depression	(Scale CC)
	60	Delusional disorder	(Scale PP)

who is evaluated fully meets the diagnostic criteria of a *DSM-IV* syndrome or disorder (to the best of the clinician's knowledge) before making a diagnosis. Exercise discretion when recommending a diagnosis.

In Summary

In this chapter, we reviewed the components of a psychological report. Although the MCMI-III is an excellent assessment tool, it is used most efficiently in the context of a comprehensive evaluation and clinical interview. All relevant findings should be used to effectively arrive at a comfort level in formulating the examinee's diagnosis. Be mindful that the singular purpose for most psychological evaluations is determining *if* treatment is necessary. It is essential for the clinician to gather as much pertinent information as possible in providing a diagnosis and subsequent treatment plan. These findings are then effectively communicated through a psychological report. Because psychological evaluations carry much weight in clinical settings and remain a matter of historical record, the clinician should strive for utmost accuracy.

Chapter by chapter throughout this book, we have taken steps together on a journey, discovering the MCMI-III from its beginnings to the present. Having followed the guidelines, we have gathered information along the road toward properly using this powerful assessment tool to arrive at our destination: to identify an accurate diagnosis of clinically disordered individuals and provide treatment planning. Yet, roads lead on to roads, and with the knowledge we have acquired, we

---

TIPS FROM "FUMBLERULES" BY WILLIAM SAFIRE (1999, p. 81)

- Don't use double negatives.
- Verbs has to agree with their subjects.
- Avoid trendy locutions that sound trendy.
- Kill all exclamation points!!!
- Don't verb nouns.
- Also, avoid awkward or affected alliterations.
- Proofread carefully to see if any words left out.

are now ready, companion book in hand, to explore ever-evolving paths of psychology. It is ultimately our role on the clinical stage that defines our direction.

Test Yourself Exercises 7

Fill in the Blanks.

1. The _____ is the primary means through which clinical assessment findings are conveyed.
2. A _____ can eliminate possible breaches and misunderstandings regarding the limits of confidentiality.
3. Objective evidence of the existence of a disease is referred to as _____ .
4. Medical conditions are reported on Axis _____ of the *DSM-IV.*
5. When organizing a report, details of mental status should be included in the section titled, _____ .
6. *Mental status* simply refers to _____ .
7. Psychosocial and environmental problems affecting the client's condition are reported on Axis _____ of the *DSM-IV.*
8. The _____ authenticates the contents of the psychological report.
9. Orientation to _____ , _____ , and _____ is a procedure used to determine the examinee's level of consciousness.
10. The singular purpose for most psychological evaluations is _____ .

Profile Exercise 1

(BR scores listed)
Demographic and situation factors: Mr. C. is a 58-year-old White bachelor and a high school graduate. He is currently a nursing home resident.
Referral question: Is psychological treatment necessary?
Exhibit 7-5 provides the MCMI-III scores for Mr. C. Use these scale scores to answer the questions in Exercise 1.

1. What do the Modifying indices suggest about Mr. C.'s response style?
2. Describe Mr. C.'s level of disturbance.
3. Discuss Mr. C.'s predominant personality style?
4. What clinical syndrome would constitute a possible *DSM-IV* Axis I diagnosis?
5. Which personality patterns constitute a possible *DSM-IV* Axis II diagnosis?
6. Discuss therapeutic implications (include referral question in your response).

EXHIBIT 7-5

MCMI-III BR Scale Scores: Profile Exercise #1: Mr. C.

Category	BR Score	Scales	
			Validity Index = 1
Modifying indices	70	Disclosure	(Scale X)
	80	Desirability	(Scale Y)
	83	Debasement	(Scale Z)
Clinical personality patterns	64	Schizoid	(Scale 1)
	79	Avoidant	(Scale 2A)
	66	Depressive	(Scale 2B)
	87	Dependent	(Scale 3)
	60	Histrionic	(Scale 4)
	37	Narcissistic	(Scale 5)
	45	Antisocial	(Scale 6A)
	43	Sadistic	(Scale 6B)
	55	Compulsive	(Scale 7)
	77	Negativistic	(Scale 8A)
	66	Masochistic	(Scale 8B)
Severe personality pathology	62	Schizotypal	(Scale S)
	68	Borderline	(Scale C)
	78	Paranoid	(Scale P)
Clinical syndromes	88	Anxiety disorder	(Scale A)
	75	Somatoform disorder	(Scale H)
	64	Bipolar: manic disorder	(Scale N)
	75	Dysthymic disorder	(Scale D)
	85	Alcohol dependence	(Scale B)
	75	Drug dependence	(Scale T)
	67	Post-traumatic stress	(Scale R)
Severe clinical syndromes	65	Thought disorder	(Scale SS)
	90	Major depression	(Scale CC)
	77	Delusional disorder	(Scale PP)

Profile Exercise 2

(BR scores listed)

Demographic and situation factors: Mr. K. is a 23-year-old White college graduate. He is currently being seen as an outpatient. Marital and drug problems were reported.

Referral question: Will the client benefit from drug rehabilitation?

Exhibit 7-6 provides the MCMI-III scores for Mr. K. use these scores to answer the questions in Exercise 2.

1. What do the Modifying indices suggest about Mr. K.'s response style?
2. Describe Mr. K.'s level of pathology.
3. Discuss Mr. K.'s predominant personality style?
4. What clinical syndrome would constitute a possible *DSM-IV* Axis I diagnosis?
5. Which personality patterns constitute a possible *DSM-IV* Axis II diagnosis?
6. Discuss therapeutic implications (include referral question in your response).

Profile Exercise 3

Exhibit 7-7 (MCMI-III scale scores) and Exhibit 7-8 (WAIS-III scale scores) are provided. Use these scores to write the psychological report for Exercise 3.

Reason for referral:

Ms. R., a 25-year-old African American female, was referred for psychological evaluation by Mr. B., a caseworker for the Department of Children and Family Services (DCFS). Information was requested concerning Ms. R.'s current level of cognitive and emotional functioning to determine suitability for unsupervised parental visitation.

EXHIBIT 7-6

MCMI-III BR Scale Scores: Profile Exercise #2: Mr. K.

Category	BR Score	Scales	
			Validity Index = 0
Modifying indices	71	Disclosure	(Scale X)
	74	Desirability	(Scale Y)
	61	Debasement	(Scale Z)
Clinical personality patterns	64	Schizoid	(Scale 1)
	74	Avoidant	(Scale 2A)
	60	Depressive	(Scale 2B)
	50	Dependent	(Scale 3)
	73	Histrionic	(Scale 4)
	88	Narcissistic	(Scale 5)
	100	Antisocial	(Scale 6A)
	90	Sadistic	(Scale 6B)
	21	Compulsive	(Scale 7)
	72	Negativistic	(Scale 8A)
	66	Masochistic	(Scale 8B)
Severe personality pathology	68	Schizotypal	(Scale S)
	70	Borderline	(Scale C)
	69	Paranoid	(Scale P)
Clinical syndromes	60	Anxiety disorder	(Scale A)
	72	Somatoform disorder	(Scale H)
	77	Bipolar: manic disorder	(Scale N)
	64	Dysthymic disorder	(Scale D)
	70	Alcohol dependence	(Scale B)
	104	Drug dependence	(Scale T)
	30	Post-traumatic stress	(Scale R)
Severe clinical syndromes	61	Thought disorder	(Scale SS)
	60	Major depression	(Scale CC)
	63	Delusional disorder	(Scale PP)

EXHIBIT 7-7

MCMI-III BR Scale Scores: Profile Exercise #3: Ms. R.

Category	BR Score	Scales	
			Validity Index = 0
Modifying indices	64	Disclosure	(Scale X)
	84	Desirability	(Scale Y)
	45	Debasement	(Scale Z)
Clinical personality patterns	30	Schizoid	(Scale 1)
	76	Avoidant	(Scale 2A)
	60	Depressive	(Scale 2B)
	20	Dependent	(Scale 3)
	46	Histrionic	(Scale 4)
	82	Narcissistic	(Scale 5)
	89	Antisocial	(Scale 6A)
	64	Sadistic	(Scale 6B)
	67	Compulsive	(Scale 7)
	81	Negativistic	(Scale 8A)
	20	Masochistic	(Scale 8B)
Severe personality pathology	62	Schizotypal	(Scale S)
	30	Borderline	(Scale C)
	72	Paranoid	(Scale P)
Clinical syndromes	78	Anxiety disorder	(Scale A)
	73	Somatoform disorder	(Scale H)
	36	Bipolar: manic disorder	(Scale N)
	79	Dysthymic disorder	(Scale D)
	80	Alcohol dependence	(Scale B)
	91	Drug dependence	(Scale T)
	68	Post-traumatic stress	(Scale R)
Severe clinical syndromes	68	Thought disorder	(Scale SS)
	66	Major depression	(Scale CC)
	68	Delusional disorder	(Scale PP)

EXHIBIT 7-8

Ms. R. IQ Scoring Summary

IQ Scores Summary			Index Scores Summary	
Verbal scale IQ	89	(low average)	Verbal comprehension	94
Performance scale IQ	95	(average)	Perceptual organization	91
Full scale IQ	91	(average)	Working memory	90
			Processing speed	96

Subtest Scores Summary

Verbal Subtests	Age SS	PR	Performance Subtests	Age SS	PR
Vocabulary	9	37	Picture completion	9	37
Similarities	9	37	Digit symbol-coding	10	50
Arithmetic	8	25	Block design	9	37
Digit span	8	25	Matrix reasoning	8	25
Information	9	37	Picture arrangement	11	63
Comprehension	6	9	Symbol search	9	37
Letter–number sequencing	9	37	Object assembly (not administered)		

Note: Difference between VIQ and PIQ = –6 (ns, frequency = 60.4%).

Appendix A
MCMI-III Interpretative Report

Theodore Millon, PhD
ID Number 43463
Female
Age 40
White
Remarried
Mental Hospital Inpatient
1/25/97

Capsule Summary

MCMI-III reports are normed on patients who were in the early phases of assessment or psychotherapy for emotional discomfort or social difficulties. Respondents who do not fit this normative population or who have inappropriately taken the MCMI-III for nonclinical purposes may have distorted reports. The MCMI-III report cannot be considered definitive. It should be evaluated in conjunction with additional clinical data. The report should be evaluated by a mental health clinician trained in the use of psychological tests. The report should not be shown to patients or their relatives.

Interpretive Considerations

The client is a 40-year-old married white female with 12 years of education. She is currently being seen as an inpatient, and she reports that she has recently experienced problems that involve loneliness and low self-confidence. These self-reported difficulties, which have occurred in the last one to three months, are likely to take the form of an Axis I disorder.

This patient's response style may indicate a tendency to magnify illness, an inclination to complain, or feelings of extreme vulnerability associated with a current episode of acute turmoil. The patient's scale scores may be somewhat exaggerated, and the interpretations should be read with this in mind.

Profile Severity

On the basis of the test data, it may be assumed that the patient is experiencing a severe mental disorder; further professional observation and inpatient care may be appropriate. The text of the following interpretive report may need to be modulated upward given this probable level of severity.

Possible Diagnoses

She appears to fit the following Axis II classifications best: Self-defeating Personality Disorder, with Dependent Personality Traits, Depressive Personality Traits, and Negativistic (Passive-Aggressive) Personality Features.

Axis I clinical syndromes are suggested by the client's MCMI-III profile in the areas of Major Depression (recurrent, severe, without psychotic features) and Generalized Anxiety Disorder

Therapeutic Considerations

Moderate stress will cause this patient to exhibit self-demeaning behavior and depressive feelings, often accompanied by an underlying irritability. Alternating between dependency and martyr-like behavior, the patient may regress from cooperation to pessimistic noncompliance. These erratic behaviors and attitudes will respond best to a short-term treatment model, with clear directions and a firm but warmly supportive stance.

RESPONSE TENDENCIES

This patient's response style may indicate a broad tendency to magnify the level of experienced illness or a characterological inclination to

MCMI-III™
ID 43463

Interpretive Report

MILLON CLINICAL MULTIAXIAL INVENTORY – III
CONFIDENTIAL INFORMATION FOR PROFESSIONAL USE ONLY

ID NUMBER: 43463   Valid Profile
PERSONALITY CODE: 8B 3 2B ** 8A * 2A 6B 6A 1 + 4" 7 5 ' ' // - ** C* //
SYNDROME CODE: A ** D ** // - ** CC * //
DEMOGRAPHIC: 43463/IM/F/40/W/R/12/LO/SC/-----/03/-----/

Category		Score		Profile BR Scores					Diagnostic Scales
		RAW	BR	0	60	75	85	115	
Modifying indices	X	118	72						Disclosure
	Y	6	30						Desirability
	Z	20	77						Debasement
Clinical personality patterns	1	6	60						Schizoid
	2A	10	69						Avoidant
	2B	17	90						Depressive
	3	17	93						Dependent
	4	9	42						Histrionic
	5	2	11						Narcissistic
	6A	6	62						Antisocial
	6B	9	65						Sadistic
	7	8	32						Compulsive
	8A	16	81						Negativistic
	8B	19	105						Masochistic
Severe personality pathology	S	3	44						Schizotypal
	C	14	79						Borderline
	P	6	63						Paranoid
Clinical syndromes	A	12	85						Anxiety disorder
	H	9	66						Somatoform disorder
	N	9	68						Bipolar: manic disorder
	D	13	77						Dysthymic disorder
	B	3	61						Alcohol dependence
	T	1	25						Drug dependence
	R	11	68						Post-traumatic stress
Severe clinical syndromes	SS	6	51						Thought disorder
	CC	12	75						Major depression
	PP	1	25						Delusional disorder

complain or to be self-pitying. On the other hand, the response style may convey feelings of extreme vulnerability that are associated with a current episode of acute turmoil. Whatever the impetus for the response style, the patient's scale scores, particularly those on Axis I, may be somewhat exaggerated, and the interpretation of this profile should be made with this consideration in mind.

The BR scores reported for this individual have been modified to account for the psychic tension and dejection indicated by the elevations on Scale A (Anxiety) and Scale D (Dysthymia).

AXIS II: PERSONALITY PATTERNS

The following paragraphs refer to those enduring and pervasive personality traits that underlie this woman's emotional, cognitive, and interpersonal difficulties. Rather than focus on the largely transitory symptoms that make up Axis I clinical syndromes, this section concentrates on her more habitual and maladaptive methods of relating, behaving, thinking, and feeling.

There is reason to believe that at least a moderate level of pathology characterizes the overall personality organization of this woman. Defective psychic structures suggest a failure to develop adequate internal cohesion and a less than satisfactory hierarchy of coping strategies. This woman's foundation for effective intrapsychic regulation and socially acceptable interpersonal conduct appears deficient or incompetent. She is subjected to the flux of her own enigmatic attitudes and contradictory behavior, and her sense of psychic coherence is often precarious. She has probably had a checkered history of disappointments in her personal and family relationships. Deficits in her social attainments may also be notable as well as a tendency to precipitate self-defeating vicious circles. Earlier aspirations may have resulted in frustrating setbacks and efforts to achieve a consistent niche in life may have failed. Although she is usually able to function on a satisfactory basis, she may experience periods of marked emotional, cognitive, or behavioral dysfunction.

The MCMI-III profile of this woman is suggestive of marked dependency needs, anxious seeking of reassurance from others, and her melancholic fear of separation from those who provide support. Dependency strivings push her to be overly compliant, to be self-sacrificing, to downplay her personal strengths and attributes, and to place herself in inferior or demeaning positions. Significant relationships appear to have become increasingly insecure and unreliable. This has resulted in increased moodiness, prolonged periods of futility and dejection, episodes of obstructive anger, and a seeking of situations in which she may act out as a martyr.

She is mostly seen as submissive and cooperative. At other times, she is thought of as alternatively petulant, self-debasing, and pessimistic. She may vacillate between being socially agreeable, sullen, aggrieved, despondent, obstructive, and contrite. She may often complain of being treated unfairly, yet she also may undermine herself and appear to court blame and criticism, behavior that keeps others on edge, never knowing if she will react in an apologetic, agreeable, or sulky manner. She may often undo the efforts of others to be helpful, frequently provoking rejection and then feeling hurt. Although struggling to be obliging and submissive, she may anticipate disillusioning relationships and often creates the expected disappointment by testing the behavior of others and questioning the genuineness of their interest and support. Self-defeating habits and an attitude that she deserves to suffer may exasperate and eventually alienate those on whom she depends. When threatened by separation and disapproval, she may express guilt and self-condemnation in the hope of regaining support, reassurance, and sympathy.

This woman may exhibit helplessness as well as experiencing anxious periods and prolonged depressive moods. Fearing that others may grow weary of her plaintive and aggrieved behavior, she may have begun to alternate between voicing self-deprecation and remorse and being petulant and bitter. A struggle between being dependently acquiescent and inducing guilt in others over what she sees as their abuse and lack of interest may now intrude into most relationships. Her seeming inability to control her sorrowful state and her feelings of being treated unjustly and being misunderstood may contribute to a persistent attitude of discontent and affective dysthymia.

AXIS I: CLINICAL SYNDROMES

The features and dynamics of the following Axis I clinical syndromes appear worthy of description and analysis. They may arise in response to external precipitants but are likely to reflect and accentuate several of the more enduring and pervasive aspects of this woman's basic personality makeup.

The self-demeaning comments and feelings of inferiority that mark this woman's major depression are part of her overall and enduring characterological structure, a set of chronic self-defeating attitudes and depressive emotions that are intrinsic to her psychological makeup. Feelings of emptiness and loneliness and recurrent thoughts of death and suicide are accompanied by expressions of low self-esteem, preoccupations with failures and physical unattractiveness, and assertions of guilt and unworthiness. Although she complains about being aggrieved and mistreated she is likely to assert that she deserves anguish and abuse. Such self-debasement is consonant with her self-image, as is her tolerance and perpetuation of relationships that foster and aggravate her misery.

Irritable and depressed much of the time, this woman appears to be experiencing a level of dysphoria that is sufficient to justify characterizing her current state as an anxiety disorder. Behavioral symptoms such as restlessness, edginess, and distractibility probably coexist with somatic signs of anxiety, such as ill-defined pains, insomnia, and exhaustion. She vacillates between keeping her dysphoric feelings in check and voicing them, thus preventing herself from stabilizing her emotions. This, in turn, precludes the opportunity for her disquiet to subside.

NOTEWORTHY RESPONSES

The client answered the following statements in the direction noted in parentheses. These items suggest specific problem areas that the clinician may wish to investigate.

Health Preoccupation

1. Lately, my strength seems to be draining out of me, even in the morning (True)
4. I feel weak and tired much of the time (True)
55. In recent weeks I feel worn out for no special reason. (True)
75. Lately, I've been sweating a great deal and feel very tense. (True)

Interpersonal Alienation

10. What few feelings I seem to have I rarely show to the outside world. (True)
69. I avoid most social situations because I expect people to criticize or reject me. (True)
99. In social groups I am almost always very self-conscious and tense. (True)
161. I seem to create situations with others in which I get hurt or feel rejected. (True)

Emotional Dyscontrol

14. Sometimes I can be pretty rough and mean in my relations with my family. (True)
22. I'm a very erratic person, changing my mind and feelings all the time. (True)

30. Lately, I have begun to feel like smashing things. (True)
34. Lately, I have gone all to pieces. (True)
83. My moods seem to change a great deal from one day to the next. (True)
87. I often get angry with people who do things slowly. (True)
124. When I'm alone and away from home, I often begin to feel tense and panicky. (True)

Self-Destructive Potential

24. I began to feel like a failure some years ago. (True)
44. I feel terribly depressed and sad much of the time now. (True)
112. I have been downhearted and sad much of my life since I was quite young. (True)
128. I feel deeply depressed for no reason I can figure out. (True)

Childhood Abuse

No items endorsed.

Eating Disorder

121. I go on eating binges a couple of times a week. (True)

POSSIBLE *DSM-IV*™ MULTIAXIAL DIAGNOSES

The following diagnostic assignments should be considered judgments of personality and clinical prototypes that correspond conceptually to formal diagnostic categories. The diagnostic criteria and items used in the MCMI-III differ somewhat from those in the *DSM-IV,* but there are sufficient parallels in the MCMI-III items to recommend consideration of the following assignments. It should be noted that several *DSM-IV* Axis I syndromes are not assessed in the MCMI-III. Definitive diagnoses must draw on biographical, observational, and interview data in addition to self-report inventories such as the MCMI-III.

Axis I: Clinical Syndrome

The major complaints and behaviors of the patient parallel the following Axis I diagnoses, listed in order of their clinical significance and salience.

296.33 Major Depression (recurrent, severe, without psychotic features)
300.02 Generalized Anxiety Disorder

Axis II: Personality Disorders

Deeply ingrained and pervasive patterns of maladaptive functioning underlie Axis I clinical syndromal pictures. The following personality prototypes correspond to the most probable *DSM-IV* diagnoses (Disorders, Traits, Features) that characterize this patient.

Personality configuration composed of the following:

301.90 Self-defeating Personality Disorder
with Dependent Personality Traits
Depressive Personality Traits and
Negativistic (Passive-Aggressive) Personality Features

Course: The major personality features described previously reflect long-term or chronic traits that are likely to have persisted for several years prior to the present assessment. The clinical syndromes described previously tend to be relatively transient, waxing and waning in their prominence and intensity depending on the presence of environmental stress.

Axis IV: Psychosocial and Environmental Problems

In completing the MCMI-III, this individual identified the following problems that may be complicating or exacerbating her present emotional state. They are listed in order of importance as indicated by the client. This information should be viewed as a guide for further investigation by the clinician.

Loneliness Low Self-Confidence

TREATMENT GUIDE

If additional clinical data are supportive of the MCMI-III's hypotheses, it is likely that this patient's difficulties can be managed with either brief or extended therapeutic methods. The following guide to treatment planning is oriented toward issues and techniques of a short-term character, focusing on matters that might call for immediate attention, followed by time-limited procedures designed to reduce the likelihood of repeated relapses.

As a first step, it would appear advisable to implement methods to ameliorate this patient's current state of clinical anxiety, depressive hopelessness, or pathological functioning by the rapid implementation of supportive psychotherapeutic measures. With appropriate consultation, targeted psychopharmacologic medications may also be useful at this initial stage.

Once this patient's more pressing or acute difficulties are adequately stabilized, attention should be directed toward goals that would aid in preventing a recurrence of problems, focusing on circumscribed issues and employing delimited methods such as those discussed in the following paragraphs.

As a first approach in a short-term therapeutic program, an effort should be made to assist the patient in arranging for a more rewarding environment and in discovering opportunities that will enhance her self-worth. Supportive therapy may be all she can tolerate in the very first sessions, that is, until she is comfortable dealing with her most painful feelings. Psychopharmacologic treatment may be considered, following appropriate consultation, as a means of diminishing her depressive feelings or controlling her anxiety. Behavior modification may also be employed to help her learn competent reactions to stressful situations. As trust in her therapist develops, she should be amenable to methods of cognitive reframing to alter dysfunctional attitudes and depressogenic social expectations; particularly appropriate would be the methods proposed by Beck and Meichenbaum. To decrease the potential of a recurrence, focused dynamic methods may be explored to rework deep object attachments and to construct a base for competency strivings. The interpersonal focus proposed by Benjamin and Klerman and group therapy procedures may provide a means of learning autonomous skills and the growth of social confidence.

An important self-defeating belief that a cognitive approach should seek to reframe is her assumption that she must appease others and apologize for her incompetence in order to assure that she will not be abandoned. What can be shown to her is that this behavior exasperates and alienates those on whom she leans most heavily. This exasperation and alienation then serve only to increase her fear and neediness. She may come to recognize that a vicious circle is created, making her feel more desperate and more ingratiating. A vigorous but short-term approach that illustrates her dysfunctional beliefs and expectations should be used to break the circle and reorient her actions less destructively. The combination of cognitive restructuring and the development of increasing interpersonal skills should prove an effective brief course of treatment.

To restate her difficulty in different terms, not only does this patient precipitate real difficulties through her self-demeaning attitudes but she also perceives and anticipates difficulties where none in fact exist. She believes that good things do not last and that the positive feelings and attitudes of those from whom she seeks support will probably end capriciously and be followed by disappointment and rejection. This cognitive assumption should be directly confronted by appropriate therapeutic techniques. What must be undone is the fact that each time she announces her defects, she convinces herself as well as others and thereby deepens her discontent and her self-image of incompetence.

Trapped by her own persuasiveness, she repeatedly reinforces her belief in the futility of standing on her own and is therefore likely to try less and less to overcome her inadequacies. This therapeutic strategy should aim at undoing this vicious circle of increased despondency and dependency.

Skillful attention is also needed to alter her ambivalence about dependency and her willingness to be used, if not abused. Unless checked, this woman may have difficulty sustaining a consistent therapeutic relationship and may subsequently deteriorate or relapse. Maneuvers designed to test the dependability of the therapist will probably be evident. To prevent such setbacks, empathic warmth should be expressed to help her overcome her fear of facing her own feelings of unworthiness. Similar support levels are necessary to undo her wish to retain her image of being a self-denying person whose security lies in suffering and martyrdom. She needs to be guided into recognizing the basis of her self-contempt and her ambivalence about dependency relationships. She should be helped to see that not all nurturant parental figures will habitually become abusive and exploitive. Efforts to undo these self-sabotaging beliefs will pay considerable dividends in short-term and possibly more substantial long-term progress.

Appendix B
Case Vignettes

Vignette Number 1:
Dysthymia in the
Schizotypal Pattern

Exhibit B-1 provides the MCMI-III scores for this vignette.

PRESENTING DESCRIPTION

Marge V. is a 42-year-old single, homeless, African American female. She was referred by the emergency room physician for psychological evaluation. She was prescribed cyclic antidepressants, however, she discontinued taking the medication. She appeared malnourished and fatigued and exhibited a flattened and constricted affect. Both behavior and dress were drab and odd. Speech was somewhat disorganized and circumstantial. She withdraws from social contact, though is content in her aloneness. She reported that she uses alcohol to calm herself, particularly when she has strange thoughts about her body "coming apart." Question 76 (Millon, 1997) on the MCMI-III, "I keep having strange thoughts that I wish I could get rid of," was keyed in the true direction. She stated that she did not feel she was worth anything after undergoing hysterectomy surgery approximately two years ago. She believes that God is punishing her and said, "Sometimes I simply feel dead inside."

MCMI-III BR Scale Scores #1: Dysthymia in the Schizotypal Pattern

Category	BR Score	Scales	
			Validity Index = 0
Modifying indices	78	Disclosure	(Scale X)
	35	Desirability	(Scale Y)
	91	Debasement	(Scale Z)
Clinical personality patterns	99	Schizoid	(Scale 1)
	87	Avoidant	(Scale 2A)
	92	Depressive	(Scale 2B)
	84	Dependent	(Scale 3)
	68	Histrionic	(Scale 4)
	33	Narcissistic	(Scale 5)
	48	Antisocial	(Scale 6A)
	48	Sadistic	(Scale 6B)
	60	Compulsive	(Scale 7)
	72	Negativistic	(Scale 8A)
	93	Masochistic	(Scale 8B)
Severe personality pathology	100	Schizotypal	(Scale S)
	70	Borderline	(Scale C)
	62	Paranoid	(Scale P)
Clinical syndromes	75	Anxiety disorder	(Scale A)
	75	Somatoform disorder	(Scale H)
	64	Bipolar: manic disorder	(Scale N)
	95	Dysthymic disorder	(Scale D)
	78	Alcohol dependence	(Scale B)
	75	Drug dependence	(Scale T)
	66	Post-traumatic stress	(Scale R)
Severe clinical syndromes	75	Thought disorder	(Scale SS)
	75	Major depression	(Scale CC)
	60	Delusional disorder	(Scale PP)

CLINICAL ASSESSMENT

The response style is suggestive of chronic turmoil. Evidence of a moderately severe level of pathology exists in Marge V.'s overall personality structure. This individual, having social anxiety and interpersonal deficits as well as unusual perceptual experiences, meets the criteria for schizotypal personality disorder. Such individuals are inclined to avoid emotional experiences, withdrawing into an ineffectual, inactive lifestyle. Ordinary stressors of life can seem overly demanding, and these individuals may experience transient psychotic episodes when overwhelmed by these stressors.

Beyond her general state of social discomfort, Marge V. is experiencing guilt, low self-esteem, and a sense of "losing herself." Because she is socially isolated, alcohol likely is a soothing elixir to relieve her fears and apprehensions. During the clinical interview, her thought processing was obscure and tangential. Rapport was difficult to maintain because of her unusual and peculiar statements and thought content. Marge. V.'s oddities were similar to schizophrenia, though absent were any delusions and hallucinations. Supportive therapy emphasizing self-worth can be helpful to connect to the individual. Psychopharmacologic medication is likely indicated. Efforts to enhance social interaction and reorient Marge cognitively should proceed according to her current ability. A primary task of intervention involves development of social management skills and the prevention of further withdrawal from her limited support systems.

DIAGNOSTIC IMPRESSIONS

Axis I: 300.4   Dysthymic Disorder
         305.00 Alcohol Abuse
Axis II: 301.22 Schizotypal Personality Disorder
                 with Schizoid Personality Traits

Vignette Number 2: Generalized Anxiety Disorder in the Avoidant Pattern

Exhibit B-2 provides the MCMI-III scores for this vignette.

PRESENTING DESCRIPTION

Esther L. is a 55-year-old divorced, White female who was referred to the clinic by her physician for complaints of anxiety. She had recurrent problems with nervousness following the birth of her first child approximately 25 years ago. She reported that she feels uncomfortable leaving her house unless accompanied by a neighbor, her only friend. Although Esther L. stated that she is extremely lonely, she does not like to socialize because she is very shy and becomes very tense when she does. She states that she worries about everything and cannot control her worries. She also has a history of hypertension and intermittent chest pain. She states that when something gets into her mind, she cannot remove it. Various words or images may enter her mind during the course of the day, and she will obsess about them for the rest of the day. She constantly cleans the house, even though she knows it is clean. She reports no suicidal ideation, however, she always feels that something bad is going to befall her. She is presently taking Xanax.

CLINICAL ASSESSMENT

This pattern is characterized by a detachment from social relationships. Esther L. chooses to isolate herself in the safety of her home, rather than risk possible rejection or embarrassment. Although such individuals withdraw from social relationships, they may become quite dependent on one or more people in their lives. Aside from a few trusted individuals, Esther L. avoids the distress of social relationships by simply detaching herself from the outside world. Millon and Davis (1996) wrote that the most common of the avoidant's symptoms is the generalized anxiety disorder, typically seen for prolonged periods of time. Tense and anxious, these individuals tend to limit involvement with external relationships. As in Esther L.'s case, well-practiced rituals, such as cleaning an already clean house, may serve to distract feelings of inner emptiness and ameliorate thoughts of inadequacy. Supportive therapeutic approaches can pave the way for further behavioral change. In conjunction with anxiety management, a variety of behavioral techniques can be used.

DIAGNOSTIC IMPRESSIONS

Axis I: 300.02 Generalized anxiety disorder
Axis II: 301.82 Avoidant personality disorder with dependent personality traits and compulsive personality features.

EXHIBIT B-2

MCMI-III BR Scale Scores #2: Generalized Anxiety Disorder in the Avoidant Pattern

Category	BR Score	Scales	
			Validity Index = 0
Modifying indices	77	Disclosure	(Scale X)
	55	Desirability	(Scale Y)
	89	Debasement	(Scale Z)
Clinical personality patterns	73	Schizoid	(Scale 1)
	101	Avoidant	(Scale 2A)
	77	Depressive	(Scale 2B)
	82	Dependent	(Scale 3)
	60	Histrionic	(Scale 4)
	62	Narcissistic	(Scale 5)
	70	Antisocial	(Scale 6A)
	65	Sadistic	(Scale 6B)
	78	Compulsive	(Scale 7)
	60	Negativistic	(Scale 8A)
	55	Masochistic	(Scale 8B)
Severe personality pathology	68	Schizotypal	(Scale S)
	67	Borderline	(Scale C)
	73	Paranoid	(Scale P)
Clinical syndromes	100	Anxiety disorder	(Scale A)
	75	Somatoform disorder	(Scale H)
	75	Bipolar: manic disorder	(Scale N)
	79	Dysthymic disorder	(Scale D)
	70	Alcohol dependence	(Scale B)
	70	Drug dependence	(Scale T)
	72	Post-traumatic stress	(Scale R)
Severe clinical syndromes	72	Thought disorder	(Scale SS)
	75	Major depression	(Scale CC)
	70	Delusional disorder	(Scale PP)

Vignette Number 3: Posttraumatic Stress Disorder in the Depressive Pattern

Exhibit B-3 provides the MCMI-III scores for this vignette.

PRESENTING DESCRIPTION

Gene P. is a 53-year-old unemployed, divorced, White male. He was referred for counseling following a consultative examination regarding his spinal column. Aside from mild osteoarthritis in the anterior spurs, the X rays were essentially negative. He stated that his back problems resulted from an injury received in Vietnam in 1970. During that tour, he was assigned to the medical brigade, a unit responsible for removal of soldiers' remains. He reported recurrent and disturbing nightmares about Vietnam, which included "demons being kicked out" and "the backyard being a graveyard." He claims he becomes overly agitated whenever he hears gunshots or fireworks on the Fourth of July. After more than 20 years, he continues to feel guilty and is unable to adapt to the distressful memories of Vietnam. He has an extensive history of alcohol dependence. He complained of memory problems, poor concentration, and nervousness. One suicide attempt was reported.

CLINICAL ASSESSMENT

The response style likely indicates an extreme tendency to magnify current turmoil. Feelings of hopelessness and a pervasive sense of guilt characterize this pattern.

Resigned to his fate, Gene P. likely copes with his turmoil through the use of alcohol, which may only serve to exacerbate an already morose state. Gene P.'s depressive symptoms began early in adulthood. This depressive pattern shares traits of the avoidant personality. Sensitive to the disapproval of others, a growing estrangement from others is inevitable. His discontent seems entwined with his chronic back problems, manifesting an unremitting, irritable mood. Although no clear organic findings were indicated, Gene P. unfortunately is unable to acknowledge the possible emotional role that his symptoms may be playing—namely, to defend against his own inadequacies. With few social supports and minimal psychological resources, along with the chronic consumption of alcohol, his symptoms will only intensify. A

MCMI-III BR Scale Scores #3: Posttraumatic Stress Disorder in the Depressive Pattern

Category	BR Score	Scales	
			Validity Index = 0
Modifying indices	74	Disclosure	(Scale X)
	51	Desirability	(Scale Y)
	84	Debasement	(Scale Z)
Clinical personality patterns	81	Schizoid	(Scale 1)
	83	Avoidant	(Scale 2A)
	97	Depressive	(Scale 2B)
	65	Dependent	(Scale 3)
	26	Histrionic	(Scale 4)
	62	Narcissistic	(Scale 5)
	80	Antisocial	(Scale 6A)
	75	Sadistic	(Scale 6B)
	41	Compulsive	(Scale 7)
	77	Negativistic	(Scale 8A)
	73	Masochistic	(Scale 8B)
Severe personality pathology	71	Schizotypal	(Scale S)
	70	Borderline	(Scale C)
	72	Paranoid	(Scale P)
Clinical syndromes	88	Anxiety disorder	(Scale A)
	85	Somatoform disorder	(Scale H)
	68	Bipolar: manic disorder	(Scale N)
	91	Dysthymic disorder	(Scale D)
	90	Alcohol dependence	(Scale B)
	82	Drug dependence	(Scale T)
	95	Post-traumatic stress	(Scale R)
Severe clinical syndromes	72	Thought disorder	(Scale SS)
	84	Major depression	(Scale CC)
	71	Delusional disorder	(Scale PP)

thorough alcohol assessment is necessary. The management of post-traumatic stress disorder should be directed toward preventing chronic disability. Behavioral–cognitive techniques coupled with relaxation therapies may be best suited in reducing the target symptoms of PTSD.

DIAGNOSTIC IMPRESSIONS

Axis I: 309.81 Posttraumatic stress disorder
305.00 Alcohol abuse
Axis II: 301.90 Personality disorder NOS (depressive personality disorder) with avoidant personality features.

Vignette Number 4: Alcoholism in the Antisocial Pattern

Exhibit B-4 provides the MCMI-III scores for this vignette.

PRESENTING DESCRIPTION

Lee H. is a 43-year-old single, unemployed, African American male referred by an affiliated homeless shelter to the treatment clinic for aftercare services. Having an extensive history of alcoholism, Lee H. has entered numerous rehabilitation programs. He described his life as "just wandering from place to place" and "doing what he wants to do." He stated that he was only staying at the shelter temporarily because of the subfreezing temperatures. Lee H. could not recall his last place of employment, nor remember his last permanent place of residence. Originally from a small town in the South, he moved to Houston when he was a teenager to live with an aunt after his parents divorced. Both parents, reportedly, were abusive toward him, especially when they drank. He felt like an orphan following his parents' divorce, but also acknowledged that he felt somewhat relieved. He started using alcohol as a teenager and presently consumes approximately one bottle of hard liquor daily.

CLINICAL ASSESSMENT

Millon refers to this personality as the nomadic antisocial pattern (Millon, 1999). This mixed pattern of antisocial, avoidant, and negativistic

EXHIBIT B-4

MCMI-III BR Scale Scores #4: Alcoholism in the Antisocial Pattern

Category	BR Score	Scales	
			Validity Index = 0
Modifying indices	77	Disclosure	(Scale X)
	59	Desirability	(Scale Y)
	85	Debasement	(Scale Z)
Clinical personality patterns	79	Schizoid	(Scale 1)
	80	Avoidant	(Scale 2A)
	68	Depressive	(Scale 2B)
	65	Dependent	(Scale 3)
	30	Histrionic	(Scale 4)
	49	Narcissistic	(Scale 5)
	95	Antisocial	(Scale 6A)
	76	Sadistic	(Scale 6B)
	26	Compulsive	(Scale 7)
	90	Negativistic	(Scale 8A)
	78	Masochistic	(Scale 8B)
Severe personality pathology	73	Schizotypal	(Scale S)
	70	Borderline	(Scale C)
	77	Paranoid	(Scale P)
Clinical syndromes	85	Anxiety disorder	(Scale A)
	85	Somatoform disorder	(Scale H)
	72	Bipolar: manic disorder	(Scale N)
	84	Dysthymic disorder	(Scale D)
	105	Alcohol dependence	(Scale B)
	82	Drug dependence	(Scale T)
	75	Post-traumatic stress	(Scale R)
Severe clinical syndromes	72	Thought disorder	(Scale SS)
	80	Major depression	(Scale CC)
	70	Delusional disorder	(Scale PP)

traits is characterized by a detachment from others and is often fueled by blatant opposition to the values of society. Underlying social withdrawal, these personalities are internally anxious and depressed, being conflicted with deep-seated feelings of anger and hostility toward a society that they feel has "abandoned" them. They are conflicted between their own inadequacies and a need for nurturance. As in the case of Lee H., most of these personalities are solitary individuals, disconnected from a "rejecting" society in general. They tend to run away from society, searching for their niches. They perceive others as unfeeling and rejecting and possibly view themselves as "throw-aways." For the most part, any attempted interpersonal relationship tends to be conflictual, further providing justification to continue an independent, itinerant existence. Ordinarily reclusive and nonaggressive, deep-seated hostilities can occasionally trigger an outward aggressive behavior. Lee H. has chosen a lifestyle through which he can deny responsibilities, caring only to wander aimlessly. Alcohol, it seems, is his one true companion. Given his pervasive personality pattern, therapeutic progress will be limited. Measures, initially, can be taken to detoxify Lee H. and, within a supportive environment, establish a sense of trust and understanding.

DIAGNOSTIC IMPRESSIONS

Axis I : 303.90 Alcohol dependence
Axis II: 301.70 Antisocial personality disorder with negativistic personality traits and avoidant personality features.

Vignette Number 5: Delusional Thinking in the Paranoid Pattern

Exhibit B-5 provides the MCMI-III scores for this vignette.

PRESENTING DESCRIPTION

Jim R., a 22-year-old unemployed, single, African American male, was admitted to a residential rehabilitation facility for cocaine abuse. He had used cocaine since age 16 and had received drug rehabilitation treatment from three different programs. Hospitalization was required for a suicide attempt, and he underwent therapy for anger management. He was diagnosed as learning disabled in early childhood, and was placed in special education, where he remained throughout high school. For approximately a year following graduation, his parents barred him from his house because of his "lifestyle." During the clinical interview, Jim R. displayed mild persecutory delusional thinking. His suspiciousness and hypersensitivity were primarily directed toward his father, demonstrated by statements such as, "Since I was a child I could not trust him." His underlying hostility toward his father was clearly expressed with distinct feelings and recollections of mistreatment by his father. He, however, could accept no blame for the relationship with his parents. He was administered the MCMI-III during his third week of treatment.

CLINICAL ASSESSMENT

This individual's style of responding to the MCMI-III is rather atypical, indicating the endorsement of antithetical items. He seeks to gain attention not only by trying to present a favorable image but also by emphasizing his troubled state. One validity item was endorsed, rendering the profile interpretation somewhat questionable.

Evidence of a moderately severe level of pathology exists. Jim R. displays a vigilant mistrust of others and generally anticipates being disillusioned by them. He is fearful of being dominated and suspicious of any efforts that may undermine his self-determination. He often feels misunderstood and views others as deceitful and hostile. There is reason to believe that he is experiencing mild symptoms of a delusional nature; however, his thinking was not of psychotic proportion, and the symptom criteria is better classified under paranoid personality disorder. His chronic abuse of cocaine also may have contributed to his heightened sensitivity and mistrust of others, thereby exacerbating his condition. He is edgy and irritable, so his use of cocaine seemingly helps to moderate his conflicting tensions, as well as gratify a resentful antisocial attitude. Although treatment can be difficult with this pattern, a gradual building of trust within the therapeutic relationship may predispose this client for additional procedures.

DIAGNOSTIC IMPRESSIONS

Axis I: 304.20 Cocaine dependence
Axis II: 301.00 Paranoid personality disorder
                 with antisocial personality traits

MCMI-III BR Scale Scores #5: Delusional Thinking in the Paranoid Pattern

Category	BR Score	Scales	
			Validity Index = 1
Modifying indices	66	Disclosure	(Scale X)
	80	Desirability	(Scale Y)
	80	Debasement	(Scale Z)
Clinical personality patterns	79	Schizoid	(Scale 1)
	77	Avoidant	(Scale 2A)
	74	Depressive	(Scale 2B)
	60	Dependent	(Scale 3)
	30	Histrionic	(Scale 4)
	75	Narcissistic	(Scale 5)
	82	Antisocial	(Scale 6A)
	61	Sadistic	(Scale 6B)
	34	Compulsive	(Scale 7)
	60	Negativistic	(Scale 8A)
	78	Masochistic	(Scale 8B)
Severe personality pathology	73	Schizotypal	(Scale S)
	79	Borderline	(Scale C)
	97	Paranoid	(Scale P)
Clinical syndromes	75	Anxiety disorder	(Scale A)
	60	Somatoform disorder	(Scale H)
	60	Bipolar: manic disorder	(Scale N)
	64	Dysthymic disorder	(Scale D)
	81	Alcohol dependence	(Scale B)
	104	Drug dependence	(Scale T)
	75	Post-traumatic stress	(Scale R)
Severe clinical syndromes	72	Thought disorder	(Scale SS)
	75	Major depression	(Scale CC)
	78	Delusional disorder	(Scale PP)

Vignette Number 6: Somatoform Disorder in the Compulsive Pattern

Exhibit B-6 provides the MCMI-III scores of this vignette.

PRESENTING DESCRIPTIONS

Wendy P. is a 29-year-old single, White female, who is employed as an accountant in a prestigious accounting firm. She was referred to the clinic by her family physician after a thorough physical examination found no physical reason for her episodes of nausea and vomiting. She stated that the nausea and vomiting began about six months ago and becomes particularly severe just before leaving for work. She states that she prides herself on attention to detail, and is overly conscientious in her work. Unfortunately, her "need to be exact" caused her to fall behind with the firm's schedule of services. She said she experienced "uncontrollable" anxiety after her supervisor counseled her about her poor performance.

CLINICAL ASSESSMENT

When interpreting BR scores of Narcissistic, Histrionic and Compulsive scales, as discussed in chapter 5, care must be exercised to differentiate between a normal, adaptive profile and the presence of pathology. Individuals with similar profiles may demonstrate compulsive tendencies, though function quite efficiently. Modifying indices depict an individual who presents in a socially adaptive manner though is somewhat defensive.

Millon (1997) recommends that higher elevations on Scale 7 tend to reflect pathology. Choca and Van Denburg (1997) suggested that spiked elevations (highest elevation of the protocol) on Scale 7 may be indicative of defensive individuals who have an air of perfectionism and tend to deny any limitations. Behind the perfectionistic facade of compulsive individuals, they contended, may be an individual who is feeling vulnerable and insecure.

Although Scale 7 correlates with adaptive measures, determining the diagnosis of significant elevations on this scale can be a daunting task for the clinician. This individual may very well be functioning normally, with no history of personality pathology and presently is undergoing a minor emotional disturbance; though evidence of a personality disorder

MCMI-III BR Scale Scores #6: Somatoform Disorder in the Compulsive Pattern

Category	BR Score	Scales	
			Validity Index = 0
Modifying indices	57	Disclosure	(Scale X)
	80	Desirability	(Scale Y)
	34	Debasement	(Scale Z)
Clinical personality patterns	50	Schizoid	(Scale 1)
	66	Avoidant	(Scale 2A)
	40	Depressive	(Scale 2B)
	53	Dependent	(Scale 3)
	37	Histrionic	(Scale 4)
	62	Narcissistic	(Scale 5)
	62	Antisocial	(Scale 6A)
	61	Sadistic	(Scale 6B)
	88	Compulsive	(Scale 7)
	27	Negativistic	(Scale 8A)
	60	Masochistic	(Scale 8B)
Severe personality pathology	46	Schizotypal	(Scale S)
	61	Borderline	(Scale C)
	45	Paranoid	(Scale P)
Clinical syndromes	60	Anxiety disorder	(Scale A)
	75	Somatoform disorder	(Scale H)
	62	Bipolar: manic disorder	(Scale N)
	41	Dysthymic disorder	(Scale D)
	61	Alcohol dependence	(Scale B)
	26	Drug dependence	(Scale T)
	31	Post-traumatic stress	(Scale R)
Severe clinical syndromes	44	Thought disorder	(Scale SS)
	52	Major depression	(Scale CC)
	25	Delusional disorder	(Scale PP)

is provided by an individual who is ambivalent and conflicted and likely denies emotional difficulties. In this case, obsessive–compulsive personality disorder is likely the appropriate Axis II diagnosis.

In general, individuals who are diagnosed as obsessive–compulsive personality disorder exhibit external perfectionist tendencies that derive from an internal conflict between hostility toward others and a fear of social disapproval. Outward behaviors are, at times, diametrically opposed to internal feelings. Wendy, most likely, displaces her anxiety into somatic symptoms. The compulsive personality may likely experience emotional distress, as well as physiological discomfort, when the defensive armor begins to break down. Treatment is sought most often as the result of physiological symptoms, oftentimes somatization or anxiety attacks.

DIAGNOSTIC IMPRESSIONS

Axis I: 300.81 Somatoform disorder, NOS
Axis II: 301.40 Obsessive–compulsive personality disorder

Appendix C
Answers to Chapter Test Sections

Chapter 1

FILL IN THE BLANKS

1. organismic, environmental
2. active–passive, pleasure–pain, subject–object
3. personality coping patterns
4. contiguous, vicarious, instrumental
5. existence, adaptation, replication, abstraction
6. intracortical–integration
7. defective
8. an "enduring pattern of inner experience and behavior that deviates markedly from the expectations of the individual's culture and is manifested in at least two of the following areas: cognitive, affectivity, interpersonal functioning, or impulse control."
9. adaptive inflexibility
10. obsessive compulsive personality

TRUE OR FALSE

1. T
2. T
3. T
4. F
5. T
6. T
7. T

8. T
9. F
10. T

Chapter 2

FILL IN THE BLANKS

1. 24, 3, 1
2. Disclosure
3. schizoid
4. H
5. SS
6. 60
7. theoretical–substantive, internal–structural, external–criterion
8. Cronbach's
9. psychiatric
10. criterion-referencing

TRUE OR FALSE

1. T
2. F
3. T
4. T
5. F
6. T
7. F
8. T
9. F
10. T

SCALE IDENTIFICATION

Z	PP
CC	A
Y	6B
3	2B
SS	S
1	X
C	2A
5	8B

P	B
H	T
6A	8A
7	4
D	N
R	

Chapter 3

FILL IN THE BLANKS

1. eighth
2. invalid, suspend
3. 1
4. Disclosure
5. X
6. a. Depressive   d. Avoidant
  b. Masochistic e. Schizotypal
  c. Borderline
7. none
8. 4, 5, 7
9. flat
10. profiling

TRUE OR FALSE

1. T
2. F
3. F
4. F
5. T
6. T
7. T
8. F
9. T
10. T

BASE-RATE TRANSFORMATION:

Validity = 0

Y	84	S	59
Z	59	C	59

1	71	P	73
2A	79	A	75
2B	59	H	69
3	60	N	68
4	42	D	75
5	5	B	78
6A	48	T	68
6B	67	R	64
7	88	SS	60
8A	79	CC	52
8B	59	PP	68

X = 108 (Raw Score); 67 (Base-rate score)

Personality code: 7**2A8A*16B3+2B8B6A4"5//-*–//

Syndrome code:-**BAD*//-*–//

Chapter 4

FILL IN THE BLANKS

1. Disclosure
2. Desirability
3. Debasement
4. setting
5. all true, all false, random
6. lowered
7. compulsive, narcissistic–compulsive
8. 34, 178
9. increases
10. fake-bad

MATCH RESPONSE STYLES

1. 9
2. 6
3. 4
4. 2
5. 3
6. 8
7. 10
8. 7
9. 1
10. 5

Chapter 5

FILL IN THE BLANKS

1. base rate
2. 75, 85
3. configural
4. 20 BR
5. the greater the extent of personality pathology
6. Histrionic, Narcissistic, Compulsive
7. the same levels
8. Compulsive
9. Narcissistic
10. Paranoid

IDENTIFY CLINICAL PERSONALITY PATTERNS/ SEVERE PERSONALITY PATHOLOGY

1. schizoid
2. compulsive
3. borderline
4. sadistic
5. paranoid
6. dependent
7. antisocial
8. avoidant
9. depressive
10. negativistic
11. narcissistic
12. schizotypal
13. masochistic
14. histrionic

IDENTIFY "CLASS-DISORDERED" CLINICAL PERSONALITY PATTERNS/SEVERE PERSONALITY PATHOLOGY

1. schizotypal
2. avoidant
3. borderline
4. depressive
5. compulsive

6. antisocial
7. negativistic
8. histrionic
9. schizoid
10. paranoid
11. narcissistic
12. dependent
13. masochistic
14. sadistic

MATCH PERSONALITY

1. avoidant–masochistic
2. schizotypal–avoidant
3. borderline–negativistic
4. avoidant–negativistic
5. schizoid–dependent
6. compulsive–schizoid
7. antisocial–narcissistic
8. histrionic–borderline
9. paranoid–antisocial
10. depressive–dependent
11. compulsive–paranoid
12. narcissistic–sadistic

Chapter 6

FILL IN THE BLANKS

1. personality pattern
2. 75, 84
3. unexplained somatic symptoms
4. Anxiety
5. Hypomanic
6. antisocial
7. dysthymic
8. Schizophrenia
9. CC
10. delusional

MATCH SYNDROMES

1. delusional disorder
2. anxiety disorder

3. drug-dependence
4. posttraumatic stress disorder
5. somatoform disorder
6. dysthymic disorder
7. thought disorder
8. bipolar: manic disorder
9. major depression
10. alcohol dependence

Chapter 7

FILL IN THE BLANKS

1. psychological report
2. signed informed consent
3. signs
4. III
5. behavioral observations
6. the examinee's general state of being
7. IV
8. clinician's signature
9. time, person, place
10. determining *IF* the examinee is in need of treatment

PROFILE EXERCISE NO. 1 (MR. C.)

Interpretive Analysis (3**2A8A*//-**P*)

1. The client's response style is atypical and indicates an inconsistency of attitude. The client seeks to gain attention and does so not only by responding in a socially desirable manner but also by exaggerating his symptoms. This configuration may indicate an agitated depression.
2. Level of disturbance is moderate to severe.
3. A markedly dependent personality structure is characterized by a dominant–submissive relationship. Insecurity, helplessness, and self-devaluation reinforce his learned dependency, though, at times, he may be apprehensive about the possibility of rejection by the nurturer. Relationships are sought, which satisfy a need for support and security. Alcohol may likely be used to counter social anxiety and underlying inner insecurities.

4. major depressive disorder
   generalized anxiety disorder
   alcohol dependence
5. dependent personality disorder with avoidant personality traits
   and passive–aggressive personality features
6. Various clinical syndromes are indicated to include generalized
   anxiety and alcoholism. Of concern, however, is the elevation on
   Scale CC. Medication may be indicated to alleviate current anxiety
   and depressive symptoms. A sustained therapeutic relationship is
   necessary, and its effectiveness will depend on encouraging an
   independent and autonomous stance on the part of the client.
   Supportive therapy may be the most efficient means of developing
   a working therapeutic relationship, as well as predispose the client
   to other techniques. One caveat in treating dependent personalities
   is an awareness on the part of the therapist to avoid enabling the
   dependent and submissive relationship, a pattern firmly embedded
   in this personality style.

PROFILE EXERCISE NUMBER 2 (MR. K.)

Interpretive Analysis (6A6B5**–*//–***–*)
1. The response style displayed no unusual test-taking tendencies,
   which may have distorted the MCMI-III results. The client approached the testing situation in an open and honest manner.
2. The client is experiencing a moderately severe mental disorder.
3. This personality structure indicates a pattern, which is markedly
   haughty, aggressive, and competitive. Similar individuals will
   assume they are "special," characterized by arrogant and self-
   indulgent features. Being antagonistic and combative, these individuals tend to control others, as well as devalue others' opinions
   and motives. Current problems may be exacerbated by marital and
   family conflict. Family members may view him as argumentative,
   insensitive, and abusive. Unless benefits are perceived or rehabilitation is mandated by authority, individuals with similar patterns
   generally resist therapeutic intervention.
4. psychoactive substance abuse
5. antisocial personality disorder with sadistic personality traits, narcissistic personality disorder
6. The presence of drug dependence should be carefully considered.
   If confirmed, drug rehabilitation is strongly recommended. Individuals with similar profiles generally are not inclined to seek
   therapy, and their unwillingness may thwart efforts of managed
   treatment. The client most likely will distance himself from the
   therapeutic process and resist attempts to explore deeper problems.

Behavior modification techniques, though, may prove to be of limited value.

PROFILE EXERCISE NUMBER 3
COMPLETE PSYCHOLOGICAL REPORT

THIS CONFIDENTIAL INFORMATION MAY NOT BE FURTHER DIS-CLOSED, RELEASED, OR SHARED, EXCEPT IN ACCORDANCE WITH THE MENTAL HEALTH AND DEVELOPMENTAL DISABILITIES CON-FIDENTIALITY ACT OF THE STATE OF TEXAS.

Name: Ms. R.   Case ID: Z987200
DOB: 03/21/74   Date of Evaluation: 03/29/99
Age: 25 years   Date of Report: 04/03/99

REASON FOR REFERRAL

Ms. R., a 25-year-old, single, African American female, was referred for psychological evaluation by Mr. B., a caseworker for Family Services. Information was requested concerning Ms. R.'s current level of cognitive and emotional functioning to determine suitability for unsupervised parental visitation.

BACKGROUND INFORMATION

Ms. R. is the mother of two children—Bryan, who is 5 years old, and Tina, who is 6. Both children are under the care and protection of Family Services. Ms. R. first came to the attention of Family Services on 04/06/95 when she left the children unsupervised without an appropriate care plan. The unsupervised condition was discovered after Bryan was admitted to the Houston Burn Trauma Center with extensive burns on both arms. There have been six indicated allegations of child neglect since that incident. Ms. R. successfully completed parenting classes at Project Hope. However, on 11/20/97 she again violated her service plan by abusing illegal drugs. On 03/20/98 guardianship was awarded to the state of Texas.

Ms. R. stated that she used heroin for approximately 5 years. One heroin overdose occurred in 1996, for which she was treated at County Hospital. She was arrested and convicted for selling a small amount of narcotics in 1997, was given probation, and remanded to Lutheran Social Services for drug and alcohol rehabilitation. Additional background information is available in her Family Services social history file.

BEHAVIORAL OBSERVATION

Ms. R. arrived on time for her scheduled 1:00 PM appointment. Ms. R. was appropriately dressed and reasonably groomed. Slight in frame, she appeared older than her stated age. No tremors or disturbance in gait were in evidence. She was alert and attentive. No suicidal ideation was reported. Affect appeared tense and apprehensive. Her moist palms were suggestive of anxiety. Mood was described as "generally happy." Speech was rapid, though fluid and coherent. Thought processing was goal-directed, with no observable evidence of a thought disorder. No bizarre mannerisms or unusual thought content was apparent. Attention was focused and direct. She was observed to be right-handed. Hearing and vision appeared to be normal. At the onset of the 3-hour evaluation, Ms. R. was somewhat guarded, though eventually relaxed, and became more cooperative as the evaluation progressed.

TESTS ADMINISTERED

Millon Clinical Multiaxial Inventory-III (MCMI-III)
Wechsler Adult Intelligence Scale-III (WAIS-III)
Luria-Nebraska Neuropsychological Screening Test
Mental Status Examination
Thematic Apperception Test

INTELLECTUAL ASSESSMENT

Ms. R. currently functions in the average range of cognitive ability, according to her performance on the WAIS-III (full-scale IQ 91; verbal IQ 89; performance IQ 95). With a 95% confidence level, Ms. R.'s full-scale IQ falls between 87 to 95 on the WAIS-III, which places her in the 27th percentile of the general population.

Verbal scale scores fell within the average range, with the exception of a relatively low score on the comprehension subtest. This score suggests that problem-solving ability, using practical reasoning, is marginal, and social acculturation, particularly in the area of ethical judgment, may be limited. Immediate and working memory is adequate.

Within the performance area, all subtest scores fell within the average range. Picture arrangement, a subtest that measures nonverbal reasoning, is a relative strength. Tasks requiring visual sequencing and organization were performed without difficulty. Overall, speed determined performance tasks requiring visual–spatial organization fell within average limits. No significant differences were demonstrated between verbal IQ and performance IQ.

Results of the Luria-Nebraska Neuropsychological Screening and the Bender-Gestalt fell within acceptable norms and suggest the absence of manifest organic impairment. Both fine and gross motor skills are intact. Memory appears adequate in all domains.

PERSONALITY ASSESSMENT

Ms. R. was administered the MCMI-III and the Thematic Apperception Test to assess emotional functioning. The MCMI-III protocol results are valid, though her test-taking attitude suggested a tendency to present herself in a favorable light. This profile configuration is characteristically found in individuals who engage in nonconforming behaviors designed to exploit their environment. An exaggerated sense of self-importance is directed by feelings of discontent—for example, believing that life has not treated her fairly.

Although seemingly sensitive to interpersonal nuances, Ms. R. tends to disregard social convention. A sanguine outlook on life—believing that "matters will work out"—most likely exists. Individuals with similar patterns tend to deny psychological distress. Often they rationalize their errant behaviors and transfer blame onto others, accepting minimal responsibility for their own actions. Ms. R. tends to avoid close interpersonal relationships, being constantly guarded and suspicious of the motivations of others. Individuals with similar profiles generally are deficient in social controls and self-discipline.

The overall diagnostic impression of this profile configuration suggests an antisocial personality pattern with narcissistic and negativistic traits. Chronic and deeply embedded substance abuse may well contribute to her irresponsible behavior. Asocial behaviors are likely fueled by underlying hostility that heightens insensitivity and indifference to the consequences of continued drug abuse. Sustained sobriety is the immediate treatment goal.

DIAGNOSTIC IMPRESSIONS
Axis I: 304.00 Opioid dependence
Axis II: 301.70 Antisocial personality disorder with narcissistic and negativistic personality traits
Axis III: None
Axis IV: Psychosocial and environmental problem: neglect of minor children
Axis V: GAF = 60 (current)

SUMMARY AND RECOMMENDATIONS

Ms. R. is a 25-year-old, single, African American female, who was evaluated to determine her suitability for unsupervised parental visitation. She currently functions in the average range of cognitive ability (WAIS-III: verbal scale IQ = 89; performance scale IQ = 95; full-scale

IQ = 91). Verbal comprehension and working-memory indices fell within average limits. Within the performance area, all scores fell within the average range, with a relative strength demonstrated in nonverbal reasoning. Overall, visual motor skills and processing speed were adequate. Results of the Luria-Nebraska Screening suggest the absence of manifest organic impairment.

Personality assessment revealed an antisocial personality pattern, with mixed narcissistic and negativistic personality traits. Nonconforming behaviors designed to exploit one's environment mark this profile pattern. Suspicious, resentful, and oppositional behaviors are indicated. Individuals with similar profiles tend to deny psychological distress. Rationalization and transference of blame in failing to accept responsibility for errant behaviors are not uncommon. Intellectually, Ms. R. is capable of understanding the demands of parenthood; however, her continued abuse of drugs interferes with being a responsible parent. Without intensive drug rehabilitation treatment, behavior modification appears unlikely.

The following recommendations are offered:

1. Both minor children should remain under the care of DCFS, and visitation with both children should continue under supervised conditions.
2. Participation in drug and alcohol aftercare, with a therapeutic focus on parenting skills.
3. A treatment plan should be designed to include a restructuring of environmental activity (e.g., education classes), in order to reinforce positive and desirable skill development.
4. Participation in Narcotics Anonymous (NA) meetings.
5. Therapeutic goals should address prosocial behaviors. Interpersonal techniques can be used to develop a responsible attitude toward shared social living.
6. Following a reasonable period of acquired sobriety, family therapy can be effectively used to reconstitute the family as a functional unit. Focus can be directed toward cooperative tasks to establish family integrity and unity.

Respectfully submitted,

Dan Jankowski, PsyD
Licensed Clinical Psychologist
#041-442-096

References

Akhtar, S. (1987). Schizoid personality disorder: A synthesis of developmental, dynamic, and descriptive features. *American Journal of Psychotherapy, 41,* 499–518.

American Psychiatric Association. (1987). *Diagnostic and statistical manual of mental disorders* (3rd ed., Rev.) Washington DC: Author.

American Psychiatric Association. (1994). *Diagnostic and statistical manual of mental disorders* (4th ed.). Washington DC: Author.

American Psychological Association. (1987). *Casebook on ethical principles of psychologists.* Washington, DC: Author.

Andreason, N. C. (1987). The diagnosis of schizophrenia. *Schizophrenia Bulletin, 13,* 9–22.

Angst, J. (1998). The emerging epidemiology of hypomania and bipolar II disorder. *Journal of Affective Disorders, 50,* 143–151.

Battaglia, M., & Bellodi, L. (1992). Schizotypal disorder. *Hospital & Community Psychiatry, 43,* 82.

Ben-Tovim, D., & Esterman, A. (1998). Zero progress with hypochondrias (Commentary). *The Lancet, 352,* 1798–1799.

Berman, S., Whyne, M., & McCann, J. T. (1995). Defense mechanisms and personality disorders: An empirical test of Millon's theory. *Journal of Personality Assessment, 64,* 132–144.

Bhatia, S. C., & Bhatia, S. K. (1997). Major depression: Selecting safe and effective treatment. *American Family Physician, 55,* 1683–1694.

Bockian, N. R., & Jungsma, A. E. (2001). *The personality disorders treatment planner.* New York: Wiley.

Brown, E. J., Heimberg, R. G., & Juster, H. R. (1995). Social phobia subtype and avoidant personality disorder: Effect on severity of social phobia, impairment, and outcome of cognitive behavioral treatment. *Behavior Therapy, 26,* 467–486.

Cassidy, F., Forest, K., Murry, E., & Carroll, B. J., (1998). A factor analysis of the signs and symptoms of mania. *Archives of General Psychiatry, 55,* 27–32.

Choca, J. P., & Van Denburg, E. (1997). *Interpretive guide to the Millon Clinical Multiaxial Inventory* (2nd ed.). Washington DC: American Psychological Association.

Clark, K. (1996). The nowhere (wo)man. An example of the defensive use of emptiness in a patient with a schizoid disorder of the self. *Clinical Social Work Journal, 24,* 153–166.

Craig, R. (1999). Essentials of MCMI-III Assessment. In S. Strack, *Essentials of Millon inventories assessment* (pp. 19, 27, 33). New York: Wiley.

Cull, A., Chick, J., & Wolff, S. (1984). A consensual validation of schizoid personality in childhood and adult life. *British Journal of Psychiatry, 144,* 646–648.

Daly, I. (1997). Mania (Seminar). *The Lancet, 349,* 1157–1160.

Dansky, B. S., Brady, K. T., Saladin, M. E., Killeen, T., Becker, S., & Roitzsch, J. (1996).Victimization and PTSD in individuals with substance use disorders: Gender and racial differences. *American Journal of Drug and Alcohol Abuse, 22,* 75–93.

den Boer, J. A. (1997, Sept.). Social phobia: Epidemiology, recognition, and treatment. *British Medical Journal, 315,* 796–800.

Dill, K. E., Anderson, C. A., Anderson, K. B., & Deuser, W. E. (1997). Effects of aggressive personality on social expectations and social perceptions. *Journal of Research in Personality, 31,* 272–292.

Epstein, R. M., Quill, T. E., & McWhinney, I. R. (1999). Somatization reconsidered. *Archives of Internal Medicine, 159,* 215–222.

Fenton, W. S., McGlashan, T. H., Victor, B. J., & Blyler, C. R. (1997). Symptoms, subtype, and suicidality in patients with schizophrenia spectrum disorders. *American Journal of Psychiatry, 154,* 199–204.

Fiester, S. J., & Gay, M. (1991). Sadistic personality disorder: A review of data and recommendations for DSM-IV. *Journal of Personality Disorders, 5,* 376–385.

Fine, M. A., Overholser, J. C., & Berkoff, K. (1992). Diagnostic validity of the passive-aggressive personality disorder: Suggestions for reform. *American Journal of Psychotherapy, 46,* 470–484.

Galletly, C. (1997). Borderline-dissociation comorbidity. *American Journal of Psychiatry, 154,* 1629.

Geberth, V. J., & Turco, R. N. (1997). Antisocial personality disorder, sexual sadism, malignant narcissism, and serial murder. *Journal of Forensic Sciences, 42,* 49–60.

Gorman, J. M. (1990). *The essential guide to psychiatric drugs.* New York: St. Martin's Press.

Grant, B. F. (1997). Prevalence and correlates of alcohol use and *DSM-IV* alcohol dependence in United States: Results of the National Longitudinal Alcohol Epidemiology Survey. *Journal of Studies on Alcohol, 58,* 464–473.

Hartlage, S., Arduino, K., & Alloy, L. (1998), Depressive personality characteristics: State dependent concomitants of depressive disorder and traits independent of current depression. *Journal of Abnormal Psychology, 107,* 349–354.

Harvard Health Letter. (July, 1998). Chronic anxiety: How to stop living on the edge (anxiety disorders). *Harvard Health Letter, 23,* 1–3.

Harvard Health Letter. (March, 1999). Dysthymia (effects of mild chronic depression). *Harvard Health Letter, 24,* 4–5.

Harvard Mental Health Letter. (June, 1996). Post-traumatic stress disorder (pt. 1). *Harvard Mental Health Letter, 12,* 1–4.

Harvard Mental Health Letter. (July, 1996). Post-traumatic stress disorder (pt. 2). *Harvard Mental Health Letter, 13,* 1–5.

Harvard Mental Health Letter. (Jan., 1999). General review: Delusions and delusional disorders-pt. 1. *Harvard Mental Health Letter, 15,* 1–3.

Harvard Mental Health Letter. (Feb., 1999). General review: Delusions and delusional disorders-pt. 2. *Harvard Mental Health Letter, 15,* 1–3.

Harvard Mental Health Letter. (April, 2000). Personality disorders (pt. 2). *Harvard Mental Health Letter, 16,* 1–5.

Hasin, D., & Paykin, A. (1999). *DSM-IV* alcohol abuse: Investigation of a sample of the at-risk drinkers in the community. *Journal of Studies on Alcohol, 60,* 181–187.

Horney, K. (1939). New ways in psychoanalysis. In K. Horney, The collected works of Karen Horney (Vol. 1, pp. 88–89, 100, 268). New York: Norton.

Jacobsberg, L. B., Hymowitz, P., Barasch, A., & Frances, A. J. (1986). *Symptoms of schizotypal personality disorder, 143,* 1222–1227.

Jansen, M., Arntz, A., Merckelbach, H., & Mersch, P. (1994). Personality disorders and features in social phobia and panic disorder. *Journal of Abnormal Psychology, 103,* 391–395.

Kessler, R. C., McGonagle, K. A., Zhao, S., Nelson, C. B., Hughes, M., Eshleman, S., Wittchen, H., & Kendler, K. (1994). Lifetime and 12-month prevalence of *DSM-III-R* psychiatric disorders in the United States: Results from the national comorbidity study. *Archives of General Psychiatry, 51,* 8–19.

Klein, D. N., & Shih, J. H. (1998). Depressive personality: Associations with *DSM-II-R* mood and personality disorders and negative and positive affectivity, 30 month stability, and prediction of course of Axis I depressive disorders. *Journal of Abnormal Psychology, 107,* 319–327.

Lamberg, L. (1998). Social phobia–not just another name for shyness. *The Journal of the American Medical Association, 280,* 1556–1558.

Lebe, D. (1997). Masochism and the inner mother. *Psychoanalytic Review, 84,* 523–540.

Leibman, M., & Salzinger, K. (1998). A theory-based treatment of psychotic symptoms in schizophrenia: Treatment successes and obstacles to implementation. *Journal of Genetic Psychology, 159,* 404–420.

Lezak, M.(1983). *Neuropsychological Assessment.* New York: Oxford University Press.

Lionells, M. J. (1984). Aggression as a hysterical mechanism. *Contemporary Psychoanalysis, 20,* 633–643.

Loevinger, J. (1957). Objective tests as instruments of psychological theory. *Psychological Reports, 3,* 635–694.

Loranger, A. (1996). Dependent personality disorder: Age, sex, and Axis I comorbidity. *Journal of Nervous & Mental Disease, 184,* 17–21.

Manning, J. S., Haykal, R. F., & Akiskal, H. S. (1999). The role of bipolarity in depression in the family practice setting. *Psychiatric Clinics of North America, 22,* 689–703.

Mendel, W. M. (1976). *Schizophrenia: The experience and its treatment.* San Francisco: Jossey-Bass.

Merikangas, K. R., & Angst, J. (1995). Comorbidity and social phobia: Evidence from clinical, epidemiologic, and genetic studies. *European Archives of Psychiatry & Clinical Neuroscience, 244,* 297–303.

Millon, A. (Director). (1993). *Millon training on personality disorders* [Video]. Published and distributed exlusively by National Computer Systems, P.O. Box 1416, Minneapolis, MN 55440.

Millon, T. (1969). *Modern psychopathology. A biosocial approach to maladaptive learning and functioning.* Philadelphia: W. B. Saunders.

Millon, T. (1981). *Disorders of personality: DSM-III: Axis II.* New York: Wiley.

Millon, T. (1990). *Toward a new personology: An evolutional model.* New York: Wiley.

Millon, T. (1994). *Millon Clinical Multiaxial Inventory-III manual.* Minneapolis, MN: National Computer Systems.

Millon, T. (1997). *Millon Clinical Multiaxial Inventory-III manual* (2nd ed.). Minneapolis, MN: National Computer Systems.

Millon, T. (1999). *Personality-guided therapy.* New York: Wiley.

Millon, T., & Davis, R. D. (1996). *Disorders of personality: DSM-IV and beyond.* New York: Wiley.

Millon, T., & Everly, Jr. G. S. (1985). *Personality and its disorders.: A biosocial learning approach.* New York: Wiley.

Morgenstern, J., Langenbucher, J., Labouvie, E., & Miller, K. J. (1997). The comorbidity of alcoholism and personality disorders in a clinical population: Prevalence rates and relation to alcohol typology variables. *Journal of Abnormal Psychology, 106,* 74–84.

Nabakov, V. (1985). *Pnin.* New York: Vintage Books. (Original work published 1957)

Nail, G. (1990, Dec.). Psychological report writing tips. Inservice presented at Mississippi State Hospital. Retrieved April 25, 2000, at http://www.gregnail@msresource.com/psy_rpt.html.

Nesse, R. M. (2000). Is depression an adaptation? *Archives of General Psychiatry, 57,* 14–20.

Othmer, E., & Othmer, S. C. (1994). *The clinical interview using DSM-IV Vol. 1: Fundamentals.* Washington, DC: American Psychiatric Press.

Overholser, J. (1996). The dependent personality and interpersonal problems. *Journal of Nervous & Mental Disease, 184,* 8–16.

Paris, J. (1997). Antisocial and borderline personality disorders: Two separate diagnoses or two aspects of the same psychopathology? *Comprehensive Psychiatry, 38,* 237–242.

Piersma, H. L., & Boes, J. L. (1997). MCMI-III as a Treatment Measure for Psychiatric Patients. *Journal of Clinical Psychology, 53*(8), 825–831.

Raine, A., Lencz, T., Bihrle, S., LaCasse, L., & Colletti, P. (2000). Reduced prefrontal gray matter volume and reduced autonomic activity in antisocial personality disorder. *Archives of General Psychiatry, 57,* 119–127.

Reich, J. H. (1993). Prevalence and characteristics of sadistic personality disorder in an outpatient veterans population. *Psychiatry Research, 48,* 267–276.

Reich, J. (1997). Antisocial traits in psychiatrically ill veterans without antisocial personality disorder: Relationship to Axis I disorders and effects on functioning. *Psychiatry Research, 71,* 77–82.

Reich, J., & Braginsky, Y. (1994). Paranoid personality traits in a panic disorder population: A pilot study. *Comprehensive Psychiatry, 35,* 260–264.

Retzlaff, P. (1998). Review of the Millon Clinical Multiaxial Inventory-III. In J. C. Impara & B. S. Plake (Eds.), *Thirteenth mental measurements yearbook* (pp. 667–668). Lincoln, NE: Buros Institute.

Rhodewalt, F., Madrian, J. C., & Cheney, S. (1998). Narcissism, self-knowledge organization, and emotional reactivity: The effect of daily experiences on self-esteem and affect. *Personality & Social Psychology Bulletin, 24,* 75–87.

Safire, W. (1999). "How to Write Good" from *Fumblerules*. In J. Winokur (Ed.), *Advice to Writers* (p. 18). New York: Pantheon Books.

Sansone, R. A., & Sansone, L. A. (1996). Dysthymic disorder: The chronic depression. *American Family Physician, 53,* 2588–2594.

Sattler, J. M. (1982). *Assessment of children's intelligence and special abilities* (2nd ed.). Boston: Allyn & Bacon.

Shapiro, D. (1965). *Neurotic Styles.* New York: Basic Books.

Southwick, S. M., Yehuda, R., Giller, E. L. (1993). Personality disorders in treatment-seeking combat veterans with post-traumatic stress disorder. *American Journal of Psychiatry, 150,* 1020–1023.

Sprock, J., & Hunsucker, L. (1998). Symptoms of prototypic patients with passive-aggressive personality disorder: *DSM-III-R* versus *DSM-IV* negativistic. *Comprehensive Psychiatry, 39,* 287–295.

Strub, R., & Black, F. (1985). *The mental status examination in neurology.* Philadelphia: F. A. Davis.

Strunk, W., & White, E. B. (1979). *The elements of style* (3rd ed.). New York: Collier Macmillan.

Thomas, V. H., Melchert, T. P., & Banken, J. A. (1999). Substance dependence and personality disorders: Comorbidity and treatment outcome in an inpatient treatment population. *Journal of Studies on Alcohol, 60,* 271–277.

Torgensen, S. (1994). Genetics in borderline conditions. *Acta Psychiatrica Scandinavica, 89,* 19–25.

Trestman, R. L., Keefe, R. S., Mitropoulou, V., Harvey, P. D., deVegvar, M. L., Lees-Roitman, S., Davidson, M., Aronson, A., Silverman, J., & Siever, L. J. (1995). Cognitive function and biological correlates of cognitive performance in schizotypal personality disorder. *Psychiatry Research, 59,* 127–136.

Trevor, T. (1997). Schizophrenia. *British Medical Journal, 314,* 108–111.

Turkat, I. D., Keane, S. P., & Thompson-Pope, S. K. (1990). Social processing errors among paranoid personalities. *Journal of Psychopathology & Behavioral Assessment, 12,* 263–269.

Turner, T. (1997). Schizophrenia. *British Medical Journal, 314,* 108–111.

West, M., Rose, S., & Sheldon-Keller, A. (1995). Interpersonal disorder in schizoid and avoidant disorders: An attachment personality perspective. *Canadian Journal of Psychiatry, 40,* 411–414

Williams, D., & Schill, T. (1994). Adult attachment, love styles, and self-defeating personality characteristics. *Psychological Reports, 75,* 31–34.

Yamada, N., Nakajima, S., & Noguchi, T. (1998). Age onset of delusional disorder is dependent on the delusional theme. *Acta Psychiatrica Scandinavica, 97,* 122–124.

Index

A

Abstraction
  as fourth phase of Millon's evolutionary
    theory, 11
Adaptation
  as second phase of Millon's evolutionary
    theory, 11
Adjustments, of base rate (MCMI-III)
  anxiety-depression (A/D) adjustment,
    49–50
  denial/compliant adjustment, 50
  disclosure adjustment, 49
  inpatient adjustment, 50
Administration (of MCMI-III)
  base-rate adjustments, 49–50
  coding, 51
  determining raw scores, 48
  equipment for, 43
  guidelines for, 42–43, 56
  location of, 42–43, 56
  profiling, 51
  scoring, 44–51
  validation, 45–49
Affect, 142
Alcohol dependence, 124–126
  and Alcohol Dependence scale, 35
  case reviews, 132–136, 181–183, 188–
    190
  and *DSM-IV* diagnostic criteria, 125–126
Alcohol Dependence scale (Scale B of
  MCMI-III), 35, 115
Amplitude, 143
Anchor base rates. *See* Base-rate scoring
Antisocial personality, 30, 86–88, 114
  and Antisocial scale, 32
  case review, 188–190

comorbidity of, 103–104
and *DSM-IV* diagnostic criteria, 87–88
mental status description, 86–87
treatment advice, 87
Antisocial scale (Scale 6A of MCMI-III), 32,
  115
Anxiety-depression (A/D) adjustment, 49–50
Anxiety disorder, 118–119
  and Anxiety Disorder scale, 35
  and *DSM-IV* diagnostic criteria, 118–119
Anxiety Disorder scale (Scale A of MCMI-
  III), 35, 145
Assessment. *See* Psychological assessment
Asperger's syndrome, 75
Autistic psychopathology, 75
Avoidant personality disorder, 77–78, 115
  and Avoidant scale, 32
  case reviews, 151–162, 184–186
  comorbidity of, 102–104
  and *DSM-IV* diagnostic criteria, 78
  mental status description, 77–78
  treatment advice, 77
Avoidant scale (Scale 2A of MCMI-III), 32,
  159

B

Back Depression Inventory (BDI), 27
Base-rate (BR) scoring, 22, 28–30, 37, 48,
  67–68
  adjustments, 49–50
  anchor prevalence points, 29
  anxiety-depression (A/D) adjustment,
    49–50
  denial/compliant adjustment, 50
  disclosure adjustment, 49
  final score, 50–51

About the Author

Dan Jankowski, PsyD, earned his doctorate in clinical psychology at the Illinois School for Professional Psychology. Currently, he is in private practice and, as adjunct professor at Roosevelt University in Chicago, teaches objective personality assessment. Among his civilian positions, he was director of Family Mental Health Services of Catholic Charities in Chicago, and as an officer in the U.S. Army, he served at various assignments in Europe, Asia, and the United States. Recently he conducted a seminar titled "Psychological Dimensions of Human Development" in the Diocese of Hyderabad in southern India and a seminar on stress management for the Macedonian officers in the former Yugoslavian republic. He is presently researching personality and individual driving habits for a future book.

DATE DUE

DEC 3 2003 .ILL			
DEC 1 1 2003			
NOV 1 5 2006			
DEC 1 1 2007 NOV 0 9 2009			
GAYLORD			PRINTED IN U.S.A.